C000179192

Web Services Testing with soapUI

Build high quality service-oriented solutions by learning easy and efficient web services testing with this practical, hands-on guide

Charitha Kankanamge

BIRMINGHAM - MUMBAI

Web Services Testing with soapUI

Copyright © 2012 Packt Publishing

All rights reserved. No part of this book may be reproduced, stored in a retrieval system, or transmitted in any form or by any means, without the prior written permission of the publisher, except in the case of brief quotations embedded in critical articles or reviews.

Every effort has been made in the preparation of this book to ensure the accuracy of the information presented. However, the information contained in this book is sold without warranty, either express or implied. Neither the author, nor Packt Publishing, and its dealers and distributors will be held liable for any damages caused or alleged to be caused directly or indirectly by this book.

Packt Publishing has endeavored to provide trademark information about all of the companies and products mentioned in this book by the appropriate use of capitals. However, Packt Publishing cannot guarantee the accuracy of this information.

First published: October 2012

Production Reference: 1191012

Published by Packt Publishing Ltd.
Livery Place
35 Livery Street
Birmingham B3 2PB, UK.

ISBN 978-1-84951-566-5

www.packtpub.com

Cover Image by Asher Wishkerman (wishkerman@hotmail.com)

Credits

Author

Charitha Kankanamge

Reviewers

Evanthika Amarasiri

Bindu Laxminarayan

Ajay Pawar

Acquisition Editor

Kartikey Pandey

Lead Technical Editors

Hithesh Uchil

Azharuddin Sheikh

Technical Editors

Vrinda Amberkar

Ankita Meshram

Prashant Salvi

Project Coordinators

Sai Gamare

Shraddha Vora

Proofreader

Maria Gould

Indexer

Monica Ajmera Mehta

Graphics

Valentina D'Silva

Aditi Gajjar

Production Coordinator

Prachali Bhiwandkar

Cover Work

Prachali Bhiwandkar

About the Author

Charitha Kankanamge is Manager, Quality Assurance and Senior Technical Lead at WSO2 with more than 9 years of experience in Software Quality Assurance. Charitha is specialized in SOA and middleware testing. He lead the WSO2 QA team since 2007. He is also a committer of the Apache Software Foundation contributing to Apache web services project. Charitha is interested in researching new technologies in software-testing space as well as new trends in agile and exploratory testing processes.

Prior to joining WSO2, Charitha has worked at Virtusa inc. for 3 years where he was involved in multiple on-site and off-shore project assignments. In his rare offline moments, he enjoys playing guitar and watching movies.

Charitha has been involved in reviewing two books, *Apache Jmeter, Emilly H. Halili* and *Quick Start Apache Axis2, Deepal Jayasinghe* both being published by Packt Publishing.

Charitha can be reached through his blog:

http://charithaka.blogspot.com

Acknowledgement

Making a book reality takes many dedicated people, and it is my great pleasure to acknowledge their contributions.

First, I'd like to thank Packt Publishers, in particular, Kartikey Pandey – Senior Acquisition Editor, who proposed me to write this book. I'm grateful for all the help I got from the editorial staff at Packt Publishers in reviewing this book, specially Hithesh Uchil – Lead Technical Editor and Sai Gamare who coordinated the progress of writing, by ensuring that I stayed on track.

This book has benefited from a great set of technical reviewers. I'd like to thank each of them for volunteering their time reviewing drafts of this book and providing valuable feedback. Specially, my colleague at WSO2 QA team, Evanthika Amarasiri who carried out in-depth quality assurance process in all chapters by executing each sample.

I sincerely thank my wife, Thushari for her patience, support, and understanding throughout the writing process. Many thanks to my beloved parents who raised me, made me the person who I am today by providing their insightful guidance in all aspects of my life.

Though I'm unable to name individually, I would like to extend my heartfelt gratitude to many colleagues at WSO2, who never hesitated to give their support to the fullest extent, whenever I requested help on various subject matters. I must thank Dr. Sanjiva Weerawarana, Founder, Chairman and CEO of WSO2, Inc. whose vision inspires me and guides me to accomplish my career aspirations.

Finally, a big thank goes to the developers and contributors of Smartbear software for making soapUI the world's best open source web services testing tool.

About the Reviewers

Evanthika Amarasiri joined 99X Techonology (former Eurocenter DDC Ltd.) in 2000 as a trainee QA Engineer. She has become competent in testing applications based on Java, C++, VB and .NET, Lotus Notes, and in mobile application testing (Symbian and J2ME). While she was working there, she studied for her B.Sc. in Information Systems at the Informatics Institute of Technology, Sri Lanka, which was affiliated to the Manchester Metropolitan University, UK. She left 99X Technology in 2006 and joined WSO2 Lanka (Pvt) Limited (in the same year) as a Software Engineer - Quality Assurance. From 2006 to date, she has worked with several leading middleware products of WSO2. During her stay at WSO2 she has gained experience and knowledge on different kinds of web technologies, operating systems, databases, application servers, and many QA testing tools. She has also gained extensive experience in functional, usability, performance testing, as well as QA test planning. By contributing to the Apache Synapse, which is a free and open source software project, she has become a committer for the same. Currently she is working as a Quality Assurance Technical Lead and is also a member of the Management Committee in the Integration Technology team of WSO2.

> I would like to thank my loving husband and my mother for all the support given while reviewing this book. Also, a special thank goes to my team mates for all the valuable inputs given, to make the review process a success. My sincere gratitude goes to Charitha, the author of the book, for selecting me as a reviewer for his book. He is a great teacher/leader who has inspired us with his work. Without his guidance and support, I would not have made this far in my career. I wish him all the best for his future endeavors.

Bindu Laxminarayan is an expert in Software Testing and Quality Assurance with expertise in Test Automation Framework Design and Development. Over the last 7 years, she has worked on various testing tools including but not limited to SOAPUI, Jmeter and selenium on RESTful and SOAP Web Services. She is currently working on Test Automation of Cloud Web Services and design patterns in Automated Testing. Over the last two years she has presented at work on StarEast Conference.

Ajay Pawar is an IBM middleware consultant having more than a decade of experience. He is Director at ePower Consultancy Services UK. Ltd.

He started his career working on technologies such as Java, Java Swing, Java EE, and then extended his experience in SOA world. He is an expert in IBM middleware tools such as WebSphere Process Server (WPS), WebSphere Integration Developer (WID), WebSphere MQ (WMQ), and Websphere Service Registry and Repository (WSRR). He has also good flair for web services testing. He is proficient in soapUI tool and he used it extensively for manual as well as automation testing.

I would like to thank my wife Hema, sweet daughter Aarohi, and a cute baby Vihaan for their constant support.

www.PacktPub.com

Support files, eBooks, discount offers and more

You might want to visit www.PacktPub.com for support files and downloads related to your book.

Did you know that Packt offers eBook versions of every book published, with PDF and ePub files available? You can upgrade to the eBook version at www.PacktPub.com and as a print book customer, you are entitled to a discount on the eBook copy. Get in touch with us at service@packtpub.com for more details.

At www.PacktPub.com, you can also read a collection of free technical articles, sign up for a range of free newsletters and receive exclusive discounts and offers on Packt books and eBooks.

http://PacktLib.PacktPub.com

Do you need instant solutions to your IT questions? PacktLib is Packt's online digital book library. Here, you can access, read and search across Packt's entire library of books.

Why Subscribe?

- Fully searchable across every book published by Packt
- Copy and paste, print and bookmark content
- On demand and accessible via web browser

Free Access for Packt account holders

If you have an account with Packt at www.PacktPub.com, you can use this to access PacktLib today and view nine entirely free books. Simply use your login credentials for immediate access.

This book is dedicated to my parents, who have raised me to be the person I am today and my beloved wife Thushari and my loving kids, Risith and Nethul.

Table of Contents

Preface

This book is all about using soapUI for functional and performance testing of service-oriented solutions. soapUI can be used to test various aspects of a service-oriented solution without merely playing the role of a web service invocation tool. We will follow a simple tutorial-style approach throughout the book in which we will explore all key features provided by soapUI based on a sample web services project. This book is ideally designed to guide readers to get more detailed insight on soapUI by doing a lot of hands-on exercises.

What this book covers

Chapter 1, Web Services Testing and soapUI, introduces soapUI by giving an overview of its history, features, and installation of soapUI in your computer. We will begin our journey towards learning soapUI by discussing some key characteristics of SOA, Web services and Web services testing in general.

Chapter 2, The Sample Project, introduces the sample web services project which will be used as the target application for functional and performance testing in the remaining chapters of the book. In this chapter, we will build a simple web services based application using Apache Axis2 open source web services framework. The primary objective of building this sample application is to use it in all demonstrations of soapUI features. As we will not discuss any topics related to soapUI or web services testing in general in this chapter, you may skip the details and download the sample web services project from http://www.PacktPub.com/support.

Chapter 3, First Steps with soapUI and Projects, serves as a guide for getting started with soapUI projects. Based on one of the web services that we built as part of the sample web services project in *Chapter 2, The Sample Project*, we will discuss the schema and WSDL of the web service in detail. We will use soapUI to invoke the operations of sample web service and discuss the SOAP requests, responses, and faults.

Chapter 4, Working with Your First TestSuite, demonstrates the basic constructs of a soapUI project—TestSuites, TestCases, and TestSteps—which prepares you for the next chapters of the book. We will also look into the validation of responses using assertions and soapUI properties.

Chapter 5, Load and Performance Testing with soapUI, covers the steps that you would have to follow when using soapUI as a load and performance testing tool. We will demonstrate the load test strategies provided by soapUI and the load test specific assertions.

Chapter 6, Web Services Simulation with soapUI, briefly describes how web services can be simulated using soapUI. We will demonstrate the usage of soapUI mock services model and static as well as dynamic mock responses.

Chapter 7, Advanced Functional Testing with soapUI, introduces the testing aspects of web services extensions such as WS-Security and WS-Addressing. We will use an improved version of the sample web services project which we built in *Chapter 2, The Sample Project* for the demonstrations in this chapter.

Chapter 8, Getting Started with REST Testing, introduces the concepts related to RESTful web services and how soapUI can be utilized in RESTful services testing. We will demonstrate the use of soapUI in RESTful services testing by using a publicly hosted sample web application.

Chapter 9, Testing Databases with soapUI, briefly describes the direct database query invocations of soapUI. In this chapter, we will discuss the database testing features provided by soapUI such as JDBC requests and assertions.

Chapter 10, JMS Testing with soapUI, demonstrates the use of JMS in soapUI. By exposing one of the sample web services over JMS transport, we will explore the JMS testing capabilities provided by soapUI.

Chapter 11, Extending soapUI with Scripting, introduces the scripting facilities given by soapUI in order to extend the default behavior of soapUI tests. We will look into the use of soapUI API methods through Groovy scripts inside our tests.

Chapter 12, Automated Testing with soapUI, demonstrates various automated testing approaches with soapUI. In this chapter, we will discuss the integration of soapUI tests with build tools such as Apache Maven.

Chapter 13, Miscellaneous Topics, introduces some useful tools integrated with soapUI such as WS-I validation tool and the utilities provided by external web services framework such as Apache Axis2. This chapter also demonstrates the use of soapUI when testing services by sending attachments.

What you need for this book

We will make use of quite a lot of open source software to run the code samples in this book. Firstly, you should install soapUI 4.0.1 or later version as explained in *Chapter 1, Web Services Testing and soapUI*. You would require MySQL and Apache Axis2-1.6.1 or later version to run the sample web services. You will also need Apache Ant to build the sample web services project. Apache Rampart, Apache Maven, Apache ActiveMQ, and Apache Wink open source libraries are required for some demonstrations as explained in the respective chapters.

Who this book is for

If you are a part of a team that builds service-oriented solutions or makes use of web services in your project, and your primary involvement is testing such a solution, then this book is the ideal reference for you. This book will help you to understand the common challenges of SOA testing and how soapUI can be utilized effective manner in testing your applications.

This book would also be a good reference for developers and QA engineers who do researches and evaluations on various commercial and open source web services testing tools. If you are an experienced software professional or a novice tester, you will quickly be able to learn the most important features of soapUI by following the simple step-by-step instructions given in this book.

Conventions

In this book, you will find a number of styles of text that distinguish between different kinds of information. Here are some examples of these styles, and an explanation of their meaning.

Code words in text are shown as follows: "The `<s:Body>` element carries the actual message payload."

A block of code is set as follows:

```
CREATE TABLE IF NOT EXISTS ROOM_T(
      room_number INT NOT NULL,
      room_type VARCHAR(100) NOT NULL,
      room_size varchar(100) NOT NULL,
      PRIMARY KEY(room_number));
```

Any command-line input or output is written as follows:

```
create database HOTEL_RESERVATION_DB;
```

New terms and **important words** are shown in bold. Words that you see on the screen, in menus or dialog boxes for example, appear in the text like this: "You can check the **Create a desktop icon** checkbox to create an icon on the desktop so can you can easily launch soapUI".

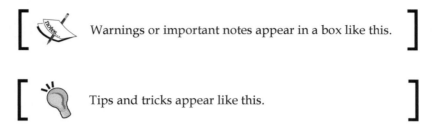

Warnings or important notes appear in a box like this.

Tips and tricks appear like this.

Reader feedback

Feedback from our readers is always welcome. Let us know what you think about this book—what you liked or may have disliked. Reader feedback is important for us to develop titles that you really get the most out of.

To send us general feedback, simply send an e-mail to feedback@packtpub.com, and mention the book title via the subject of your message.

If there is a topic that you have expertise in and you are interested in either writing or contributing to a book, see our author guide on www.packtpub.com/authors.

Customer support

Now that you are the proud owner of a Packt book, we have a number of things to help you to get the most from your purchase.

Downloading the example code

You can download the example code files for all Packt books you have purchased from your account at http://www.PacktPub.com. If you purchased this book elsewhere, you can visit http://www.PacktPub.com/support and register to have the files e-mailed directly to you.

Errata

Although we have taken every care to ensure the accuracy of our content, mistakes do happen. If you find a mistake in one of our books—maybe a mistake in the text or the code—we would be grateful if you would report this to us. By doing so, you can save other readers from frustration and help us improve subsequent versions of this book. If you find any errata, please report them by visiting http://www.packtpub.com/support, selecting your book, clicking on the **errata submission form** link, and entering the details of your errata. Once your errata are verified, your submission will be accepted and the errata will be uploaded on our website, or added to any list of existing errata, under the Errata section of that title. Any existing errata can be viewed by selecting your title from http://www.packtpub.com/support.

Piracy

Piracy of copyright material on the Internet is an ongoing problem across all media. At Packt, we take the protection of our copyright and licenses very seriously. If you come across any illegal copies of our works, in any form, on the Internet, please provide us with the location address or website name immediately so that we can pursue a remedy.

Please contact us at copyright@packtpub.com with a link to the suspected pirated material.

We appreciate your help in protecting our authors, and our ability to bring you valuable content.

Questions

You can contact us at questions@packtpub.com if you are having a problem with any aspect of the book, and we will do our best to address it.

1
Web Services Testing and soapUI

Web services are one of the key building blocks of service-oriented solutions. Because of their usage and importance in the enterprise applications, the project teams are expected to be knowledgeable and familiar with the technologies which are associated with web services and **service-oriented architecture(SOA)**. The testing aspect of web services in particular is one of the key topics which needs to be discussed when you work with web services.

Web servics testing can be performed using many approaches. The client APIs included in web service frameworks such as Apache Axis2 can be used to programatically invoke web services. In addition to that, number of properitory and open source tools are avaialble to test web services automatically. soapUI is one such free and open source testing tool that suppots functional and non-functional evaluations of web services.

We will discuss the following topics in this chapter which will provide you with an introduction to the basic concepts of SOA, web services testing, and soapUI:

- Overview of some of the key characteristics of web services
- The role of web services in SOA
- Approaches of testing web services
- Web services testing challenges
- Introduction to soapUI
- Installing soapUI

SOA and web services

SOA is a distinct approach for separating concerns and building business solutions utilizing loosely coupled and reusable components. SOA is no longer a nice-to-have feature for most of the enterprises and it is widely used in organizations to achieve a lot of strategic advantages. By adopting SOA, organizations can enable their business applications to quickly and efficiently respond to business, process, and integration changes which usually occur in any enterprise environment.

Service-oriented solutions

If a software system is built by following the principles associated with SOA, it can be considered as a service-oriented solution. Organizations generally tend to build service-oriented solutions in order to leverage flexibility in their businesses, merge or acquire new businesses, and achieve competitive advantages. To understand the use and purpose of SOA and service-oriented solutions, let's have a look at a simplified case study.

Case study

Smith and Co. is a large motor insurance policy provider located in North America. The company uses a software system to perform all their operations which are associated with insurance claim processing. The system consists of various modules including the following:

- Customer enrollment and registration
- Insurance policy processing
- Insurance claim processing
- Customer management
- Accounting
- Service providers management

With the enormous success and client satisfaction of the insurance claims processed by the company during the recent past, Smith and Co. has acquired InsurePlus Inc., one of its competing insurance providers, a few months back.

InsurePlus has also provided some of the insurance motor claim policies which are similar to those that Smith and Co. provides to their clients. Therefore, the company management has decided to integrate the insurance claim processing systems used by both companies and deliver one solution to their clients.

Smith and Co. uses a lot of Microsoft(TM) technologies and all of their software applications, including the overall insurance policy management system, are built on .NET framework. On the other hand, InsurePlus uses J2EE heavily, and their insurance processing applications are all based on Java technologies. To worsen the problem of integration, InsurePlus consists of a legacy customer management application component as well, which runs on an AS-400 system.

The IT departments of both companies faced numerous difficulties when they tried to integrate the software applications in Smith and Co. and InsurePlus Inc. They had to write a lot of adapter modules so that both applications would communicate with each other and do the protocol conversions as needed.

In order to overcome these and future integration issues, the IT management of Smith and Co. decided to adopt SOA into their business application development methodology and convert the insurance processing system into a service-oriented solution.

As the first step, a lot of wrapper services (web services which encapsulate the logic of different insurance processing modules) were built, exposing them as web services. Therefore the individual modules were able to communicate with each other with minimum integration concerns. By adopting SOA, their applications used a common language, XML, in message transmission and hence a heterogeneous systems such as the .NET based insurance policy handling system in Smith and Co. was able to communicate with the Java based applications running on InsurePlus Inc.

By implementing a service-oriented solution, the system at Smith and Co. was able to merge with a lot of other legacy systems with minimum integration overhead.

Building blocks of SOA

When studying typical service-oriented solutions, we can identify three major building blocks as follows:

- Web services
- Mediation
- Composition

Web services

Web services are the individual units of business logic in SOA. Web services communicate with each other and other programs or applications by sending messages. Web services consist of a public interface definition which is a central piece of information that assigns the service an identity and enables its invocation.

The service container is the SOA middleware component where the web service is hosted for the consuming applications to interact with it. It allows developers to build, deploy, and manage web services and it also represents the server-side processor role in web service frameworks. A list of commonly used web service frameworks can be found at `http://en.wikipedia.org/wiki/List_of_web_service_frameworks`; here you can find some popular web service middleware such as **Windows Communication Foundation (WCF)**, Apache CXF, Apache Axis2, and so on. We will use Apache Axis2 as the service container for sample projects within the context of this book. Apache Axis2 can be found at `http://axis.apache.org/`.

The **service container** contains the **business logic**, which interacts with the **service consumer** via a **service interface**. This is shown in the following diagram:

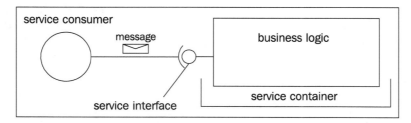

Mediation

Usually, the message transmission between nodes in a service-oriented solution does not just occur via the typical point-to-point channels. Instead, once a message is received, it can be flowed through multiple intermediaries and subjected to various transformation and conversions as necessary. This behavior is commonly referred to as message mediation and is another important building block in service-oriented solutions. Similar to how the service container is used as the hosting platform for web services, a broker is the corresponding SOA middleware component for message mediation. Usually, **enterprise service bus** (**ESB**) acts as a broker in service-oriented solutions.

Composition

In service-oriented solutions, we cannot expect individual web services running alone to provide the desired business functionality. Instead, multiple web services work together and participate in various service compositions. Usually, the web services are pulled together dynamically at the runtime based on the rules specified in business process definitions. The management or coordination of these business processes are governed by the **process coordinator**, which is the SOA middleware component associated with web service compositions.

We looked into the primary building blocks of service-oriented solutions and the corresponding SOA middleware components. Next, we are going to discuss some of the distinguished elements associated specifically with web services. These are SOAP messaging, **Web Services Description Language (WSDL)**, message exchanging patterns, and RESTful services.

Simple Object Access Protocol

Simple Object Access Protocol (SOAP) can be considered as the foremost messaging standard for use with web services. It is defined by the **World Wide Web Consortium (W3C)** at `http://www.w3.org/TR/2000/NOTE-SOAP-20000508/` as follows:

> *SOAP is a lightweight protocol for exchange of information in a decentralized, distributed environment. It is an XML based protocol that consists of three parts: an envelope that defines a framework for describing what is in a message and how to process it, a set of encoding rules for expressing instances of application-defined datatypes, and a convention for representing remote procedure calls and responses.*

The SOAP specification has been universally accepted as the standard transport protocol for messages processed by web services. There are two different versions of SOAP specification and both of them are widely used in service-oriented solutions. These two versions are SOAP v1.1 and SOAP v1.2.

Regardless of the SOAP specification version, the message format of a SOAP message still remains intact. A SOAP message is an XML document that consists of a mandatory SOAP envelope, an optional SOAP header, and a mandatory SOAP body.

The structure of a SOAP message is shown in the following diagram:

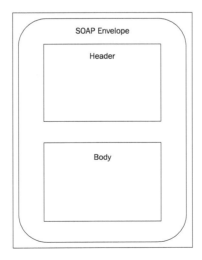

The SOAP Envelope is the wrapper element which holds all child nodes inside a SOAP message.

The SOAP Header element is an optional block where the meta information is stored. Using the headers, SOAP messages are capable of containing different types of supplemental information related to the delivery and processing of messages. This indirectly provides the statelessness for web services as by maintaining SOAP headers, services do not necessarily need to store message-specific logic. Typically, SOAP headers can include the following:

- Message processing instructions
- Security policy metadata
- Addressing information
- Message correlation data
- Reliable messaging metadata

The SOAP body is the element where the actual message contents are hosted. These contents of the body are usually referred to as the message payload.

Let's have a look at a sample SOAP message and relate the preceding concepts through the following diagram:

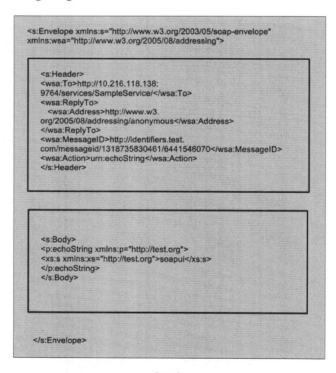

In this example SOAP message, we can clearly identify the three elements; envelope, body, and header. The header element includes a set of child elements such as `<wsa:To>`, `<wsa:ReplyTo>`, `<wsa:Address>`, `<wsa:MessageID>`, and `<wsa:Action>`. These header blocks are part of the WS-Addressing specification. Similarly, any header element associated with WS-* specifications can be included inside the SOAP header element.

The `<s:Body>` element carries the actual message payload. In this example, it is the `<p:echoString>` element with a one child element.

> When working with SOAP messages, identification of the version of SOAP message is one of the important requirements. At first glance, you can determine the version of the specification used in the SOAP message through the namespace identifier of the `<Envelope>` element. If the message conforms to SOAP 1.1 specification, it would be `http://schemas.xmlsoap.org/soap/envelope/`, otherwise `http://www.w3.org/2003/05/soap-envelope` is the name space identifier of SOAP 1.2 messages.

Alternatives to SOAP

Though SOAP is considered as the standard protocol for web services communication, it is not the only possible transport protocol which is used. SOAP was designed to be extensible so that the other standards could be integrated into it. The WS-* extensions such as WS-Security, WS-Addressing, and WS-ReliableMessaging are associated with SOAP messaging due to this extensible nature. In addition to the platform and language agnosticism, SOAP messages can be transmitted over various transports such as HTTP, HTTPS, JMS, and SMTP among others. However, there are a few drawbacks associated with SOAP messaging. The performance degradations due to heavy XML processing and the complexities associated with the usage of various WS-* specifications are two of the most common disadvantages of the SOAP messaging model. Because of these concerns, we can identify some alternative approaches to SOAP.

REST

Due to the complexities accompanied with the SOAP model, **Representational State Transfer (REST)** architecture has emerged as a result. RESTful web services can be considered as a lightweight alternative to the bulky and complex SOAP based web service standards. In RESTful web services, the emphasis is on point-to-point communication over HTTP, primarily using plain old XML (POX) messages. We will discuss RESTful web services in detail in *Chapter 8, Getting started with REST Testing*.

Java Script Object Notation

Java Script Object Notation (JSON) is a lightweight data exchange format similar to XML. It is based on a subset of JavaScript language. JSON uses key value pairs to represent data which are carried inside the message. The following example shows how the XML payload of a SOAP message can be represented in JSON:

```
<p:echoString xmlns:p="http://test.org">
    <data>soapui<data>
</p:echoString>
```

The corresponding JSON format of the preceding XML payload is represented by:

```
{"p:echoString":{"@xmlns":{"p":"test.org"}, "data":{"$":"soapui"}}}
```

You may refer to `http://www.json.org` for more details about JSON.

Web Services Description Language

According to the WSDL 1.1 specification, WSDL is defined as:

> *WSDL is an XML format for describing network services as a set of endpoints operating on messages containing either document-oriented or procedure-oriented information. The operations and messages are described abstractly, and then bound to a concrete network protocol and message format to define an endpoint. Related concrete endpoints are combined into abstract endpoints (services)*

In simple terms, WSDL provides a formal definition of the web service through abstract and concrete definitions of the interface. The following diagram shows the main structure of a WSDL document:

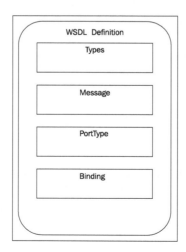

WSDL is an XML document with a `<definitions>` element at the root and the child elements, `<types>`, `<message>`, `<portType>`, and `<binding>`. These can be explained as follows:

- The `<types>` element is used to define the data types used by the web service usually through a XML schema. The schema can be defined inline as a child element of `<types>` or can be imported from an external URL.

- The `<message>` element defines an abstract representation of all the messages used by the web service. A message consists of logical parts, each of which is associated with a definition within some type in the XML schema of the web service. The following image is an example of a message:

```
<wsdl:message name="echoStringRequest">
<wsdl:part name="parameters" element="ns:echoString"/>
</wsdl:message>
<wsdl:message name="echoStringResponse">
<wsdl:part name="parameters" element="ns:echoStringResponse"/>
</wsdl:message>
```

- The `<portType>` element is an abstract representation of the operations and message exchange patterns used in the web service. Operations represent a specific action performed by a web service and which can be related to the public methods used by a program. Operations have input and output parameters and those are represented as messages. Hence, an operation consists of sets of input and output messages. This is evident from the following image:

```
<wsdl:portType name="SampleServicePortType">
<wsdl:operation name="echoString">
<wsdl:input message="ns:echoStringRequest" wsaw:Action="urn:echoString"/>
<wsdl:output message="ns:echoStringResponse" wsaw:Action="urn:echoStringResponse"/>
</wsdl:operation>
</wsdl:portType>
```

In the preceding example, the `SampleServicePortType` element includes a single child element, `<wsdl:operation name="echoString">`, which itself includes two child elements to define the input and output messages processed by the `echoString` operation.

- The `<binding>` element connects the abstract web service interface defined by `<portType>` and `<message>` elements into a physical transport protocol. A binding represents a particular transport technology that the service uses to communicate. For example, SOAP v1.1 is one such commonly used binding.

We will discuss about the WSDL in detail in *Chapter 2*, *The Sample Project*, using the one that is used in the sample project.

Message exchanging patterns

As we have already discussed, the web services communicate with each other and the other programs by sending messages. If we consider two SOAP processing nodes, the communication pattern between the two entities can be defined as a **message exchanging pattern** (**MEP**). The primary message exchanging patterns are:

- Request-response
- Fire and forget

In a request-response pattern, when a source entity (service requester) transmits a message to a destination (service provider), the provider should respond to the requester. This is the most commonly used message exchanging pattern and we will use this in most of the examples in this book.

In the following diagram, a service requester sends a SOAP request message to a service provider:

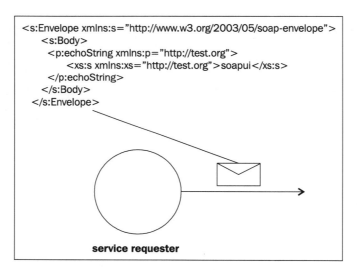

Upon receiving the SOAP request message, the service provider responds with a SOAP response as shown in the following diagram:

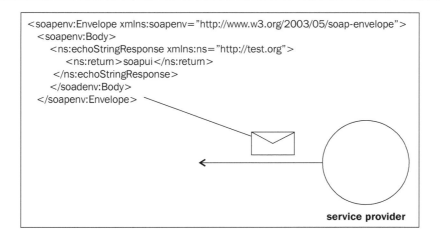

```
<soapenv:Envelope xmlns:soapenv="http://www.w3.org/2003/05/soap-envelope">
  <soapenv:Body>
    <ns:echoStringResponse xmlns:ns="http://test.org">
      <ns:return>soapui</ns:return>
    </ns:echoStringResponse>
  </soadenv:Body>
</soapenv:Envelope>
```

service provider

When a response to a request message is not expected from a web service (or service provider), it is known as a fire and forget message exchange pattern. For example, if we send a ping request to a web service, we do not expect a response message back.

SOAP Faults

Before concluding our discussion on web services and the associated concepts, we should look at the fault handling mechanism of web services. Faults can be returned by web services due to various reasons. For example, if the request message does not conform to the XML schema of web service, the service responds back with a SOAP Fault. The SOAP Fault element is used to carry such faults occurred during web service communication. This element must be included inside body of a SOAP message. A typical SOAP 1.1 Fault message consists of the following child elements:

- `faultcode`: The `faultcode` element is used to define the type of the fault. For example, if the problem of message transmission is due to the server, the associated faultcode is `Server`. Similarly, we can use `VersionMismatch`, `MustUnderstand` and `Client` error codes as appropriate.

- `faultstring`: The `faultstring` element is intended to provide a human readable explanation about the fault.

- `faultactor`: The `faultactor` element provides an indication about the responsible party who caused the fault to occur in the message path.

- `detail`: The `detail` element is used to carry application specific error information related to the body element. For example, if the payload of the SOAP request is unable cannot be processed by web service, the associated response should include the detail element inside the SOAP Fault.

In the case of SOAP v1.2 messaging, `faultcode` is renamed to `Code` and `faultstring` is renamed to `Reason`. In addition to that, a SOAP v1.2 Fault message can include the optional child elements, `Node`, `Role`, and `Detail`. A detailed explanation of SOAP 1.1 Faults can be found at `http://www.w3.org/TR/2000/NOTE-SOAP-20000508/#_Toc478383507`. SOAP 1.2 Faults are explained in detail at `http://www.w3.org/TR/soap12-part1/#soapfault`.

Approaches of testing web services

We discussed a set of concepts most associated with web services. Now, it is time to look in to the testing aspects of web services. As we noticed, web services are loosely coupled and autonomous components which are individual units of business logic in SOA. This facilitates a distinguished approach for testing web services. Because of the loosely coupled nature, the services do not maintain tight, cross-service dependencies with each other. Therefore, once a particular web service is implemented, it can be tested independent from others.

This gives the ability to testers to follow a component level testing methodology. Before moving into various integrations, a web service can be tested to verify both functional and non-functional requirements. Once the service is enhanced with different attributes such as security policies, then such a service can also be tested individually to ensure that it functions properly before taking the integration scenarios into account. This gives great flexibility for testers and provides agility to testing processes.

We can identify a set of common approaches for testing web services as follows:

- Unit testing
- Functional testing of web services
- Integration testing of web services
- Performance testing

Let's discuss each of these approaches in detail.

Unit testing of web services

A web service is a unit of business logic and it consists of one or more operations. These operations must be tested individually in order to make sure the intended business problems are addressed by web service operations. Therefore, similar to how individual methods in a computer program are tested as units, web service operations must also be unit tested. Unit tests can be developed using the unit test framework associated with the programming language which is used to implement the web services. For example, if web services are written in Java, JUnit framework can be used as the unit testing framework. Generally, it is the responsibility of the author of the web service to write a sufficient number of unit tests to cover the logic of the web service operations.

Functional testing

Once a web service is deployed in a service container, it is subjected to a comprehensive functional verification. The purpose of functional testing of a web service is to ensure that the expected business functionality is given by the web service. There are many approaches to perform functional testing as explained below.

Tool assisted testing

The primary objective of using tools for web service testing is to support the automatic generation and submission of web service requests. As the web service interface is a machine readable XML document, it is not an easy task to read the WSDL and derive tests manually. Therefore, tools can be used to point to the WSDL and generate the corresponding requests automatically, so that the testers can send them to the service with or without alterations. soapUI is a good example of such a testing tool, which can be used in functional testing of web services.

Using client APIs provided by service container middleware

The life for a web service is given by the service container middleware where the service is hosted. Usually, the middleware providers ship the associated client API libraries which can be used to invoke web services programmatically without using any third party tool.

Integration testing of web services

Web services do not essentially run alone. Instead they are integrated with multiple components such as brokers or service coordinators. Once a service is integrated or joined with another component, we should carry out tests to make sure that such integrations do not break the system. For example, in a service-oriented solution, if a service consumer application sends a message to a web service but the message does not conform to the advertised schema of the web service. In this case, the web service usually responds with a SOAP fault. However, if we want to take such a request and transform the request SOAP message such that it is valid according to the schema, then we do not want to ask the consumers of our web service to change the client applications as the service schema is modified. This type of message transformation is achieved by using a broker component, in other words, enterprise service bus (**ESB**) middleware. According to the transformation rules defined in the enterprise service bus, the request is converted into the correct format and forwarded to the web service. This is a typical example of web service integration. In order to test this type of integration, the request message should be forwarded to the ESB component instead of directly sending it to the web service. Tools such as soapUI can easily be used to send the messages to desired target locations appropriately.

Performance testing of web services

Once we are satisfied with the functional aspects of the web service, it should be tested thoroughly for performance. This includes load and stress testing the web service as well as measuring the performance under various conditions. We can use various open source or commercial tools in web services performance testing. Apache JMeter (found at `http://jmeter.apache.org/`) is a good example of an open source testing tool which can be used to test web services. The functional tests which we create on soapUI can easily be extended to test the performance of web services. We will discuss the performance testing capabilities of soapUI in detail in *Chapter 5, Load and Performance Testing with soapUI*.

The common challenges of Web services testing

When compared to traditional testing approaches, there are some unique challenges associated with web services testing.

Use of external web services

The autonomous and loosely coupled nature of web services introduces a greater level of scalability and extensibility to the system. All services included in a system are not necessarily built in-house. Some web services can be developed and hosted by third parties. These services can be dynamically discovered and used according to the business requirements. Though this accelerates the delivery of solutions, testing such a system becomes complex because the quality assurance and availability of the third party services are out of your control.

Implications of using complex standards and protocols

Web services, especially SOAP-based services can use various WS-* specifications. When testing web services which adhere to specifications such as WS-Security, the tester should possess a fair amount of knowledge about the standards and concepts to carry out testing effectively. This introduces a higher learning curve for testers to get started with the testing of web services.

Web services can also be exposed over multiple transport protocols. Thus, testing is not limited to one particular transport such as HTTP. The same web service can be made accessible over transports such as JMS or VFS which requires changes in the testing setup as well as a different set of test scenarios.

Headless nature of web services

In traditional web application testing, test scenarios can be identified quite easily by studying the GUI of the components. As we discussed previously, the operations of web services are exposed to the outside world via machine-readable service contracts (such as WSDLs). Thus, during the early stages of web services development, testers need to use WSDLs as the reference for the derivation of test scenarios which can be difficult as compared to exploring a GUI.

As we proceed with the chapters of this book, we will learn how soapUI addresses some of the aforementioned challenges and make the life of a web services tester easier.

We have discussed the fundamentals of SOA and web services testing. Now, we are ready to explore the world of web services testing with soapUI.

What is soapUI?

The primary objective of designing testing tools is to assist people in testing software by reducing the time taken by test execution. There are different types of tools which can be used for functional and non-functional testing. Some of the tools are designed to automate user interface based interactions and some are used to derive various types of requests messages automatically and transmit them to applications with or without modifications. Some tools support both of these aspects.

soapUI is a tool which can be used for both functional and non-functional testing. It is not limited to web services, though it is the de-facto tool used in web services testing. In web services testing, soapUI is capable of performing the role of both client and service. It enables users to create functional and non-functional tests quickly and in an efficient manner by using a single environment.

The first release of soapUI (v1.0) was in October 2005. Ole Lensmer, while working in a project related to SOA, felt the need for a testing tool to support agile development. Therefore, he started to develop soapUI in his spare time. Eventually, the project was open sourced and the community grew. Ever since, a number of versions have been released with various new features and enhancements and the newest version of soapUI is 4.0.1 at the time of writing this book.

The originator of soapUI, Ole Lensmer was managing the project releases through a company called Eviware for the past few years. In July 2011, Eviware was acquired by SmartBear Software (`http://smartbear.com/`) and now soapUI is part of SmartBear Software.

soapUI is a free and open source utility, which means you can utilize the various features provided by the tool freely as well as you are allowed to make modifications to the source code of soapUI and suit it according to your requirements. soapUI is licensed under the terms of the GNU **Lesser General Public License (LGPL)**. It has been implemented purely using Java platform hence it runs on most operating systems out of the box.

It should be noted that soapUI is also distributed as a non-free commercial version known as soapUI Pro, which basically provides users with custom utilities and enhanced production level testing capabilities. All our discussions and examples are based on the free version of soapUI for your convenience.

soapUI v4.0.1 was the newest version at the time of writing the book. Therefore, it is used throughout the context of this book. However, we will not discuss any version specific topics, so the older 3.x versions of soapUI can also be used to try out the sample projects and demonstrations.

Capabilities of soapUI

The primary goal of the authors of soapUI is to provide users with a simple and user-friendly utility which can be used to create and run functional as well as non-functional tests through a single test environment. Based on that objective, soapUI has become the world's leading SOA and web service testing tool. soapUI can be installed with no configuration overhead in most of the common operating systems which allow users to start using the tool without spending time on configuring various installation prerequisites.

By using the easy-to-use Java Swing-based GUI, you can start creating functional tests with zero coding. Eventually, the same functional tests can be used for load and performance testing through the same test environment. This gives users a great flexibility since all functional and non-functional tests can be managed through a single point of access.

Let's look at some of the important features of soapUI which we are planning to discuss in the following chapters.

- **Complete coverage of functional aspects of web services and web applications**: soapUI supports most of the standards used in web applications, such as message transmission through HTTP, HTTPS transport as well as JMS. It also supports testing SOAP and RESTful web services. Specifically, soapUI supports most of the web service specifications such as WS-Security, WS-Addressing, among others.

- **Service mocking**: Using soapUI mock services, you can simulate the web services before they are actually implemented. This gives you the ability to test the web service consumer applications without waiting until the web service providers are implemented.

- **Scripting**: Either using Groovy or JavaScript, soapUI allows you to do various pre- or post-processing test configurations such as dynamic mock responses, initialize or cleanup tests, dynamic mock operation dispatching, and so on.

- **Functional testing** : soapUI lets you do functional verifications against web services, web applications, and JDBC data sources. You can validate responses of your tests using various in-built and custom assertions. It also allows you to add conditional test steps to control the test execution flow.

- **Performance testing**: With just a few clicks, you can generate performance and load tests quickly using soapUI.

- **Test automation**: soapUI can be integrated into automated test frameworks such as JUnit, and the tests can also be launched through Apache Maven and Apache Ant build frameworks. It can also be integrated into continuous integration tools such as Hudson or Bamboo.

In addition to the preceding features, the proprietary version of soapUI, soapUI Pro, provides users with data-driven testing capabilities, HTTP recording, and test reporting facilities which are not in scope of this book.

Installing soapUI

We looked at the major features provided by soapUI and discussed the tool in general. It is time to explore the easy and straightforward soapUI installation on some of the popular operating systems.

System requirements

To be able to run soapUI, you should have **Java Development Kit (JDK)** v1.6 running in your system. As soapUI is implemented in Java, it runs on many operating systems including Windows XP, Windows Vista, Windows 7, Windows Server 2003, Windows Server 2008, various Linux flavors such as Ubuntu, Red Hat, Fedora, SuSE, and CentOS, and Mac OS X v10.4 or higher.

We can summarize the system requirements to install and run soapUI as follows:

Operating System	Java version	Memory	Processor	Disk Space
Microsoft Windows XP Microsoft Windows Vista Microsoft Windows Server 2003 and Microsoft Windows Server 2008	JDK v1.6.x	512 MB (minimum)	1 GHz or higher, 32 or 64-bit processor	200 MB hard disk space (minimum)

Operating System	Java version	Memory	Processor	Disk Space
Linux: Ubuntu Red Hat Fedora CentOS and SuSE	JDK v1.6.x	512 MB (minimum)	1 GHz or higher, 32 or 64-bit processor	240 MB hard disk space (minimum)
Mac OS: Mac OS X v10.4 or higher Mac OS X Server v10.4 or higher	JDK v1.6.x	512 MB (minimum)	1 GHz or higher, 32 or 64-bit processor	140 MB hard disk space (minimum)

Let's discuss the installation procedure of soapUI in each of the preceding operating systems in detail.

Installing soapUI on Linux

soapUI is distributed as two different installers for your convenience. You could either download the binary archive (ZIP) of the installer or the installer script.

First, we will look at the installation procedure of the binary archive. Perform the following steps:

1. Download the Linux binary zip version (for example `soapui-4.0.1-linux-bin.zip`) of the latest soapUI release from `http://www.soapui.org`.

2. Extract the downloaded binary distribution into a directory in your local file system, for example `/home/user/soapui`.

 We will refer to the extracted directory as `SOAPUI_HOME`.

3. Go to `SOAPUI_HOME/bin` and run the `soapui.sh` startup script as follows: `./soapui.sh`. This will launch the soapUI graphical user interface.

> If you encounter a **Permission denied** error when running the
> `soapui.sh` script, make sure to change the file permission
> mode by granting executable privileges to the user by
> executing the `chmod` command as `chmod 755 soapui.sh`.

You can also install soapUI using the Linux installer by performing the
following steps:

1. Download a soapUI Linux installer (for example `soapUI-x32-4_0_1.sh`)
   from `http://www.soapui.org`.

2. After the file is downloaded, give executable permissions by running the
   command, `chmod 755 soapUI-x32-4_0_1.sh`.

3. Run the installer as follows: `./soapUI-x32-4_0_1.sh`.

4. This will launch the installer UI as shown in the following screenshot:

Now, you can proceed through the installation wizard. You will be asked to accept
the license agreement at the next step of the wizard. Simply click on **I accept the
agreement** option and click on **Next**. You will be required to specify a destination
directory for soapUI to be installed.

At the next step of the installation wizard, you can select which components you need to include in soapUI, such as; Hermes JMS, soapUI source files, and tutorials. Simply accept all options and click on **Next**. You will be prompted with the license agreement for Hermes components at the next step. Accept the license agreement and click on **Next** to proceed through the wizard. Then, you will be asked to specify a directory for soapUI tutorials. Enter a location which is in your filesystem and click on **Next**. You will be asked for a directory where soapUI symlinks are created for executables such as the soapui.sh file. Enter a directory and click on **Next**. You can check the **Create a desktop icon** checkbox to create an icon on the desktop so can you can easily launch soapUI. Finally, click on the **Next** button to start the installation.

The soapUI installation screen will look like the following screenshot:

soapUI installation on Windows

Similar to the preceding installation procedure on Linux, soapUI can be installed on a Windows operating system either using Windows installer or Windows binary archive.

Let's look at the installation steps of Windows binary archive. They are as follows:

1. Download the Windows binary zip version (for example `soapui-4.0.1-windows-bin.zip`) of the latest soapUI release from `http://www.soapui.org`.

2. Extract the downloaded binary distribution into a directory in your local filesystem, for example `C:/soapui`.

> We will refer to the extracted directory as `SOAPUI_HOME`.
> This will launch the soapUI GUI.

3. Go to `SOAPUI_HOME/bin` and run the `soapui.bat` startup script by executing the command: `soapui.bat`.

The steps for soapUI installation using the Windows installer are almost the same as the steps given in the Linux installer. You just need to double-click on the installer (`soapUI-x32-4_0_1.exe`) and it will launch the soapUI installation wizard.

Installing soapUI on MacOS

soapUI installation on Mac OS is straightforward and similar to the preceding steps which we described for Linux and Windows installers.

A glance at soapUI user interface

soapUI is a self-explanatory testing tool. The easy-to-use user interface makes it simple to work with soapUI for any type of user. With a few clicks, you can start testing a web service or a web application with minimum effort. This highly usable and flexible user interface helped soapUI to become the most user-friendly and easier SOA and web service testing tool among the testing community.

Once soapUI is launched, you will be shown the starter user interface as shown in the following screenshot:

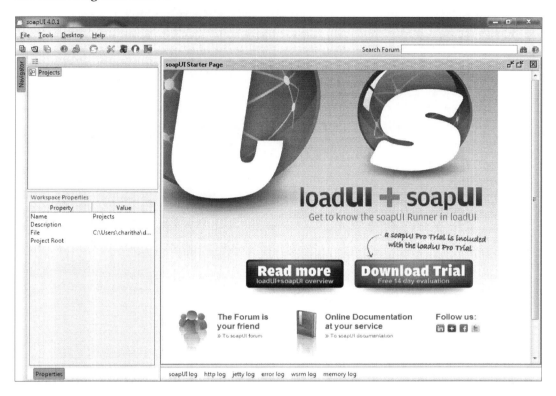

In soapUI, all tests are organized under a central element, known as **Projects**. Just by right-clicking on the **Projects** node in the left-hand side pane in soapUI GUI, a new soapUI project can be created as shown in the following screenshot:

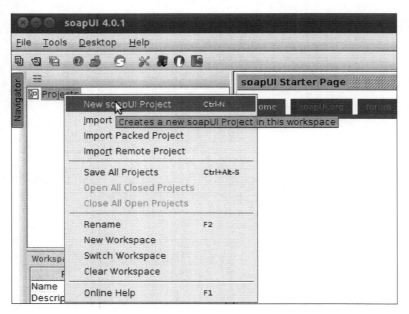

I will leave it to you to navigate through the rest of the UI elements on your own before starting with sample projects. You will find a lot of materials on the soapUI official website related to these features. We will explore through the soapUI user interface as we proceed through the demonstrations and samples in the rest of the chapters.

Summary

Web services are the individual units of business logic in SOA. In order to test web services, we must possess a good understanding about SOA and web services as well as the associated technological components. This chapter has been dedicated to build that foundation.

We started to look into soapUI, the world's leading and most complete SOA and web services testing tool. We discussed the primary goals and objectives of using soapUI in web services testing. We looked at a bit of history of soapUI and its distribution models. Finally, the steps of installing soapUI on Linux, Windows, and Mac OS were explained.

Now, we have soapUI running on our systems. Let's get our hands dirty with a sample project in the next chapter.

2
The Sample Project

In this book, we follow a hands-on approach for learning web services testing with soapUI. We strongly recommend you to have your computer with you while reading the book and try out the test scenarios which will be described throughout this book.

In this chapter, we will be covering the following topics:

- Getting the project environment ready
- Designing the web services
- Implementing the web services
- Deploying the web services

As the first step of hands-on learning, we will introduce a sample project in this chapter. Our objective is to build a simple yet comprehensive project which covers the considerable amount of features related to web services testing. We will design and build a sample project with a few web services. We start from scratch, following the code-first web service development approach where we write Java classes first and then deploy them in a web service container.

 There are two ways of developing web services; contract-first and code-first approaches. In a contract-first approach, the web service definition or the WSDL is created initially and the service implementation is done after that. In a code-first approach, the service implementation classes are developed at the beginning and usually the WSDL is automatically generated by the service container in which the web service is deployed. In our sample project, we will follow the second approach, code-first web service development, since it is relatively easier when creating web services from scratch.

We will not discuss any testing aspects within this chapter. Our focus is to build the foundation for the later chapters in this book, where we plan to use soapUI to test the sample project. If you think that you can move ahead with soapUI without spending time on the web services sample project, you will just use the outcome of the project, which are a set of web services.

Downloading the example code

You can download the example code files for all Packt books you have purchased from your account at http://www.PacktPub.com. If you purchased this book elsewhere, you can visit http://www.PacktPub.com/support and register to have the files e-mailed directly to you.

If you decided to skip the sample project and just use the resulting web services, the following steps will help you to quickly deploy and use the web services with soapUI:

1. Download the web services sample from http://www.PacktPub.com/support. Extract WebServicesSample-Deliverable.zip to your local file system. You will find HotelReservation.aar file and dbscripts folder at the root of the extracted folder.

2. Run dbscripts/HotelReservationDBSchema.sql on your MySQL database server to create the sample database and tables.

3. Modify the values of mysql.host, mysql.port, mysql.username, and mysql.password properties in mysql.properties file which can be found inside conf folder of HotelReservation.aar.

4. Deploy HotelReservation.aar in Apache Axis2 (see *Deploying web services* section at the end of this chapter to find out how to deploy web services in Apache Axis2) and use it in all the soapUI tests which we will be working in the rest of the chapters.

5. You can refer to the README.txt of WebServicesSample-Deliverable.zip for more information about the installation procedure.

The problem domain

Our project will be based on a hypothetical Hotel Reservation System, which is targeted for use by an administrative staff of a hotel. The system consists of three basic functions as follows:

1. Guest management

2. Room management

3. Reservation management

Let's look at the high level architecture of the sample hotel reservation application that we are going to discuss in this chapter:

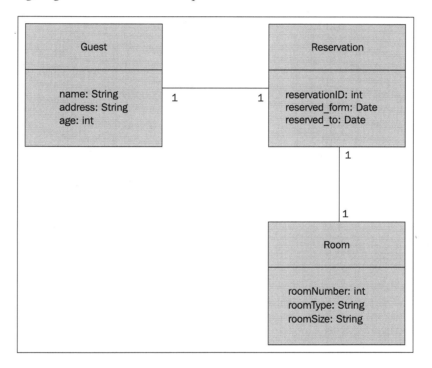

The hotel reservation system comprises of three fundamental entities; Guest, Room, and Reservation. Each guest is identified by name, address, and age. The rooms are identified by room number, room type, and room size. A room reservation is done by assigning a guest to a room.

We are not going to make our project too complicated since our focus is to derive a set of web services for testing with soapUI in the next chapters. Therefore, we deliberately omit some interrelationships between these entities. For example, we assume that a guest can do only one reservation at a time.

Project pre-requisites

Before starting to implement the project, let's make the project environment ready.

Java

We are going to develop the sample project using Java. Therefore, make sure to install JDK1.6 or later version in your machine.

Apache Ant

We will be using Apache Ant to build our project. Of course, you may use any build tool you prefer.

You can download the latest version of Apache Ant from `http://ant.apache.org/bindownload.cgi` and follow the installation guide to set up Ant on your machine.

MySQL

MySQL will be used as the database management system in our sample project. All data used in sample hotel reservation system will be stored in a MySQL database. Therefore, we should set up MySQL in our machines. We can download MySQL from `http://www.mysql.com/downloads/mysql/` and follow the instructions given in the installation guide to set it up on your machine.

Setting up Apache Axis2

There are numerous web service frameworks which can be used in web services development and deployment. Apache CXF (`http://cxf.apache.org/`) and Apache Axis2 (`http://axis.apache.org/axis2/java/core/`) are two examples of popular open source web service frameworks. The pure RESTful web service frameworks such as RESTeasy (`https://www.jboss.org/resteasy/`) can also be used in web services implementation.

We will use Apache Axis2 web services framework in our sample project because Apache Axis2 is primarily a SOAP based web services engine and our sample project is focused on a set of SOAP-based web services. Let's set up Axis2 on our machine according to the following steps:

1. You can download the binary distribution of Apache Axis2 from `http://axis.apache.org/axis2/java/core/download.cgi`. Download the binary and extract it into a folder in your file system.

 Apache Axis2-1.6.1 was the latest version at the time of writing the book. You may download the same or the latest version.

2. Let the extracted folder of the Axis2 binary distribution be `AXIS2_HOME`. Open a command window or shell and change the directory to `AXIS2_HOME/bin`.

3. Export the `AXIS2_HOME` environment variable as follows:

   In Linux:

   ```
   export AXIS2_HOME=/home/user/axis2-1.6.1
   ```

   In Windows:

   ```
   set AXIS2_HOME=/home/user/axis2-1.6.1
   ```

4. Start Axis2 server by executing `axis2server.sh` or `axis2server.bat` as follows:

   ```
   sh axis2server.sh
   ```

Setting up project source directories

As of now, we have configured the Java runtime environment, Apache Ant, MySQL database management system, and Apache Axis2. Now, we are going to set up the source folder structure of our sample web services development project so that we can start adding code.

1. Create a directory in your file system, let's name it as `sample-project`.

2. Create the following sub-directories under the `sample-project` folder:

   - **src**: It is used to store the java source files
   - **build**: The ant `build.xml` file will be stored here
   - **conf**: It is used to store all configuration files

Designing the web services

Our sample hotel reservation system is implemented using SOAP-based web services. As per the three basic entities used in the system, we can plan to have three web services explained as follows:

- **GuestManagementService**:

  `GuestManagementService` will be used to add, delete, or retrieve the details of guests in system. This web service consists of the following methods:

    - `addGuest` (name, address, age)
    - `getGuestDetails` (name)
    - `deleteGuest` (name)

- **RoomManagementService**:

  Adding, deleting, and retrieving the details of rooms are managed by the `RoomManagementService` which includes the following methods:

    - `addRoom` (roomNumber, roomType, roomSize)
    - `getRoomDetails` (roomNumber)
    - `deleteRoom` (roomNumber)

- **ReservationService**:

  `ReservationService` is used to manage the room reservations of the system, such as creating a new reservation, finding out the reservation details of a particular room, and removing an existing reservation. The following methods are included in this web service:

    - `addReservation` (roomNumber, guestName, reserved_from, reserved_to)
    - `getReservationDetails` (roomNumber)
    - `removeReservation` (reservationID)

Creating the database

We use a MySQL database to store the information in our sample hotel management system. Let's create the database and add three tables corresponding to the previous three entities.

1. Open a MySQL shell or an editor and enter the following statement:

   ```
   create database HOTEL_RESERVATION_DB;
   ```

2. Add the following three tables to the database:

```
USE HOTEL_RESERVATION_DB;

CREATE TABLE IF NOT EXISTS GUEST_T(
         name VARCHAR(100) NOT NULL,
             address VARCHAR(200),
             age INT NOT NULL,
             PRIMARY KEY(name));

CREATE TABLE IF NOT EXISTS ROOM_T(
             room_number INT NOT NULL,
             room_type VARCHAR(100) NOT NULL,
             room_size varchar(100) NOT NULL,
             PRIMARY KEY(room_number));

CREATE TABLE IF NOT EXISTS RESERVATION_T(
         res_id INT NOT NULL AUTO_INCREMENT,
             guest_name VARCHAR(100) NOT NULL,
             room_no INT NOT NULL,
             reserved_from DATE NOT NULL,
             reserved_to DATE NOT NULL,
             PRIMARY KEY(res_id),
             FOREIGN KEY(guest_name) references
GUEST_T(name),
             FOREIGN KEY(room_no) references ROOM_T(room_
number));
```

Now, we have the database schema ready for our system. Let's proceed with implementing the web services.

Implementing the web services

As we have seen under *Designing the web services* section, we are going to use three different web services to handle the guest, room, and reservation management functions. We have also discussed that three MySQL tables are used to store information in each of these web services. Let's put together all these elements and start to implement our system.

First, we should define the guest, room, and reservation Java beans which are used as data transferring objects in our system.

The complete source of all Java bean classes can be found at `src\com\sample\reservation\dto` folder of the code bundle.

- **Guest.java**:

  `Guest.java` is a Java bean which represents a guest entity in our system. The class consists of the name, address, and age variables as well as their corresponding getter/setter methods.

```
 package com.sample.reservation.dto;

public class Guest {

    private String name;
    private String address;
    private int age;

    public Guest(String name, String address, int age) {
        }

    public Guest() {

    }

    public String getName() {
    }

    public void setName(String name) {
    }

    public String getAddress() {
        }

    public void setAddress(String address) {
    }

    public int getAge() {
        }

    public void setAge(int age) {
    }
}
```

- This is a simple Java bean and the code itself explains the purpose of this particular class. You may save this class under the src folder according to the package structure.

  Similarly, let's add Room and Reservation bean classes.

- **Room.java**:

  Room.java is a Java bean which represents a room entity in our system. The code for the same is as follows:

```java
package com.sample.reservation.dto;

public class Room {

    private int roomNumber;
    private String roomType;
    private String roomSize;

    public Room(int roomNumber, String roomType, String roomSize)
{


    }

    public Room(){

    }

    public int getRoomNumber() {
            }
    public void setRoomNumber(int roomNumber) {
    }

    public String getRoomType() {
    }

    public void setRoomType(String roomType) {

    }

    public String getRoomSize() {

    }

    public void setRoomSize(String roomSize) {

    }
}
```

- **Reservation.java**:

Reservation.java is a Java bean for the reservation entity in our system. The code for the same is as follows:

```
package com.sample.reservation.dto;


public class Reservation {

    private int reservationID;
    private String guestName;
    private int roomNumber;
    private Date reserved_from;
    private Date reserved_to;


    public Date getReserved_from() {
    }

    public void setReserved_from(Date reserved_from) {
    }

    public Date getReserved_to() {
    }

    public void setReserved_to(Date reserved_to) {

    }



    public int getReservationID() {

    }

    public void setReservationID(int reservationID) {
    }

    public String getGuestName() {
    }
```

```
    public void setGuestName(String guestName) {
    }

    public int getRoomNumber() {

    }

    public void setRoomNumber(int roomNumber) {

    }
}
```

Since we have the three Java beans ready, the method signatures of the three web service classes, which we are going to implement shortly, will look like the following. These classes will be exposed as web services in our sample application.

- **GuestManagementService**:

    `GuestManagementService` class consists of `addGuest`, `getGuestDetails`, and `deleteGuest` methods.

    ```
    public class GuestManagementService {



    //A new guest is added to the system by invoking this method. The
    //method returns true if the guest is added successfully.
        public boolean addGuest(String name, String address, int age){

        }

    //Details of an existing guest are retrieved using this method
        public Guest getGuestDetails(String guestName){

        }

    //An existing guest is deleted by invoking this method. We can
    //implement this method to return a boolean similar to addGuest()
    //method. However, inorder to demonstrate IN-ONLY message exchange
    //pattern, let's keep it void.
        public void deleteGuest(String guestName){

        }
    }
    ```

- **RoomManagementService**:

RoomManagementService includes three methods, addRoom, getRoomDetails, and deleteRoom as follows:

```
public class RoomManagementService {

//A new room is added to the system by invoking this method.
//The method returns true if the room is added successfully

    public boolean addRoom(int roomNumber, String roomType, String roomSize){

    }

//Details of an existing room are retrieved using this method

    public Room getRoomDetails(int roomNumber){

    }

// An existing room can be deleted by invoking this method

    public void deleteRoom(int roomNumber){

    }
}
```

- **ReservationService**:

ReservationService consists of addReservation, getReservationDetails, and removeReservation methods follows:

```
public class ReservationService {

//A hotel room is reserved for a guest by invoking this method
    public boolean addReservation(int roomNumber, String guestName, Date reserved_from, Date reserved_to){

    }
//Details of an existing reservation can be found out by calling
//this method
public Reservation getReservationDetails(int RoomNumber) {

    }
```

```
// An existing reservation can be deleted by invoking this method

public void removeReservation(int reservationID) {

}

}
```

Web services fault handling

Did we think about the scenarios such as trying to add a guest who is already available in GUEST_T table? Or did we try to delete a non-existing room? We need to handle these exceptional cases and provide users with meaningful errors. We can implement exception classes associated with each of the above web service classes as follows.

Create a new package, com.sample.reservation.exception and add the following three exception classes:

- **Exception 1**:

```
public class GuestManagementException extends Exception {

    private String message;

    public GuestManagementException() {

    }

    public GuestManagementException(String message) {

        super(message);

    }

    public String getMessage() {

        return super.getMessage();

    }

    public void setMessage(String message) {

        this.message = message;

    }

}
```

- **Exception 2**:

```
public class RoomManagementException extends Exception {

    private String message;

    public void setMessage(String message) {

        this.message = message;

    }

     public String getMessage() {

        return super.getMessage();

    }

    public RoomManagementException() {

    }

    public RoomManagementException(String message) {

        super(message);

    }


}
```

- **Exception 3**:

```
public class ReservationManagementException extends Exception{
     public ReservationManagementException() {
     }

     public ReservationManagementException(String message) {
         super(message);
     }

    public String getMessage() {
         return super.getMessage();
```

```
    }

    public void setMessage(String message) {
        this.message = message;
    }
    private String message;

}
```

Managing database operations

It is a recommended programming practice to manage all database interactions through a separate module or a class. Therefore, we can have a class dedicated to database storage handling tasks. Let this class be `Storage.java` and have it under a new package, `com.sample.reservation.database`.

The `Storage.java` class is used to establish the connection to the database and execute SQL queries in each method invocation of the web service implementation classes. For example, if the `addGuest()` method of `GuestManagementService` is called, the corresponding `addGuest()` method of the `Storage` class handles the database interactions. Similarly, for all the methods in web service implementation classes, we can have the corresponding methods in `Storage.java` class.

Let's have a look at how we handle the **CRUD (Create Read Update Delete)** operations associated with the `GuestManagementService` using `Storage.java` The complete source code of `Storage.java` class can be found at `src\com\sample\reservation\database\Storage.java` in the code bundle.

```
public class Storage {

//First, we need to establish the jdbc connection with HOTEL_
//RESERVATION_DB
//We will read the MySQL database connection details from a property
//file, which will be placed at the conf directory of Web Service
//Archive file (HotelReservation.aar)
    private Connection getConnection(){
//JDBC connection handling logic will be inserted here
//We read username, password, hostname(or IP) and port of mysql
//database from mysql.properties file which is placed at the conf
//directory of the web service archive.
    }

//The method corresponding to addGuest() in GuestManagementService.
```

```
        // This is used to add a new guest to GUEST_T table

    public boolean addGuest(Guest guest) {
        //Check whether the guest already exists before adding a new
//guest
        if (getGuestDetails(guest.getName()) == null) {
            //Execute INSERT SQL Query to add a new row to
//GUEST_T table
            String sqlStatement = "INSERT INTO GUEST_T VALUES ('"
+ guest.getName()
                    + "','" + guest.getAddress() + "', " + guest.
getAge() + ")";
            statement.execute(sqlStatement);
    }
//The method corresponding to the getGuestDetails() in
//GuestManagementService.

    // This is used to get details of a particular guest from
//GUEST_T table

    public Guest getGuestDetails(String name)  {
        //Execute SELECT SQL Query to retrieve the corresponding row
//from GUEST_T table

        String sqlStatement = "SELECT * FROM GUEST_T WHERE name = '" +
name + "'";
    }
     //The method corresponding to the deleteGuest() in
//GuestManagementService
    //This is used to delete a guest from GUEST_T table
    public void deleteGuest(String name) {
        if (getGuestDetails(name) != null) {

            //Execute DELETE SQL Query to retrieve the
//corresponding row from GUEST_T table

            String sqlStatement = "DELETE FROM GUEST_T WHERE name
= '" + name + "'";
    }
}
```

As `Storage.java` is a JDBC connection handler, it simply manages all the database related transactions involved in our sample project. If a database related error is thrown during these transactions, we handle those errors via a separate exception class, `StorageException.java`.

The complete source code of `StorageException.java` class can be found at `src\com\sample\reservation\exception\StorageException.java` in the code bundle.

Now, you should be able to compile the classes we have implemented up to now. If you are working on this project using an integrated Java development environment (IDE), such as Eclipse, you can compile the project very easily. Make sure to add the MySQL JDBC driver jar to the classpath since it is required to establish the MySQL database connection. You can download the MySQL JDBC driver from `http://www.mysql.com/downloads/connector/j/`.

If you do not wish to use any Java IDE, you could use the ant build script (`build.xml`) given in `build` folder of the code bundle.

 Before making all the service implementation classes available as real web services, it is recommended to test the `Storage.java` class separately to ensure that the database transactions are done properly. You can add a simple Junit test to test each method of `Storage.java`.

Completing the web service implementation classes

Under *Designing web services* section, we looked at the method signatures of all the three web service classes, `GuestManagementService`, `RoomManagementService`, and `ReservationService`. It is time to conclude our discussion on web service implementation classes since we have all the dependent classes ready by now. As an example, we will look at the implementation of `GuestManagementService.java`.

 The complete source code of all the three web service implementation classes can be found under `src\com\sample\reservation` folder of the code bundle.

```
public class GuestManagementService {

    //Adding a new guest to the system.
    //We create a new Guest object and call addGuest() operation of
    //Storage class to insert the new guest record to GUEST_T table

    public boolean addGuest(String name, String address, int age)
```

```
            Guest guest = new Guest();
            guest.setName(name);
            guest.setAddress(address);
            guest.setAge(age);

            Storage storage = new Storage();

                storage.addGuest(guest);
                return true;
                    }

        }


        //retrieving the details of a guest.
        //By calling getGuestDetails() method of Storage class
        // we get the corresponding guest record from GUEST_T table

        public Guest getGuestDetails(String guestName)     {
            Storage storage = new Storage();

                Guest guest = storage.getGuestDetails(guestName);
                  return guest;
                      }


        //Deleting an existing guest.
          //We call deleteGuest() method of Storage class to delete a guest
    //from GUEST_T table

        public void deleteGuest(String guestName)   {

            Storage storage = new Storage();


                Guest guest = storage.getGuestDetails(guestName);
                storage.deleteGuest(guest.getName());
        }
```

Deploying web services

Though we developed all the Java classes included in our sample hotel reservation system, we have not made them web services yet. In other words, still, our three web service implementation classes cannot be invoked by a web service client, such as soapUI. In this section, we make a deployable artifact so that we can deploy the services in a service container such as Apache Axis2.

There are multiple ways of deploying a web service in the Apache Axis2 SOAP engine. We will use the service archive-based deployment mechanism where we create a deployable archive with all service artifacts and copy that into the Axis2 server's deployment folder. In this mechanism, the deployable artifact is known as an `Axis2 Archive` (aar).

In order to deploy an Axis2 service as an `aar` file, a deployment descriptor should be included with it. The Axis2 deployment descriptor is known as `services.xml` and must be placed inside the `META-INF` folder of the `aar` file. The `services.xml` tells the Axis2 engine the details such as what services are included in the service archive, what operations are exposed through the web service, and so on.

Since we have three different web services, we can either deploy them as three Axis2 archives (aar) or include everything in a single archive. In our sample project, we will bundle all service implementation classes and the dependencies to a single service archive. Since we follow the second approach, we need to consider the Axis2 service group concept where we can associate multiple services inside a group and deploy together.

With all these details, the `services.xml` of our web services look like the following.

Note that only the `GuestManagementService` is shown here. The complete `services.xml` file can be found in `conf` folder in the code bundle.

```xml
<serviceGroup name="HotelReservation">
    <service name="GuestManagementService"
            targetNamespace="http://sample.com/reservation/guest">
        <description>
            Guest management web service
        </description>
        <schema schemaNamespace="http://sample.com/reservation/guest/
types"
                elementFormDefaultQualified="true">
            <mapping namespace="http://sample.com/reservation/guest/
types"
                    package="com.sample.reservation.dto"/>
        </schema>
        <messageReceivers>

            <messageReceiver mep="http://www.w3.org/2006/01/wsdl/in-
only"
                            class="org.apache.axis2.rpc.receivers.
RPCInOnlyMessageReceiver"/>
            <messageReceiver mep="http://www.w3.org/2006/01/wsdl/in-
out"
```

```
                                class="org.apache.axis2.rpc.receivers.
RPCMessageReceiver"/>
        </messageReceivers>
        <parameter name="ServiceClass">com.sample.reservation.
GuestManagementService</parameter>
        <operation name="addGuest" mep="http://www.w3.org/2006/01/
wsdl/in-out">
            <actionMapping>urn:addGuest</actionMapping>
            <messageReceiver class="org.apache.axis2.rpc.receivers.
RPCMessageReceiver"/>
        </operation>
        <operation name="getGuestDetails" mep="http://www.
w3.org/2006/01/wsdl/in-out">
            <actionMapping>urn:getGuestDetails</actionMapping>
            <messageReceiver class="org.apache.axis2.rpc.receivers.
RPCMessageReceiver"/>
        </operation>
        <operation name="deleteGuest" mep="http://www.w3.org/2006/01/
wsdl/in-only">
            <actionMapping>urn:deleteGuest</actionMapping>
            <messageReceiver class="org.apache.axis2.rpc.receivers.
RPCInOnlyMessageReceiver"/>
        </operation>
    </service>
</serviceGroup>
```

Here, all web services are grouped under the `<serviceGroup>` element. You can find that the service implementation class is described as a parameter, `<parameter name="ServiceClass">`. A complete explanation of `services.xml` descriptor is beyond the scope of this book. You can find more information on this at `http://axis.apache.org/axis2/java/core/docs/axis2config.html#Service_Configuration`.

After completing `services.xml` for all the three web services, make sure to copy it to `conf` folder in our project structure.

We should also make sure to update the following properties in `conf/mysql.properties` file which we use to read the database connection details:

`mysql.host`: It is the host name or IP address of the mysql database server

`mysql.port`: It is the port in which mysql server is running

`mysql.username`: It is the root user of mysql database

`mysql.password`:It is the password of the root user

Now, we are ready to build the whole project and generate an `Axis2 archive` (aar) file. For that, you can use the ant `build.xml` given under `build` folder of the code bundle. Copy the `build.xml` to the `build` sub-folder in your project folder. When you run `ant` command from `build` directory, it will create `HotelReservation.aar` under the project root directory with the following structure:

```
├── com
│   └── sample
│       └── reservation
│           ├── database
│           │   └── Storage.class
│           ├── dto
│           │   ├── Guest.class
│           │   ├── Reservation.class
│           │   └── Room.class
│           ├── exception
│           │   ├── GuestManagementException.class
│           │   ├── ReservationManagementException.class
│           │   ├── RoomManagementException.class
│           │   └── StorageException.class
│           ├── GuestManagementService.class
│           ├── ReservationService.class
│           └── RoomManagementService.class
├── conf
│   └── mysql.properties
└── META-INF
    ├── MANIFEST.MF
    └── services.xml
```

Once you have `HotelReservation.aar`, you are ready to deploy it in Apache Axis2. You can copy `HotelReservation.aar` to AXIS2_HOME/repository/ services folder.

Take a look at the following example:

```
cd sample-project
    cp HotelReservation.aar /home/user/axis2-1.6.1/repository/
services/
```

> At this point, make sure to copy the MySQL JDBC driver which you may have downloaded from http://www.mysql.com/ downloads/connector/j/ to AXIS2_HOME/lib folder to facilitate jdbc connectivity between web service implementation classes and MySQL database.

If you have already started the server, the services will automatically be deployed. If not, simply restart the Axis2 Server. Open a web browser and access `http://localhost:8080/axis2/services/`, you will find the three web services as shown in the next screenshot:

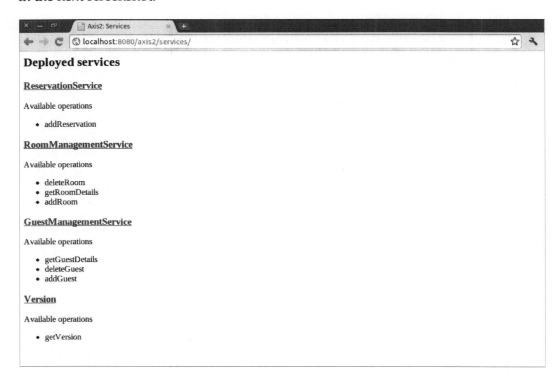

You should be able to see the WSDLs of each of these web services by accessing following URLs:

`http://localhost:8080/axis2/services/GuestManagementService?wsdl`

`http://localhost:8080/axis2/services/RoomManagementService?wsdl`

`http://localhost:8080/axis2/services/ReservationService?wsdl`

Summary

We dedicated this chapter to create a sample project, which used a few web services to implement a simple hotel room reservation system. We started from scratch and created three **Plain Old Java Objects** (**POJOs**). Then we exposed them as web services by deploying in Apache Axis2. These three web services, namely GuestManagementService, RoomManagementService, and ReservationService will be used throughout this book. All our discussions of soapUI will be based on these services. Hence, even if you did not follow the sample project, it is advisable to download WebServicesSample-Deliverable.zip from http://www.PacktPub.com/support, follow the instructions given in README.txt to deploy HotelReservation.aar on Apache Axis2, and get the services ready to try out the soapUI samples which we will discuss in the next chapters.

3
First Steps with soapUI and Projects

As we have completed building our sample web services project, it is time to discover the testing aspects of web services with soapUI. In this chapter, we will look into the basics of web services testing using the features provided by soapUI. We plan to cover the following topics in this chapter:

- Detailed study of the sample guest management web service
- How to build a soapUI project to invoke operations of the sample service
- Study SOAP requests, responses, and faults using the sample service

Invoking web services through soapUI is pretty straightforward as compared to most of the other alternative tools such as Apache JMeter. What we will be focused on is how soapUI features can be utilized in an effective manner so that we can achieve the maximum test coverage in web services testing. In order to fulfill our objectives, it is essential to have a good understanding about the functional aspects of the web services which are going to be tested, as well as the fundamental mechanism of the SOAP request and response handling in soapUI.

Understanding the web services definition

In the previous chapter, we developed three different web services, as follows:

- `GuestManagementService`
- `RoomManagementService`
- `ReservationService`

Out of these three services, we will focus on the WSDL of the
`GuestManagementService` in this chapter. Once you are familiar with interpreting
`GuestManagementService`, you will be able to follow up with the other two services.

If you have not already done so, make sure to start axis2server by running
`axis2server` startup script (`axis2server.bat` or `axis2server.sh`) from
`AXIS2_HOME/bin`.

Open a browser and navigate to `http://localhost:8080/services/`
`GuestManagementService?wsdl`. You will find the structure of the WSDL
of the service similar to the following diagram:

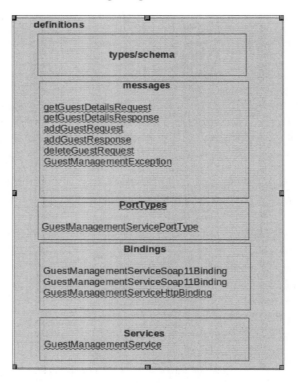

We will look into each of the key elements shown in the preceding diagram
depicting the WSDL structure of the web service.

Schema

First, notice the schema section of the WSDL under the `wsdl:types` element, where
the data types used by web service are explicitly defined. We are not going to dig deep
into the schema of our web service, but let's have a look at the `addGuest` element.

The `addGuest` element has the following XML fragment:

```
<xs:element name="addGuest">
<xs:complexType>
<xs:sequence>
<xs:element minOccurs="0" name="name" nillable="true"
type="xs:string"/>
<xs:element minOccurs="0" name="address" nillable="true"
type="xs:string"/>
<xs:element minOccurs="0" name="age" type="xs:int"/>
</xs:sequence>
</xs:complexType>
</xs:element>
```

We can identify the three elements associated with the `addGuest` root element, `name`, `age` and `address`, in the preceding portion of the schema. If you recall the data types which we defined when implementing `GuestManagementService` in the previous chapter, these data types given in the schema corresponded to what we described there. When we invoke the service, we should send a message which conforms to the service schema. In short, if we send the age of a guest as a string value, the service will respond with a fault since one of the data types of our request does not match with the schema definition. Similarly, I will leave you to go through the other elements defined in the schema of the `GuestManagementService`.

Now, we should understand the other elements in our WSDL. A better way to understand the WSDLs is to start with the `portType` element which defines the service interface.

portType

Let's have a look at the `GuestManagementServicePortType` element. We can identify the abstract definitions of the three operations exposed by `GuestManagementService` under that element, as follows:

- `addGuest`
- `deleteGuest`
- `getGuestDetails`

Under these operations, the input, output, and fault messages which are exchanged between service consumer and provider are defined. As you can see, each of the operations include a fault message. The `addGuest` and `getGuestDetails` operations are defined as request-response MEP since both of them consist of input and output messages. The `deleteGuest` operation is a one-way operation as it does not have an output message. You can correlate this behavior to the method signatures of these operations given in the `GuestManagementService` implementation class.

As we have looked into the `portType` element in the WSDL of our web service, we can proceed with understanding another important element in the service definition.

binding

The `binding` elements describe the concrete details of using a `portType` with a given protocol. In other words, a `portType` element is an abstract definition of a service interface, which does not provide information on how messages are represented on the wire. The `binding` elements associate the `portType` elements with concrete wire protocol definition. There are three bindings which can be identified in our WSDL. These are as follows:

- SOAP 1.1 binding
- SOAP 1.2 binding
- HTTP binding

In our service, both SOAP 1.1 and SOAP 1.2 bindings use HTTP transport only. You can notice it in the following element:

```
<wsdl:binding name="GuestManagementServiceSoap11Binding" type="tns:Gue
stManagementServicePortType">
<soap:binding transport="http://schemas.xmlsoap.org/soap/http"
style="document"/>
```

You will also observe that the default style of the service is given as `document`.

If we study the SOAP 1.1 binding further, we can identify that all three operations of the `GuestManagementService` are defined with concrete message details. For example, `addGuest` operation is described under the SOAP 1.1 binding element as follows:

```
<wsdl:operation name="addGuest">
<soap:operation soapAction="urn:addGuest"  style="document"/>
<wsdl:input>
<soap:body use="literal"/>
</wsdl:input>
<wsdl:output>
<soap:body use="literal"/>
</wsdl:output>
<wsdl:fault name="GuestManagementServiceGuestManagementException">
<soap:fault use="literal" name="GuestManagementServiceGuestManagement
Exception"/>
</wsdl:fault>
</wsdl:operation>
```

As shown in the preceding XML fragment, `urn:addGuest` is the `soapAction` HTTP header defined for the `addGuest` operation. Similarly, all other operations include a `soapAction` HTTP header.

The `addGuest` operation emulates request-response MEP. Therefore, it includes input and output elements. As these requests and responses are SOAP messages, they consist of the `<soap:body>` element. This element defines how the message parts appear inside the SOAP body of the SOAP envelope. The type of encoding that is used to translate the abstract message parts into a concrete representation is specified by the `use` attribute of the SOAP body element.

In short, the `addGuest` operation uses `document/literal` SOAP style/`use` attributes. Therefore, the input message (request) for the `addGuest` operation can be represented as follows:

```
<soapenv:Envelope xmlns:soapenv="http://schemas.xmlsoap.org/soap/
envelope/">
<soapenv:Body>
<a:addGuest xmlns:a="http//sample.com/reservation/guest/types">
<name>John</name>
<address>Colombo, Sri Lanka</address>
<age>32</age>
</a:addGuest>
</soapenv:Body>
</soapenv:envelope>
```

Because the `addGuest` operation is defined as `document` style, the SOAP body simply includes an instance of the `addGuest` element defined under the XML schema of `GuestManagementService`.

A further explanation on all WSDL bindings are out of the scope of this book. Hence, we will limit our discussion on SOAP 1.1 binding to what we have discussed and proceed with the `<wsdl:service>` element.

Service

According to the WSDL 1.1 specification, a service groups a set of related ports together. In our WSDL, we can identify three ports or endpoints described as follows:

```
<wsdl:service name="GuestManagementService">
<wsdl:port name="GuestManagementServiceHttpSoap11Endpoint" binding="tn
s:GuestManagementServiceSoap11Binding">
<soap:address location="http://localhost:8080/
axis2/services/GuestManagementService.
GuestManagementServiceHttpSoap11Endpoint/"/>
```

```
0</wsdl:port>
<wsdl:port name="GuestManagementServiceHttpSoap12Endpoint" binding="tn
s:GuestManagementServiceSoap12Binding">
<soap12:address location="http://localhost:8080/
axis2/services/GuestManagementService.
GuestManagementServiceHttpSoap12Endpoint/"/>
</wsdl:port>
<wsdl:port name="GuestManagementServiceHttpEndpoint" binding="tns:Gues
tManagementServiceHttpBinding">
<http:address location="http://localhost:8080/axis2/services/
GuestManagementService.GuestManagementServiceHttpEndpoint/"/>
</wsdl:port>
</wsdl:service>
```

Under the `service` element, each `port` is assigned to a particular binding and defines the `address` details specific to that binding. For example, the SOAP 1.1 binding of `GuestManagementService` is exposed at the location, `http://localhost:8080/axis2/services/GuestManagementService.GuestManagementServiceHttpSoap11Endpoint`.

Therefore, if you want to invoke `GuestManagementService` by sending a SOAP 1.1 request, you should use the preceding URL.

So far, we have discussed all the important details specific to our web service. We have even constructed a sample SOAP request by adhering to the WSDL of service. However, deriving SOAP requests by hand is a time consuming and complex approach. On the other hand, in a web service equation, the consuming applications of web services should be able to send as well as receive and interpret the SOAP messages. As a result of this, we should use a tool which has the ability to invoke web services and interpret service responses at minimum.

The most trivial use case of soapUI is to support SOAP message delivery. We are going to look into our first soapUI project so that we can send the first SOAP request to `GuestManagementService`.

Creating a soapUI project

All your work which you carry out with soapUI is based on projects. Therefore, projects can be considered as the central masterpiece in soapUI. Whatever you do, except the activities related to tools such as Axis2 WSDL2Java, perform under a project. Let's create our first soapUI project. Perform the following steps to create a project:

1. Start soapUI.

2. Select **File | New soapUI Project** from the main menu.

In a fresh soapUI instance, if you add a new project in this way, the project is added under the default **workspace**. If you want to add the project into a different workspace, you can do so by creating a new workspace or use an existing workspace. We will discuss more about workspaces in the next chapter.

3. Once the **New soapUI Project** dialog box is launched as shown in the following screenshot, enter `HotelReservationProject` as the name of the project. In our example, the initial WSDL will be the definition of `GuestManagementService`. We can find out the web service definition by appending the `?wsdl` suffix at the end of the endpoint URL. Therefore, enter `http://localhost:8080/axis2/services/GuestManagementService?wsdl` as the initial WSDL as shown in the following screenshot:

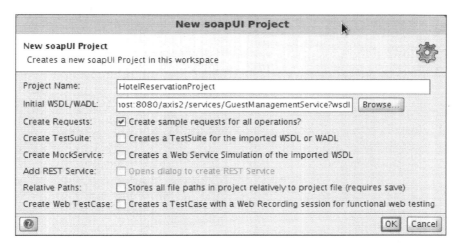

 You should also keep in mind that it is not mandatory to have an initial WSDL for creating a new soapUI project. You can create a soapUI project without an initial WSDL and add WSDL later. Also, if you create the project for testing a RESTful web service or a web application, having an initial WSDL does not make sense. However, an initial WSDL will make testing easier for a novice user if the project is used purely for SOAP based web services testing.

4. You will also find a few selections in the **New soapUI Project** dialog box such as **Create Requests**, **Create TestSuite**, **Create MockService** and so on. We will look into all these options within the next chapters. For now, just select the default option.

5. With the default **Create Requests** option, soapUI generates sample requests for all operations exposed in your web service. In other words, with this option selected, we should be able to see the SOAP requests generated by soapUI which can be used to invoke `addGuest`, `getGuestDetails`, and `deleteGuest` operations of the `GuestManagementService`.

6. Now, we can save our new soapUI project by clicking on **Saves all projects in the current workspace** icon which can be found on the main tool bar. Or else, we can select the project and press *Ctrl + S* to save the individual project. Either way, soapUI saves the project in your filesystem with the name, `<project name>-soapui-project.xml`.

Once the new soapUI project is created with an initial WSDL, you can find that soapUI automatically generates requests for all operations under the two SOAP bindings. In our example, we should be able to see six requests divided among **GuestManagementServiceSoap11Binding** and **GuestManagementServiceSoap12Binding**.

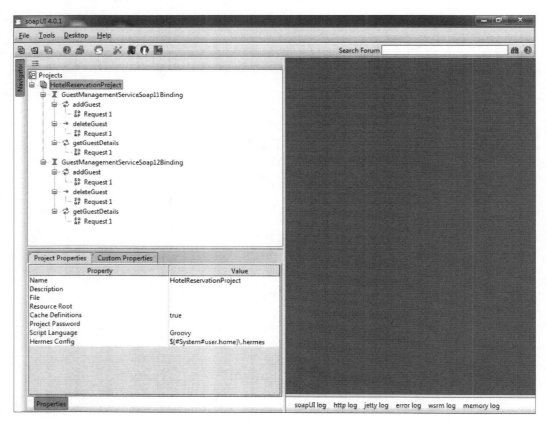

When adding a WSDL or creating a project with an initial WSDL, soapUI scans through all SOAP bindings which appear in the WSDL and finds out the operations exposed by the service. Then it generates the requests corresponding to those operations according to the XML schema of the service.

As we have just discussed, when we have the WSDL of the web service with all bindings, portTypes, service elements, and schema, it is possible to derive a SOAP request by hand. What soapUI does is it handles all the complexities and gets it done for you.

Let's look at the addGuest request generated by soapUI in the following screenshot:

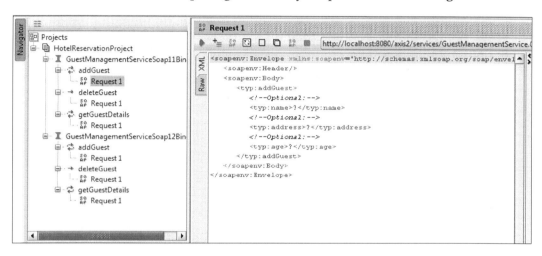

As you can see in the preceding image, the SOAP 1.1 request message is shown at the left-hand side pane of the request editor. You can open the request editor by double-clicking on the corresponding SOAP request in the project tree at the right-hand side pane or by right-clicking on the SOAP request and selecting **Show Request Editor**. Compare the request payload (the <typ:addGuest> element) of this message with the request which we have derived by hand at the end of the *Understanding the web service definition* section. You will find both of them to be similar.

Invoking the guest management web service

Before going deep inside SOAP requests, we will look into invoking our sample web service. We will invoke the addGuest operation and add a new guest in our sample hotel reservation system. Next, we will get the details of the added guest by calling getGuestDetails operation. Finally, we will delete the guest by invoking the deleteGuest operation. This can be performed as described in the following steps:

1. Select **Request1** which appears under the **addGuest** operation, shown in the left-hand side pane in the soapUI project.

2. In the request editor, which appears at the right-hand side, you will find the SOAP 1.1 request which is supposed to be used in invoking the addGuest operation.

3. The inputs which should be specified by the user are denoted by **?** in the request editor. Replace them with the appropriate input values as shown in the following XML fragment:

```
<soapenv:Envelope xmlns:soapenv="http://schemas.xmlsoap.org/soap/
envelope/" xmlns:typ="http//sample.com/reservation/guest/types">
    <soapenv:Header/>
    <soapenv:Body>
        <typ:addGuest>
            <!--Optional:-->
            <typ:name>Saman</typ:name>
            <!--Optional:-->
            <typ:address>Colombo, Sri Lanka</typ:address>
            <!--Optional:-->
            <typ:age>24</typ:age>
        </typ:addGuest>
    </soapenv:Body>
</soapenv:Envelope>
```

4. By default, soapUI automatically adds the endpoint associated with SOAP 1.1 binding and gives it as the default endpoint for you to direct the request. This is shown in the following screenshot:

If you carefully look at this endpoint, it is the same endpoint which you can find at the `<wsdl:port name="GuestManagmentServiceHtt pSoap11Endpoint">` element under the `<wsdl:service>` element in `GuestManagementService` WSDL. soapUI allows you to edit this endpoint or target your request to a totally different endpoint.

In the situations where your web service container is changed, you will need to change the default endpoint location. For example, say you decide to move away from the Axis2 SOAP engine and use a different service container. In such a case, you can change the endpoint easily through the soapUI request editor. Also, when the same web service is deployed across multiple environments such as Development, Testing, or Production, you can change the target endpoint and submit the request to the service which is deployed in a particular environment.

5. For now, let's proceed with the defaults. Click on the run icon which appears at the top-left corner in the soapUI request pane to submit the request to the given endpoint.

6. Once the request is sent to the endpoint, you will notice the response appears at the right-hand side pane of the soapUI request editor as shown in the following screenshot:

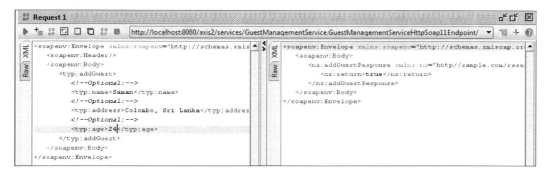

We get the response with `<ns:return>true</ns:return>` as the SOAP body, if a guest is successfully added to the system. Compare this behavior with the method signature of `addGuest` method in the `GuestManagementService` implementation class where we have defined `boolean` as the return value.

Now, we have added a new guest to the system. Let's check if it has actually been added to the system by calling the `getGuestDetails` operation. Perform the following steps to check if a guess has been added to the system:

1. Select **Request1** which appears under the **getGuestDetails** operation in the left-hand side pane in soapUI project.

2. The request editor will show the corresponding SOAP 1.1 request. Replace **?** with the name of the guest which we have added to the system, as shown in the following XML fragment:

```
<soapenv:Envelope xmlns:soapenv="http://schemas.xmlsoap.org/
soap/envelope/" xmlns:typ="http//sample.com/reservation/
guest/types">
   <soapenv:Header/>
   <soapenv:Body>
      <typ:getGuestDetails>
         <!--Optional:-->
         <typ:guestName>Saman</typ:guestName>
      </typ:getGuestDetails>
   </soapenv:Body>
</soapenv:Envelope>
```

3. Click on the run icon to submit the request to the default SOAP 1.1 endpoint.

4. The response will contain the corresponding guest details as follows.

```
<soapenv:Envelope xmlns:soapenv="http://schemas.xmlsoap.org/
soap/envelope/">
   <soapenv:Body>
      <ns:getGuestDetailsResponse xmlns:ns="http//sample.
com/reservation/guest/types">
         <ns:return xsi:type="ns:Guest" xmlns:ax21="http://
exception.reservation.sample.com/xsd" xmlns:xsi="http://www.
w3.org/2001/XMLSchema-instance">
            <ns:address>Colombo, Sri Lanka</ns:address>
            <ns:age>24</ns:age>
            <ns:name>Saman</ns:name>
         </ns:return>
      </ns:getGuestDetailsResponse>
   </soapenv:Body>
</soapenv:Envelope>
```

7. We have invoked both `addGuest` and `getGuestDetails` operations using soapUI. The only remaining operation to be invoked is `deleteGuest`.

Similar to the `addGuest` and `getGuestDetails` operations, select **Request1** under the **deleteGuest** operation in the left-hand side pane of soapUI. Replace **?** of `guestName` element with the name of the guest which we have added to the system, as shown in the following XML fragment:

```
<soapenv:Envelope xmlns:soapenv="http://schemas.xmlsoap.org/soap/
envelope/" xmlns:typ="http//sample.com/reservation/guest/types">
    <soapenv:Header/>
    <soapenv:Body>
        <typ:deleteGuest>
            <!--Optional:-->
            <typ:guestName>Saman</typ:guestName>
        </typ:deleteGuest>
    </soapenv:Body>
</soapenv:Envelope>
```

8. Submit the request to the default SOAP 1.1 endpoint by clicking on the run icon.

This time, you will not get any SOAP response back. Why do we expect this behavior? Think about how we implemented the `deleteGuest` operation in the `GuestManagementService` implementation class. There, we specified the method as void:

```
public void deleteGuest(String guestName){ }
```

If you invoke the `getGuestDetails` operation again for the deleted guest, you can ensure that the guest has actually been removed from the system.

Now, we have invoked all operations of the `GuestManagementService` using soapUI. Similarly, you can try out the other two web services (`RoomManagementService` and `ReservationService`) as well. It will be a good idea to further look into some of the preceding requests and response messages to get a better understanding about web service invocation, as well as the important features provided by soapUI for request and response handling.

A detailed look at SOAP requests and responses

We invoked three operations in `GuestManagementService` using soapUI. As we have observed, `addGuest` and `getGuestDetails` operations are examples for request-response MEP, whereas the `deleteGuest` operation emulates a one-way pattern.

Add another guest to the system by running an `addGuest` operation. In the request editor, switch to the **Raw** tab from the default XML view in both request and response. This is shown in the following screenshot:

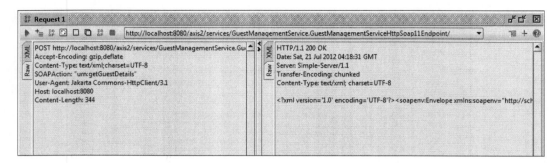

The **Raw** view of the request shows the HTTP header block. In the response pane, the **Raw** view shows the HTTP headers as well as the HTTP body, which includes the SOAP response message. We can see that the HTTP 200 successful response code in the response message.

In request HTTP headers, take a note of the **User-Agent** header. Since soapUI uses the Jakarta Commons HttpClient component from the Apache HTTP Components project as the request submission client, the value is set to **Jakarta Commons-HttpClient/3.1**.

By default, a soapUI request uses **UTF-8** encoding as the character set, hence you can see it as a part of the **Content-Type** header:

```
Content-Type: text/xml;charset=UTF-8
```

You can change these properties as you wish through the **Request Properties** pane in soapUI, shown in the following screenshot:

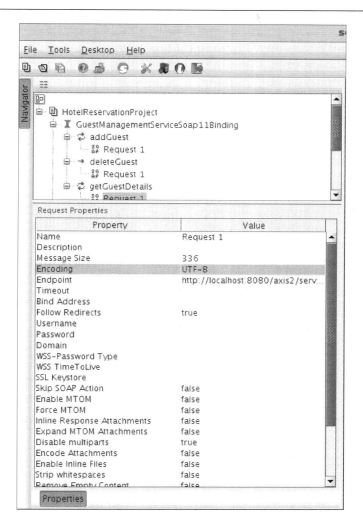

It is best to name each of the requests meaningfully without using the default **Request1** for each of the requests. You can edit the request name as well through the **Request Properties** pane.

If we invoke the `deleteGuest` operation, an empty response can be observed in the **XML** view of the request editor. If you look at the **Raw** view of the response, you will be able to find the following HTTP header:

```
HTTP/1.1 202 Accepted

Date: Sat, 31 Dec 2011 02:02:38 GMT

Server: Simple-Server/1.1

Transfer-Encoding: chunked
```

Can you explain why this response does not have a body? As we discussed earlier, `deleteGuest` uses one-way MEP, therefore the service does not return a response upon receiving a request SOAP message. Instead, in one-way messaging, the service should respond back with **HTTP 202 Accepted** status if the request is accepted by the service and no error has occurred.

So far, we have explored requests and responses which conform to SOAP 1.1 specification. All requests which are categorized under **GuestManagementServiceSoap12Binding** are SOAP 1.2 messages. You can find it out simply by looking at the namespace URL of the `Envelope` element in the SOAP message:

```
<soap:Envelope xmlns:soap="http://www.w3.org/2003/05/soap-envelope">
```

When you submit a SOAP 1.2 request to the `GuestManagementService`, it responds back with a SOAP 1.2 response.

Generating SOAP Faults

We discussed a few of the positive scenarios associated with the `GuestManagementService` of our sample hotel reservation system. Our discussion on soapUI requests and responses cannot be concluded until we explore the failure scenarios related to the web service. What will happen if we try to add an existing guest to the system? We have implemented our service implementation class to handle these types of scenarios such that the service responds with a fault in case of a failure.

We will look into a possible failure case where an existing guest is going to be added to the system.

In a preceding example, where we added the guest called **Saman**, submit the same request again. As the guest has already been added to the system, the `GuestManagementService` should respond back with a fault. (Look at how we handled the fault in the *Web services fault handling* section of *Chapter 2, The Sample Project*) Note that we implemented our sample service in a way so that it throws an error if we invoke the `addGuest` operation with a name of an existing guest. We did that just for the simplicity of our sample application and you should not interpret it as a behavior of a real production system. The SOAP Fault corresponding to the `addGuest` operation will be as follows:

```
<soapenv:Envelope xmlns:soapenv="http://schemas.xmlsoap.org/soap/
envelope/">
    <soapenv:Body>
        <soapenv:Fault>
            <faultcode>soapenv:Server</faultcode>
            <faultstring>Guest already Exists</faultstring>
            <detail>
                <ns:GuestManagementServiceGuestManagementException
xmlns:ns="http//sample.com/reservation/guest/types">
                    <GuestManagementException xsi:type="ax21:GuestM
anagementException" xmlns="http//sample.com/reservation/guest/
types" xmlns:ax21="http://exception.reservation.sample.com/xsd"
xmlns:xsi="http://www.w3.org/2001/XMLSchema-instance">
                        <ax21:message>Guest already Exists</ax21:message>
                    </GuestManagementException>
                </ns:GuestManagementServiceGuestManagementException>
            </detail>
        </soapenv:Fault>
    </soapenv:Body>
</soapenv:Envelope>
```

If you look at the **Raw** view of the SOAP Fault, you will find the following HTTP header block:

```
HTTP/1.1 500 Guest already Exists
Date: Fri, 30 Dec 2011 14:35:41 GMT
Server: Simple-Server/1.1
Transfer-Encoding: chunked
Content-Type: text/xml; charset=UTF-8
```

You can see the HTTP 500 response with the error message, **Guest already Exists**.

Similarly, you may try out the other possible faulty scenarios with the rest of the web services in our sample system in order to familiarise yourself with the SOAP Fault handling.

Summary

We looked into our first soapUI project in this chapter. Out of the three web services which we implemented in the previous chapter, the guest management web service was used to add a new guest to the system, view the details of the guest, and delete the guest from the system. We invoked all these operations of our sample service using soapUI. We studied the request generated by soapUI and related it to the contents of WSDL of GuestManagementService. We also had a detailed discussion on two different views of requests and responses presented by soapUI. In the **Raw** view, we were able to see the message with HTTP headers, and the **XML** view showed just the SOAP envelope of the message. We also discussed about failure cases of web service invocations and had a look at a SOAP Fault.

We are going to extend our project to a full comprehensive test suite in the next chapter.

4

Working with Your First TestSuite

In the previous chapter, we discussed the basics of soapUI projects. When you are testing an individual service or a complete service-oriented solution, it is not just sufficient to create a project with multiple SOAP requests and manually execute and validate the responses of them one by one. Instead, we should follow some mechanism to execute our tests in a well organized manner, so that, we could minimize some unnecessary delays and focus on achieving a greater level of test coverage.

soapUI **TestSuites** are one of the key building blocks in a project which allow us to structure and execute functional tests. In this chapter, we will look into the following high-level topics of building a comprehensive test suite in order to test our sample hotel room reservation system:

- Creating a TestSuite
- Running the TestSuite
- Adding test assertions
- Adding properties to the tests

A sample test scenario

We have built a sample hotel reservation system in *Chapter 2, The Sample Project*, and invoked one of its services in *Chapter 3, First Steps with soapUI and Projects*. However, we did not do a complete end-to-end workflow with our system. Let's think about the following scenario:

A new guest has arrived to the hotel. An operator of the hotel reservation system registers the new guest in system, looks for a room, and reserves it for the guest.

This is the preliminary use case of our sample system. All three web services which we discussed previously, GuestManagementService, RoomManagementService, and ReservationService take part in this scenario. How are we going to test this particular scenario using soapUI? Will it be enough to create a project and add SOAP requests to execute the relevant operations of each web service individually, as we did in *Chapter 3, First Steps with soapUI and Projects*?

The answer will be yes, if we need to execute this particular scenario once and for all. However, we do not live in a world where software is built in a single run, tested once and used in production. Instead, there are a large number of iterations per release cycle as well as multiple versions. In such cases, if we do not maintain our tests in a reusable and structured manner, we will end up in a chaos.

We are going to use some of the important constructs of soapUI to build a comprehensive test suite to verify the preceding scenario. Open soapUI and start our journey of exploring more exciting features!

Creating a TestSuite

A soapUI functional test consists of three key elements as follows:

- **TestStep**: A TestStep is the foundation of any functional test. It is used to manage the execution flow of the test and validate the test results. A TestStep is directly associated with a TestCase.
- **TestCase**: In a soapUI project, a TestCase is a collection of TestSteps organized for testing some functionality of the service under test.
- **TestSuite**: A TestSuite is a collection of TestCases which work together as a logical unit to test some specific functionality.

The structure of these elements in a soapUI project can be represented in a diagram as follows:

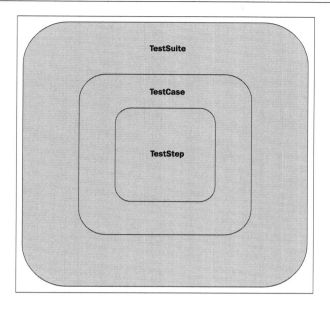

We will discuss each of these elements in detail while we go through our sample TestSuite. Without spending more time on theoretical aspects, let's start to build our soapUI project.

Our first scenario, as we just described, is a relatively simple one. Open the **HotelReservationProject** in soapUI which we have created in the previous chapter. We have already added the WSDL of GuestManagementService there.

 In this exercise, we will remove the SOAP 1.2 binding from each web service as we do not have to bother about SOAP versions at this moment. Therefore, you may remove GuestManagementServiceSoap12Binding (interface) from the project.

In addition to the WSDL of `GuestManagementService`, we will need to add the rest of the WSDLs of our sample hotel reservation system by performing the following steps:

1. Right-click on the **HotelReservationProject** and select **Add WSDL**. You will be prompted to specify the URL or **Browse** in the file system for a WSDL. This is shown in the following screenshot:

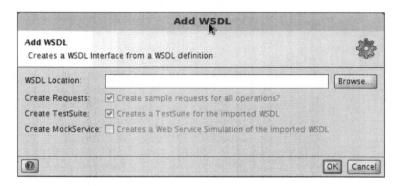

2. We are going to add WSDL URL of the `RoomManagementService`. The WSDL which has been automatically generated by Apache Axis2, can be accessed by navigating your web browser to `http://localhost:8080/axis2/services/RoomManagementService?wsdl`. Once you have made sure that the WSDL is accessible in the browser, specify the WSDL URL of `RoomManagementService` (`http://localhost:8080/axis2/services/RoomManagementService?wsdl`) as the **WSDL location**.

3. Uncheck the **Create TestSuite** check box so that we can manually add a TestSuite as we preferred.

>
> If we select the **Create TestSuite** option, soapUI automatically generates a test suite for the imported WSDL. soapUI scans through the WSDL and extracts all the operations. Then it generates test cases for each of the operations. By default, one TestCase for each operation is created. So, if you have five operations in the WSDL, you will automatically get five TestCases.

4. Leave the **Create Requests** check box checked and click on **OK**.

5. Now, you will notice that the `RoomManagementService` interface is also added to our project. Make sure to remove the **RoomManagementServiceSoap12Binding** from the project. Similarly, repeat the preceding steps to add `ReservationService` as well.

6. As of now, our project structure will be similar to the following screenshot:

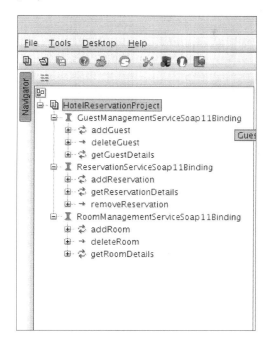

Under each service interface, you can see the operations corresponding to the operations defined in the respective WSDL. soapUI represents the MEP used by a particular operation using two distinct icons as shown in the following screenshot:

As **addGuest** operation uses request-response MEP, it is denoted by two circular arrow heads. The **deleteGuest** operation is denoted by a single arrow head since it is a one-way operation.

Now, think about our first test scenario again and decompose it into a few steps for clarity.

- Add a few hotel rooms to the system
- Upon the arrival of a new guest, a receptionist at the hotel registers the new guest in the system
- Finally, the receptionist reserves an available room for the guest

This particular scenario involves a few web service calls. New rooms can be added to the system by invoking `RoomManagementService`. Guest registration can be done through `GuestManagementService`. Finally the room reservation will be done by calling `ReservationService`. Though these three web services are logically related to each other, we have implemented our system in a way that they can be invoked independently.

Adding TestCases

We are ready to test our scenario. First, we are going to check whether the `RoomManagementService` works as expected. We can add a single TestCase to test each of the operations in `RoomManagementService` or we can add separate TestCases for operations. The choice depends on the functionality of service or operations. If the service has a large number of operations it will be a good idea to add a separate TestCase for each operation. In our case, we have a maximum number of three operations per service. Therefore, we may add one TestCase for a service. For the sake of completeness of the topic, we are going to follow the first approach where we add a separate test case for each operation; this gives us three test cases. Perform the following steps to generate TestCases:

1. Right-click on **RoomManagementServiceSoap11Binding** in the left-hand side menu of the project and select **Generate TestSuite**. Then the Generate TestSuite window will be seen as shown in the following screenshot:

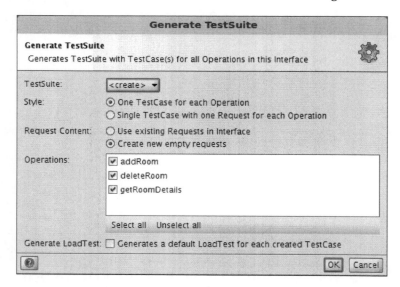

2. Accept the default options and click on **OK**, so that we will have one test case for each operation.

3. Specify `RoomManagementServiceTestSuite` as the name of the TestSuite.

4. Now, we will have a TestSuite with three TestCases as follows:
   - **addRoom TestCase**
   - **deleteRoom TestCase**
   - **getRoomDetails TestCase**

5. Each of these TestCases consist of one TestStep. We will look into each of the TestCases in the following sections.

addRoom TestCase

addRoom is our preliminary TestCase which is used to add a new room record into the system. Initially, we do not include any additional TestSteps into this TestCase. We accept the default test steps generated by soapUI and proceed.

The addRoom TestCase editor can be opened by double-clicking on **addRoom TestCase** in the left-hand side menu or right-clicking on the TestCase and selecting **Show TestCase Editor**. If you open the TestCase Editor in either of these ways, it will be similar to the following screenshot:

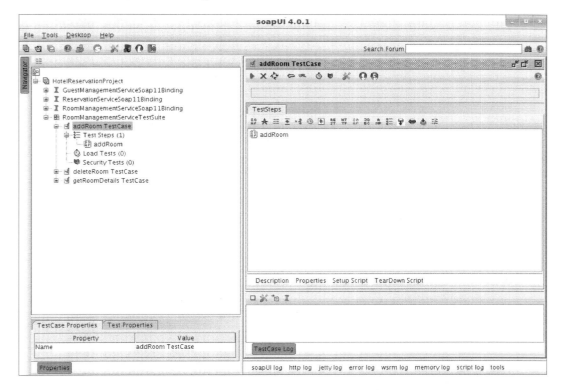

You can see that our TestCase includes one TestStep named **addRoom**. If you double click on the **addRoom** TestStep, you will recognize it as a usual SOAP request.

SOAP request is one of the different set of TestSteps included in soapUI TestCases. soapUI provides you with various TestSteps which perform different types of test execution tasks. For example, HTTP Request TestStep can be used to send a raw HTTP message to a web page or a service. If you want to hold the execution of the current TestCase for a specified time, you can use Delay TestStep. JDBC Request TestStep can be used to invoke a SQL query in a database while running the TestCase.

As we are exploring soapUI in detail within the context of this book, we will use almost all of these TestSteps given in soapUI. For the moment, let's use the default SOAP request TestStep as follows:

1. Double-click on the **addRoom** TestStep which is under **addRoom TestCase** in the left-hand side menu of the project. This will open the SOAP request which can be forwarded to the **addRoom** operation in `RoomManagementService`.

2. Replace the **?** entries with appropriate values. For example:

```
<typ:roomNumber>101</typ:roomNumber>
<typ:roomType>Standard</typ:roomType>
<typ:roomSize>Double</typ:roomSize>
```

As we are ready with everything needed to test, we can run the **addRoom TestCase** now. However, we will wait until we have completed the rest of the operations in `RoomManagementService`.

If you look at the structure of the **RoomManagementServiceTestSuite**, the test cases are organized by soapUI under a specific order. **addRoom TestCase** is at the top and **getRoomDetails TestCase** is at the bottom. When running the TestSuite, soapUI executes the TestCases sequentially as they appear in the tree view of the TestSuite. Therefore, when we run **RoomManagementServiceTestSuite**, **addRoom TestCase** will be executed first. After that, the **deleteRoom TestCase** will be executed. Finally, the **getRoomDetails TestCase** will be executed.

Therefore, if were to execute this in the default order, after you add a room, it will be deleted instantly by the execution of **deleteRoom TestCase**. When the **getRoomDetails TestCase** executes at last, you always get a SOAP Fault since the particular room does not exist. Because of this, you should reorganize the order of execution of TestCases by moving the **getRoomDetails TestCase** to follow the **addRoom TestCase** in the TestSuite tree view of the soapUI project.

You can do this by clicking on the **getRoomDetails TestCase** and dragging it to be placed after **addRoom Test Case**.

getRoomDetails TestCase

Similar to the **addRoom TestCase, getRoomDetails TestCase** also consists of a single SOAP request TestStep. Perform the following steps to update the **getRoomDetails** TestStep:

1. Double click on the **getRoomDetails** TestStep. The SOAP request, which will be sent to the **getRoomDetails** operation, will be opened up.

2. Replace **?** with the same room number we specified in the previous TestCase as follows:

```
<typ:roomNumber>101</typ:roomNumber>
```

deleteRoom TestCase

We can execute the whole TestSuite once we complete the configuration of **deleteRoom TestCase. deleteRoom TestCase** includes a single SOAP request TestStep. The room which has been added after executing **addRoom TestCase** is supposed to be removed from the system by executing the **deleteRoom TestCase**. Therefore, follow the same steps as in the preceding TestCases and specify the same room number which has been previously added in the SOAP request:

```
<typ:roomNumber>101</typ:roomNumber>
```

Running the first TestSuite

In the preceding section, we have added three TestCases under the **RoomManagementService TestSuite**. SoapUI provides users with the facility to execute each TestCase individually as well as everything together.

In each TestCase, you will find the small green arrow icon which can be used to execute the TestCase alone as shown in the following screenshot:

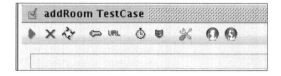

Instead of executing each TestCase one by one, we are going to execute the whole TestSuite by performing the following steps:

1. Double-click on **RoomManagementServiceTestSuite** in the left-hand side menu of our soapUI project. This will open a detailed view of the TestSuite where you can see three TestCases which consists of the TestSuite.

2. We have completed updating all our TestSteps in the preceding section. Therefore, just click on the run icon (the small green arrow) which appears at the top-left corner of the TestSuite view.

3. Once the test execution is over, you will see something similar to the following screenshot:

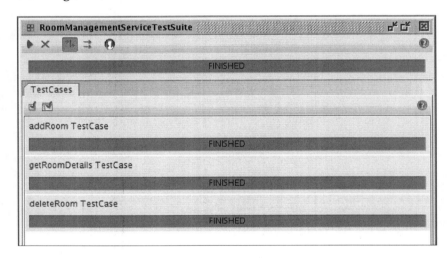

4. All TestCases are marked in green denoting the success of the test. If you double-click on the green bars, the associated TestCase will be opened. Then click on the relevant TestStep. You can see the SOAP requests and responses which were submitted to the web service.

5. If you check the response of the SOAP request TestStep of **addRoom TestCase**, you will notice that the room has been added correctly to the system. Similarly, if you check the SOAP response of **getRoomDetails TestCase**, it will include the information of the added room as follows:

```
<ns:return xsi:type="ns:Room" xmlns:ax23="http://exception.
reservation.sample.com/xsd" xmlns:xsi="http://www.w3.org/2001/
XMLSchema-instance">
        <ns:roomNumber>101</ns:roomNumber>
        <ns:roomSize>Double</ns:roomSize>
        <ns:roomType>Standard</ns:roomType>
    </ns:return>
```

With this, we can confirm that the room has been added to the system.

Now, is this the correct approach of verifying the success or failure of our test? Do we need to open the response messages of each and every request in TestSteps to find out what goes wrong or not? If this is the way we verify the status of tests, can this be considered as automated testing? If the preceding is all we can get from soapUI, what is the advantage of including SOAP requests under TestSuites and TestCases instead of directly sending them as we did in *Chapter 3, First Steps with soapUI and Projects*?

By now, we all have a lot of questions like these. We expect to find answers for all of these concerns before ending this chapter.

Let's do another simple test. In the preceding **RoomManagementService TestSuite**, disable **deleteRoom TestCase** (right-click on the test case and select the **Disable Test Case** option).

Add another room (for example, room number 102) by executing the TestSuite. After executing the test, you will notice that the new room is added to the system. Now, execute the TestSuite again.

The test is successful again! You will notice that both **addRoom TestCase** and **getRoomDetails TestCase** are shown as passed with a green status bar. Click on the finished **addRoom TestCase** and double-click on **addRoom** TestStep. This will open the SOAP request and response as we saw earlier. This time, you will notice that we got a SOAP Fault as the response as we tried to add a room which has already been added. The SOAP Fault would be as follows:

```
<soapenv:Fault>
        <faultcode>soapenv:Server</faultcode>
        <faultstring>Room already Exists</faultstring>
```

Though we got a SOAP Fault, why does soapUI show it as a passed test?

soapUI does not read our mind. We need to instruct it to fail tests if some conditions are not satisfied. In other words, we need to have a mechanism to validate the responses which we get as a result of TestStep execution. We can validate them by manually reading the responses as we did before. However, when executing complex test suites automatically, we cannot look and read each and every response manually to figure out the status of tests. Test assertions come into action in this situation.

Adding test assertions

Assertions allow users to validate the responses by comparing some properties of the message with expected values. In soapUI, assertions are applied to TestSteps. There are many predefined assertions available for us to use in soapUI tests. Some assertions are applicable only for a specific set of TestSteps whereas some are common for any TestStep.

You can add any number of assertions to a TestStep. After the TestStep is executed, all of the associated assertions are applied to the response. The TestStep is failed if any of the assertions fail.

Let's continue our discussion on assertions with our sample TestSuite.

We are going to add an assertion to addRoom TestStep in our project as follows:

1. Open **addRoom** TestStep by double-clicking on **addRoom** TestStep under the **addRoom TestCase** in soapUI project.

2. You will notice the **add an assertion to this item icon** at the top-left corner of TestStep editor. Click on that icon. The **Select Assertion** dialog box will open as shown in the following screenshot:

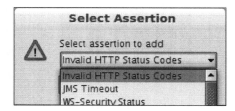

3. You can find all assertions provided by soapUI in the preceding dialog box. During the course of this book, we will cover most of these assertions. In this example, let's use a few simple assertions.

Not SOAP Fault assertion

First, let's check whether we get a valid SOAP response instead of a fault. For that, we need to add a Not SOAP Fault assertion which evaluates the response to check whether it is a SOAP Fault or a valid SOAP response. If the response is a SOAP Fault, the TestStep will be marked as failed. To add a Not SOAP Fault assertion, perform the following steps:

1. Select **Not SOAP Fault** assertion from the **Select Assertion** drop down and click on **OK**.

2. Execute the **RoomManagementService TestSuite** again. This time the status of the TestSuite will be marked as failed in a red color. You will also notice that the reason for the TestSuite failure is the **addRoom TestCase**.

3. Select the **addRoom TestCase** and open the **addRoom** TestStep. The assertion result will be given at the bottom of the TestStep result view as shown in the following screenshot:

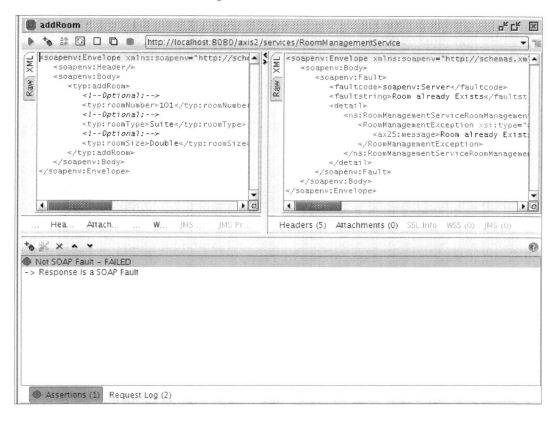

4. As you can see, we got a SOAP Fault as we tried to add an existing room to the system. We added an assertion, Not SOAP Fault, to check whether the response is a SOAP fault or not. In this case, the assertion evaluated the test to be failed as the response was a fault.

5. We know that if we execute this particular TestSuite again and again without any modification, we should get a SOAP Fault as we did earlier. Now, let's check whether we get the correct fault string in SOAP Fault. In order to check that, we can use multiple assertions. We will use XPath Match assertion first.

XPath Match assertion

An XPath Match assertion is used to compare the result of an XPath expression with a predefined value. We are going to check the SOAP response of the **addRoom** TestStep to evaluate whether it contains the expected fault string in case of a SOAP Fault.

1. In the same **addRoom** TestStep which we just used, select the **XPath Match** assertion from the **Select Assertion** dialog box.

2. Specify the XPath expression and expected result as follows:

   ° **XPath Expression**: `//soapenv:Fault/faultstring`

   ° **Expected Result**: `Room already Exists`

   The XPath Match Configuration window will look like the following screenshot:

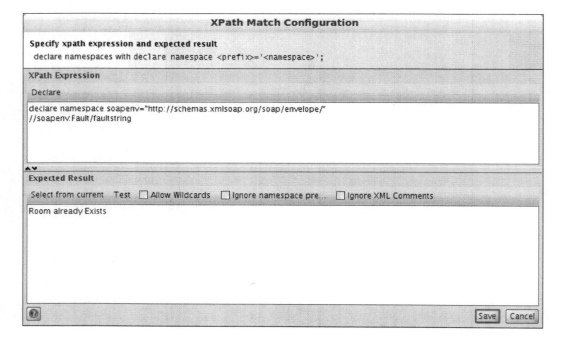

3. When you specify the XPath expression as shown in the preceding screenshot, make sure to declare any namespace prefix which you use in the expression. In our case, we declare the namespace prefix of `soapenv` as follows:

   ```
   declare namespace soapenv="http://schemas.xmlsoap.org/soap/
   envelope/"
   ```

4. Note that all namespaces must be declared before they are used in the XPath expression.

5. If you are adding an XPath assertion based on a valid response message, the namespaces can automatically be declared by selecting the **Declare** button in the XPath expression editor. soapUI adds all namespace declarations of the current message to the XPath expression.

6. You can specify the expected result of the evaluation of the XPath expression in the **Expected Result** editor. According to the SOAP Fault message in our example, the expected output of the `//soapenv:Fault/faultstring` expression is a string value, `Room already Exists`.

> Similar to the namespace declaration, if you specify the expected result based on a valid response message, the result can automatically be retrieved by clicking on **Select from current** button in the **Expected Result** editor. soapUI evaluates the XPath expression which is specified in the XPath expression editor against the current message and returns the expected result.

7. After configuring the XPath expression and the expected result, click on **Save** to add the new assertion into the **addRoom** TestStep.

8. Execute the **RoomManagementService TestSuite** again. In the **addRoom** TestStep, you could observe two assertion results; a Not SOAP Fault assertion with a failed status and an XPath Match assertion with a pass state.

9. Here, the XPath Match assertion has been evaluated to `true`, as we got a SOAP Fault with the fault string, **Room already Exists**.

10. We have added two assertions for the **addRoom** TestStep. We have tested both of them for the failure case. If we execute this TestStep again with a new room number value, we will get a failure for XPath Match assertion as it checks the content of a SOAP Fault message. For now, just disable this XPath assertion by right-clicking on the assertion.

11. You can add another XPath assertion to check the success case of our test. For that, you can simply check the content of the SOAP response by an expression as follows:

    ° **XPath Expression**: `declare namespace ns='http//sample.com/reservation/room/types';`

       `//ns:addRoomResponse/ns:return`

    ° **Expected Result**: true

The Contains assertion

The Contains assertion is another simple and straightforward assertion which can be used to verify the existence of some text in response messages. Let's add a Contains assertion to the **getRoomDetails** TestStep in our example by performing the following steps:

1. In the getRoomDetails TestStep, select the Contains assertion from the Select Assertion dialog box.

2. The **Contains Assertion** dialog box will be shown where we can specify the content to be checked in response.

3. The response of **getRoomDetails** can always contain a string value, **Standard**, **Luxury** or **Suite** depending on the room type. Therefore, we can check the existence of those strings using a regular expression as follows:

    ° Regular Expression: **(?s).*(Standard | Suite | Luxury).***

The **Contains Assertion** window would look like the following screenshot:

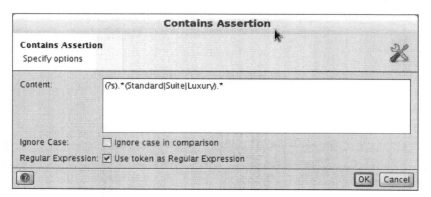

4. In the Contains assertion, the content which we look for can either be a string value or a regular expression. If we use a regular expression as in this example, we must check the **Use token as Regular Expression** check box, otherwise the expression we specify as the content will be considered as a pure string value.

5. Execute the **RoomManagementService TestSuite** again with a new room number. The **getRoomDetails** TestStep will be marked as passed.

6. We have done some preliminary modifications in our first TestSuite. However we are not done yet. We have not executed our whole test scenario yet. Before doing that, let's discuss another important construct in soapUI functional tests – properties.

Adding properties to soapUI tests

Properties can be considered as place-holders in a soapUI project. Properties are used to parameterize the execution of tests. In soapUI, properties can be defined at many levels in a project. You can define the properties which are common to your project at the project level. TestSuite and TestCase specific properties can be defined at their respective levels. Let's dive into the details of properties with our example project.

In our project, the project specific properties can be defined in the **Custom Properties** tab as shown in the following screenshot:

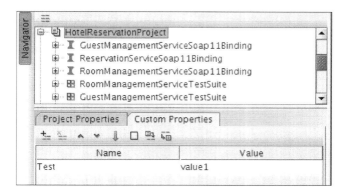

For example, we can define a property called **Test** at the project level as shown in the preceding screenshot. This property can be accessed from anywhere in our project through property expansions. For example, $\{#Project#Test\}.

A property can also be considered as a variable in a computer program. If we want to define something which can be used somewhere else, we can use properties. Therefore, in our sample **HotelReservation** project, we can make use of the properties at various levels.

We have organized our project into TestSuites, and each TestSuite deals with one web service. So, the web service specific properties can be defined at the TestSuite level by performing the following steps:

1. Select **RoomManagementService TestSuite** in the left-hand side menu in our soapUI project. You would observe the **Test Properties** tab at the bottom where we can define custom properties specific to the TestSuite.

2. In **RoomManagementService TestSuite**, we have three test cases and three test steps. In all these elements, we send the SOAP request message to a common web service endpoint. Also, the web service endpoint always consists of the following format :http://<host>:<port>/axis2/services/<serviceName>.

3. Without repeating this everywhere in our TestSuite, we can easily define some properties at the TestSuite level so that in case the service is moved into a different host or different environments, or the port or service name is changed, we do not need to change these in all the references in our project. We can simply change the value of properties.

4. Add three properties under **RoomManagementService TestSuite** as follows:

```
host = localhost
httpport = 8080
servicename = RoomManagementService
```

5. Now, we can access these properties through property expansions from anywhere in our TestSuite. For example, go to each of the three TestSteps and open the associated requests, **addRoom**, **getRoomDetails**, and **deleteRoom**. Go to the **Test Properties** tab of the request and edit the endpoint (or you can choose the **[edit current..]** option from the endpoint URL) as: `http://${#TestSuite#host}:${#TestSuite#httpport}/axis2/services/${#TestSuite#servicename}`.

Reading property values from a file

Usually, the properties are managed externally to the projects so that the property values can be updated without affecting the project settings. In soapUI, without defining the property value at the TestSuite, TestCase or TestStep level, we can read them from an external file. To read the properties from an external file, perform the following steps:

1. Go back to the **Test Properties** section under the **RoomManagementService TestSuite**.

2. Remove the existing values of all three properties.

3. Create a file called `roommgtservice.properties` in the filesystem. The content of the property file can be key-value pairs as follows:

```
host=localhost

httpport=8080

servicename=RoomManagementService
```

4. Click on **Loads property values from an external file** icon which appears at the **Test Properties** tab as shown in the following screenshot:

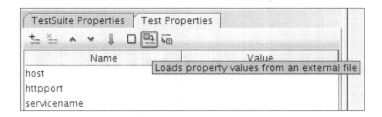

5. The **Load Properties** dialog box will be opened. Browse for the **roommgtservice.properties** file (the one just created) in your filesystem and click on **OK**.

6. If the properties are loaded successfully, a message will be prompted as: **Added/Updated 3 properties from file**.

7. Replace the endpoint URL with the property expansions as we did earlier. Execute a TestStep (for example, **getRoomDetails**) and see the HTTP headers. You will notice that the endpoint URL is constructed by reading the properties from the file.

 Note that the preceding property values are not dynamically loaded from the property file into the soapUI project. If you make an update in the property file, you should reload the file in order to reflect the change.

Transferring property values between TestSteps

Think about a scenario where you need to extract some value from a response message and include it in the subsequent request(s). In such a case, we need to have a mechanism to retrieve a specified value and transfer it to the other elements of the project. soapUI brings this functionality through the Property Transfer TestStep.

Let's walk through our sample project to understand this important feature. We still have not associated TestSuites for GuestManagementService and ReservationService. In order to complete our end-to-end room reservation scenario, let's add TestSuites for both these services by performing the following steps:

1. As we did in the *Creating a TestSuite* section, add two TestSuites, one each for GuestManagementService and ReservationService.

2. Now, you will have three TestSuites with each having three TestCases.

3. Add a new room by executing the **addRoom TestCase** of the **RoomManagementService TestSuite**. Specify the room details as follows:

```
room_number=201
room_type=Suite
room_size=Double
```

4. Add a new guest by executing the **addGuest TestCase** of the **GuestManagementService TestSuite**. Specify the following details for the new guest:

```
name=saman
address=Colombo
age = 32
```

5. Now, we need to reserve a room for the new guest by invoking `ReservationService`. We can do this by executing the **addReservation TestCase** of the **ReservationService TestSuite**. You can specify the following inputs in the addReservation SOAP request:

```
Room Number=201
Guest Name=Saman
Reserved From = 2012-01-25
Reserved To = 2012-01-27
```

What are we going to do here? We have implemented the reservation service in a way so that we would use it to explore some interesting features in soapUI. Therefore, let's assume the checkout procedure of our system is as follows:

The new guest Saman has requested to check out from the hotel. The reception of the hotel finds out which hotel room was occupied by the guest. Then they access our hotel reservation application and do a web service call to get the reservation details associated with the room number. Then, the hotel staff verify that the guest had occupied the specified room, the check-in and check-out dates, and so on.

Finally, the hotel staff remove the associated reservation record.

Think about this scenario with the web services we used in our system. The details associated with a reservation is obtained by calling the `getReservationDetails` operation of `ReservationService`. In order to remove the reservation from the system, we will call the `removeReservation` operation. The `removeReservation` operation can only be invoked with a `reservationID`. The `reservationID` is an auto generated identity primarily used as the key of a particular reservation. By invoking the `getReservationDetails` operation, we can get the `reservationID` and then use that particular ID to invoke the `removeReservation` operation.

As a tester of this system, you can manually call each of these operations and do what is necessary. But how should we use soapUI to correlate the requests and responses like these?

Our objective is to execute **getReservationDetails TestCase** and extract the reservationID from the response, then use that reservationID value in removeReservationTestCase. So, we are going to define a property which is common to both **getReservationDetails TestCase** and **removeReservation TestCase**. The ideal place to define this property is at the TestSuite level. To achieve this, perform the following steps:

1. Select **ReservationService TestSuite** from the soapUI project tree and click on the **Test Properties** tab.

2. Add a new property resID and keep the empty value.

3. Now, select the **getReservationDetails TestCase**. We are going to create a **Property Transfer** TestStep which will be used to transfer a specified value from a previous TestStep to the subsequent requests. Right-click on the **TestStep** element and select **Add Step | Property Transfer**.

4. You will be asked to specify a name for the step. Enter Reservation Property Transfer.

5. The **Reservation Property Transfer** window will be opened for us to add one or more transfers as shown in the following:

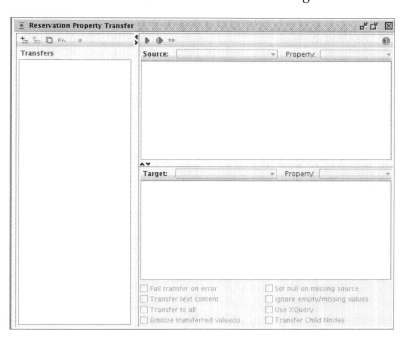

Here, in the property transfer window, the left-hand side pane lists down the transfers configured in this TestStep. Let's add a new transfer and discuss the rest of the features associated with it.

6. Click on the **Adds a new property transfer** icon at the top-left corner in the preceding property transfer window. You will be prompted to enter a name for the transfer. Enter `ReservationIDTransfer`.

7. Once the transfer is created, you can use **Source** and **Target** panes to specify the relevant XPath expressions to extract and replace property values. First, let's have a look at the Source pane. In the drop-down box next to Source, you can see various levels of soapUI projects which can be used as the source of property transfers. By default the closest TestStep will be shown. In our case, it is the **getReservationDetails** TestStep. The drop-down list next to Property shows the source property which is used in the transfer, which can either be request, response, or service endpoint.

8. We will select **Response** as we need to extract the `reservationID` from the response message. The Source pane would look like the following screenshot:

9. Now, we need to specify the XPath expression to extract a value from the **getReservationDetails** SOAP response. The response will be similar to the following:

```
<soapenv:Envelope xmlns:soapenv="http://schemas.xmlsoap.org/soap/
envelope/">
    <soapenv:Body>
        <ns:getReservationDetailsResponse xmlns:ns="http//sample.
com/reservation/res/types">
            <ns:return xsi:type="ns:Reservation" xmlns:ax25="http://
exception.reservation.sample.com/xsd" xmlns:xsi="http://www.
w3.org/2001/XMLSchema-instance">
                <ns:guestName>saman</ns:guestName>
                <ns:reservationID>16</ns:reservationID>
                <ns:reserved_from>2012-01-25</ns:reserved_from>
                <ns:reserved_to>2012-01-27</ns:reserved_to>
                <ns:roomNumber>201</ns:roomNumber>
            </ns:return>
        </ns:getReservationDetailsResponse>
    </soapenv:Body>
</soapenv:Envelope>
```

As we already have this response in soapUI (if not, run getReservationDetails TestStep once), we can declare namespaces associated with the XPath expression by clicking on the **ns** icon on the toolbar of the property transfer window. Once you are done with it, specify the XPath expression as `//ns:getReservationDetailsResponse/ns:return/ns:reservationID`.

10. Now, we need to specify the target where we want to transfer the value extracted from the above XPath expression. We can use the Target pane at the bottom of the property transfer window for that.

11. Similar to the Source, we can select one of the levels of the soapUI project to which the property value must be transferred to. In our example, we need to transfer the property value to the **resID** property which we have defined at the TestSuite level. Select **ReservationServiceTestSuite** as the Target and select **resID** from the drop-down list next to Property. With this, our property transfer configuration will be like the following screenshot:

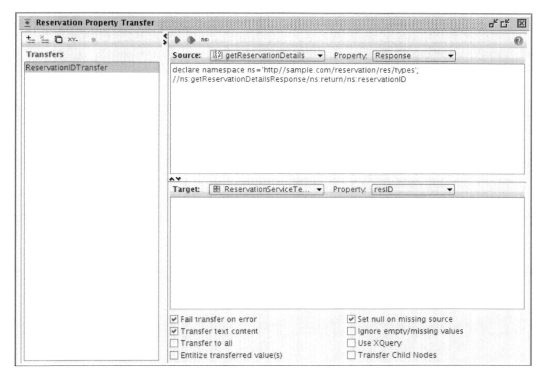

In soapUI, the properties can be transferred to various targets based on the requirement. If we want to transfer the extracted value from a response to the subsequent requests, then we can specify the XPath expression of the request as the target.

But in our example, we do not transfer the `reservationID` to another request in the same TestCase. Instead, we extract a value from a TestStep in **getReservationDetails TestCase** and pass it to the **removeReservation** TestStep which is inside **removeReservation TestCase**. In other words, we do not pass property values in between TestSteps in the same TestCase level. Because of this reason, we created a property which is common to both TestCases and assigned the property a value.

12. We have completed the property transfer settings. Now, we can parameterize the value of the `<typ:reservationID>` element in removeReservation SOAP request to read **resID** TestCase level property from the preceding property transfer. To do that, update the removeReservation SOAP request of the removeReservation TestCase as follows:

    ```
    <typ:reservationID>${#TestSuite#resID}</typ:reservationID>
    ```

13. Select the **ReservationTestSuite** and click on the run icon in the detailed TestSuite view (Make sure to disable addReservation TestCase since we have already added the same reservation previously). You will see that all TestCases will be executed. Have a look at the **Test Properties** tab at the TestSuite. You will notice that a value is assigned to the **resID** property, which is the autogenerated `reservationID` given in the **getReservationDetails** response.

We went through all the services in our sample hotel room reservation system and explored various functional testing features of soapUI. As an exercise, you could put all those together and create a comprehensive TestSuite with various assertions and try on your own.

Summary

Functional testing is a key for a success of any software development project. We can do functional testing manually or using automated tools. soapUI provides users with support for functional testing through various approaches. In this chapter we looked at building our first functional TestSuite to test the sample application which we developed in *Chapter 2, The Sample Project*. We discussed the basic constructs of any soapUI project, TestSuites, TestCases, and TestSteps. We made use of different types of assertions to verify the output of the tests. Finally, we looked into the soapUI properties and the transferring of property values between requests and responses.

The next chapter will be an extension of this and we are planning to discuss some advanced topics of web services testing using soapUI.

5
Load and Performance Testing with soapUI

Web services testing cannot be concluded merely focusing on the functional aspects of the system. It is always required to do an assessment about the non-functional requirements expected from a service-oriented solution. Regardless of the architectural style being used, non-functional aspects must be fulfilled by a system. No matter how intuitive the user interface of your application is, if it counts in minutes to load the pages or crashes when multiple users access it, your users will not think again to use such an application. In most of the situations, non-functional requirements such as performance and scalability are validated using tools. soapUI, being the de-facto utility for functional testing of service oriented solutions, can also be used in non-functional testing. There are some key advantages of using soapUI over other open source tools, such as Apache Jmeter, for non-functional testing:

- Without redesigning separate tests for non-functional testing, soapUI allows you to extend the existing functional TestCases as load tests and execute them with a minimum set of configurations
- soapUI provides us with set of pre-built load testing strategies which can be used out of the box in non-functional testing
- soapUI can seamlessly be integrated into loadUI (http://www.loadui.org/), which is a complete open source load testing solution

We will examine the following topics in this chapter:

- Introduction to the performance testing aspects of web services
- Planning for web service performance testing
- Working with load tests in soapUI
- Performance test statistics and reporting in soapUI
- Using load test assertions

Non-functional testing of web services

There are multiple non-functional requirements expected from the web services which are included in your SOA. A few of these non-functional aspects can be:

- Scalability
- Usability
- Performance
- Extensibility
- Reliability

Web services are dealt with relatively complex XML message processing. As one of the promises of using web services is to communicate with heterogeneous systems, there are a lot of heavy XML serialization/de-serialization tasks used. These complexities multiply by greater levels when the messages are enriched with various **Quality of Service (QoS)** options such as the WS-* headers. For example, when SOAP messages are secured with message-level security policies such as encryption, the SOAP engine has to process all security headers in addition to the raw SOAP message in order to dispatch the message to the correct method of the service implementation class. With these facts, we can argue that there can be a considerable slowness introduced by SOAP web services. Because of that, it is essential to test the non-functional aspects such as performance and scalability of web services before moving them into production.

When testing a service-oriented solution, it is of utmost importance to test your web services individually to assess both functional as well as non-functional requirements. Before integrating the web services with the rest of the consuming applications or other web services, you should carry out sufficient level of non-functional testing. In most cases, when you publish a web service for consumers, you are expected to define a valid **Service-level Agreement (SLA)**. Hence, it is important to do performance or scalability tests with individual web services beforehand and verify whether the published SLA figures are realistic and achievable.

We can identify many reasons for the poor performances of web services and service-oriented solutions. These include the following:

- Issues of SOA middleware used in your solution
- Architectural and design issues of web services
- Issues of message routing and transform rules

Your overall service-oriented solution can fail and underperform if you choose an SOA middleware which itself suffers from various performance drawbacks. Even if your middleware vendor advertises attractive figures about performance, you should do a comprehensive set of non-functional testing in your SOA with the selected middleware stack.

Even if you use the best commercial or open source SOA middleware stack, if you design the solution wrong, you will experience a lot of performance drawbacks. If the WSDL of the web service is not designed correctly or the service implementation is not done appropriately according to the volume of messages transferred in your system, you can expect various performance issues.

Performance degradation of a service-oriented solution is not resulted merely due to the web services. As we discussed in *Chapter 1, Web Services Testing and soapUI*, the configurations used in other key building blocks of an SOA, such as broker and process coordinator, can also contribute to the performance problems. If there are routing algorithms which are not tuned properly, the overall throughput of message processing in your solution can be affected.

Performance testing

Out of the various non-functional requirements, which we have discussed above, our focus will be on performance testing during this chapter.

 As defined on Wikipedia (http://en.wikipedia.org/wiki/ Software_performance_testing), performance testing is in general testing that determines how a system performs in terms of responsiveness and stability under a particular work load.

Load testing is a specific form of performance testing that is conducted to assess the behavior of the system under a specific load. In soapUI, though we generally use the term "load testing" for all types of non-functional testing, we can do all types of performance assessments of web services such as load, stress, and endurance.

Planning for web service performance testing

As with any types of testing, performance testing must also be planned properly in order to achieve the correct results. Web service performance test planning can be described in a set of steps, as follows:

- Identify the expected performance requirements
- Study the service contract
- Analyze service integration scenarios
- Identify message volume, size, and transmission rate

The expected performance requirements can be specific to your needs. For example, your SLA of a web service includes a phrase stating that the published web service must serve the consumer within 5 ms at peak hours, or the service should be available (up and running) 99.99 percent of the time. Depending on the SLA, you should plan for what types of performance tests need to be done. If the SLA defines 99.99 percent up time, you must plan for a sufficient round of endurance tests to make sure there are no memory leaks or threading issues when the service runs over a long period.

One of the major promises of using web services in SOA is to achieve loose coupling through well-defined interfaces. As we have discussed in previous chapters, the web service contract, WSDL plays a major role in your SOA. The performance of your web services are directly related to the design constraints of the WSDLs. Therefore, it is important to study the message exchange patterns, operations, bindings, and transports defined in the WSDL to decide the most appropriate performance testing mechanism.

Though it is recommended to start with assessing the performance of individual web services first, we cannot expect that the web services stay alone as silos in a typical service oriented solution. One web service can be consumed by multiple applications in various different ways. We need to identify these integration patterns when deciding the performance testing approaches.

There can be multiple types of message exchanging between web services. SOAP, pure XML messages or JSON messages can be a few examples. Even with one particular message type, there can be different payload sizes. Some messages can transmit large binary attachments. Some can include custom SOAP or HTTP headers. Millions of messages can be consumed by web services per day. Likewise, we need to have a good understanding about message consumption and volume in web services when planning performance tests.

Using soapUI for performance testing

Let's look at how soapUI can help to achieve the performance objectives of your web services. As we discussed above, performance testing of web services is not just running SOAP or XML messages in a loop to overload the service. It should be a well-planned activity which must be aligned with the performance expectations of the overall service-oriented solution. As soapUI supports multiple message formats such as SOAP and JSON through a single interface, you can run multiple types of performance tests. In your SOA, you can have different types of services, some with pure SOAP, some with JSON, and some with plain old XML over HTTP. You do not want to maintain completely different test scripts or tools to verify performance of web services, which consumes different message types. soapUI allows you to have everything in a common place and maintain tests from a single interface.

Once your service is secured with a WS-Security policy such as token authentication, soapUI allows you to extend your functional security tests to performance tests in no time. This helps you to assess the performance impact on your services after applying WS-Security policies.

Also, soapUI allows users to configure various load testing options such as introducing delays in between threads to simulate real-world use cases and run tests in burst mode to stress test services.

We will look into how soapUI can be used in performance testing in the following sections. As we did before, we will be proceeding with our sample hotel reservation application and discuss various performance testing aspects provided by soapUI.

Working with load tests in soapUI

In *Chapter 4*, *Working with Your First TestSuite*, we created a TestSuite for the **RoomManagementService** interface. Similarly, create another TestSuite for **GuestManagementService** and name it GuestManagementServiceTestSuite. We are going to load test the **getGuestDetails** operation in the **GuestManagement** service. To do this, follow these steps:

1. In **HotelReservationProject**, select the **getGuestDetails** TestCase under **GuestManagementServiceTestSuite**. You will notice the **Load Tests (0)** node there.

   Right-click on it or press *Ctrl* + *N* to create a new load test. You will be asked to enter a name for the load test; specify getGuestDetailsLoadTest as the name.

2. The detailed view of **getGuestDetailsLoadTest** will be opened as shown in the following screenshot. There is only one TestStep, **getGuestDetails**, in the load test. This is because the **getGuestDetails** TestCase includes a single TestStep. If your TestCase contains a number of different TestSteps such as SOAP requests, property transfer, and JDBC requests, all of them will be added automatically to the corresponding load test.

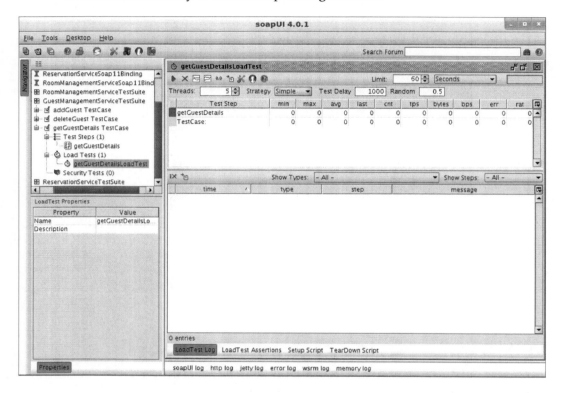

Let's run this test with the default option and look at the results. You can execute the test by clicking on the green arrow icon at the load test toolbar. When you start the test, the progress will be indicated at the upper-right corner.

Limit of a load test

Limit defines the load test execution interval. There are two variables for limit; the **limit value** and **limit type**. In the 4.0.1 Version of soapUI, there are three limit types; **Total Runs**, **Seconds** and **Runs per Thread**, as shown in the following screenshot:

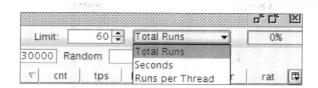

The **Total Runs** limit type is used to set the number of times the TestCase needs to be executed during each load test run. If we set **60** total runs, you will notice that the TestCase is executed 60 times. Therefore, if a particular TestCase has N TestSteps, all N steps will be executed 60 times.

If we set the limit type as **Seconds**, the test will be run till the specified time is over. If we set 60 seconds as the limit, the test will be over in one minute. Once the test is started, you can see a log similar to the following in the load test log which is at the bottom of the load test window:

```
LoadTest started at Sat Mar 31 14:21:25 IST 2012
```

Once the test is finished, the following log message will be shown:

```
LoadTest ended at Sat Mar 31 14:22:25 IST 2012
```

This implies that if you select the limit in seconds, the test will be run for the specified duration.

The individual message-specific logs that print in the soapUI log are disabled during load tests to preserve memory and resource usage. You will notice the INFO:Disabling logs during loadtests message in the soapUI log when running load tests.

The **Runs per thread** limit type can be used to set TestCase runs per threads as needed. For example, if we set the limit as 5 runs per thread and the thread count is 2, TestCase will run 10 times.

Threads in a soapUI load test

Threads act as virtual users in a load test. If the thread count is set as N, soapUI creates N number of clones of the associated TestCase and executes them. You can set as many threads as required based on the capability of handling resources of the system in which soapUI runs on.

Load test strategies of soapUI

SoapUI allows you to simulate different types of load on web services using multiple load test strategies. In the free version of soapUI 4.0.1, we can identify the following types of load test strategies:

- Simple
- Burst
- Thread
- Variance

Each of these strategies has corresponding strategy type variables such as **Test Delay** and **Random**, as shown in the following screenshot:

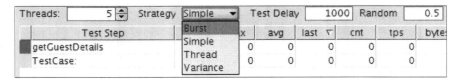

Simple load strategy

The default load test strategy of a soapUI load test is simple. In our **getGuestDetailsLoadTest** example, we made use of the simple strategy. In simple strategy, **Test Delay** defines the delay between each test run. Random is used to set the relative amount of randomization for test delay. If **Test Delay** is **1000** ms and **Random** is **0**, each test will be executed in intervals of 1 second. If **Random** is **1**, all tests will be executed in random delay between each other relative to the **Test Delay** value.

Let's summarize the simple load strategy using our **getGuestDetailsLoadTest** example. Set the load test parameters as follows:

- **Threads = 2**
- **Strategy = Simple**
- **Test Delay = 5000**
- **Random = 0**
- **Limit = 30 seconds**

Now, run the test and observe the results. You will notice that the cnt value (total number of times a TestStep executed) is increased by 2 in intervals of 5 seconds. As we have defined two threads, **getGuestDetails** TestCase will be executed by these two threads at 5 second intervals (the test delay is 5000 ms and there is no randomization).

First you will notice that the cnt value is 2 as two threads started immediately. Then after 5 seconds, cnt will be 4. Likewise the TestCase will be executed in 5 second intervals by two threads for 30 seconds. If we set **Random** as **1**, all test runs will be executed with a random delay between each other.

> The simple load strategy is ideal for web service benchmarking. With the **Random** value set to **0** , you can assess the performance of your web service in successive SOA middleware version upgrades or web service updates, and check whether there are any performance degradation issues due to version upgrades.

You can also carry out stress tests with a simple load strategy. By setting no randomization and **Test Delay** as **0**, you can simulate a burst in the target web service.

Burst load strategy

Burst load strategy can be used to generate a rapid load on the target web service. With this mode, TestCases are executed in bursts without a pre-defined delay between each of them.

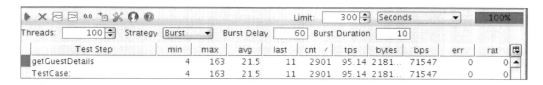

Test Step	min	max	avg	last	cnt	tps	bytes	bps	err	rat
getGuestDetails	4	163	21.5	11	2901	95.14	2181...	71547	0	0
TestCase:	4	163	21.5	11	2901	95.14	2181...	71547	0	0

If you change the load strategy to burst, the associated load strategy parameters are displayed at the right as shown in the preceding screenshot. **Burst Delay** represents the delay between bursts. In our example, the burst delay is set to 60 seconds, which means there will be a 1 minute delay in between each burst run. **Burst Duration** is used to define the number of seconds that the burst runs on the target service. We have defined 10 seconds for the burst. In other words, soapUI goes into sleep mode during the 60 second burst delay and does not send any requests to the target web service. After 60 seconds, the configured number of threads will start to run and generate a sudden traffic for 10 seconds (burst duration).

Let's run the test and observe the results. Make sure you have set the burst mode load testing parameters as follows. It is important to set enough thread count for burst mode as we want to generate a relatively large traffic in a short period of time on the target service.

- **Threads = 100**
- **Strategy = Burst**

- **Burst Delay = 60 seconds**
- **Burst Duration = 10 seconds**
- **Limit = 300 seconds**

You will notice that, as you start the test, there will be no updates on traffic for 60 seconds. After 60 seconds, you will notice a sudden increase of message count (cnt) which will last for 10 seconds. Next, there will be another 60 seconds sleep time. This will continue for 5 minutes.

 The recommended stress testing approach is to use burst mode in soapUI load testing. You can overload the web services and find out breaking points in your services by using burst load testing strategy.

Thread load strategy

Thread load strategy is another useful approach for simulating load. In this strategy, the thread count will be increased gradually from start threads values to end threads values. If you want to monitor the behavior of web services with an increasing thread count, this approach is ideal:

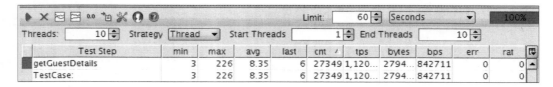

Let's reconfigure our sample **getGuestDetailsLoadTest** with the thread strategy:

- **Threads = 10**
- **Strategy = Thread**
- **Start Threads = 1**
- **End Threads = 10**
- **Limit = 60 seconds**

As the limit value is set to 60 seconds and the start and end thread values are 1 to 10, we can assume that each thread runs for at least 6 seconds. Run the test and monitor the behavior. While the test is running, you could observe that the **Threads** value at the left of the strategy bar is increased from 1 to 10 in intervals of nearly 6 seconds.

Variance strategy

As the name implies, this strategy varies the number of threads over time. Within a defined interval, the number of threads will decrease and increase as per the given variance value simulating a more realistic load on the target web service.

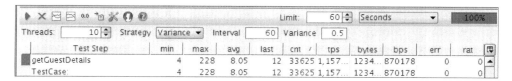

We can look at the behavior of our load test with variance strategy. Reconfigure **getGuestDetailsLoadTest** with the following values and run the test:

- **Threads = 10**
- **Strategy = Variance**
- **Interval = 60**
- **Variance = 0.5**
- **Limit = 60 seconds**

Once you start the test, the thread count shown at the upper-left corner of the strategy bar will be increased from 10 to 15, within 12 seconds. Next, the thread count will be decreased to 5. Finally, the test will be completed with the original thread count (10). The thread count varied by 5 since we set the variance value as 0.5.

As we have used direct JDBC calls without optimizing queries in our sample hotel reservation system, you may encounter JDBC errors such as `com.mysql.jdbc.exceptions.jdbc4.CommunicationsException` when stress testing the system with an increased number of threads. Adjust the thread count to a relatively small value in order to avoid these failures while trying out samples in this chapter.

Note that, though we have changed the same test with different strategies for the sake of demonstration, you can have four different load tests, each with a different load strategy. Then you can run all of these load tests sequentially to generate extensive load on the system.

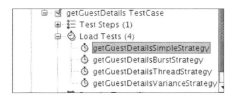

A closer look at the load test report and statistics of soapUI

We have already seen the load test results produced by soapUI under different load strategies. However, we did not discuss what each of the figures is and the usage of different statistics graphs. In simple words, after each load test execution, soapUI produces a **statistics table** with the following fields for each TestStep as well as summary for the overall TestCase:

- min: This defines the minimum response time taken by TestStep
- max: This defines the maximum response time
- avg: This defines the average response time
- last: This defines the average response time for the last run
- cnt: This defines the total number of times a TestStep has been executed
- tps: This defines the number of transactions per second
- bytes: This defines the total bytes transferred
- bps: This defines the bytes per second
- err: This defines the number of errors occurred
- rat: This defines the percentage of failed requests

You could run multiple load tests with different strategies and collect the statistics such as tps, bps, and avg and use them as baseline performance metrics for your web services.

In addition to the statistics table, you will find the **LoadTest Log** tab at the bottom of the load test window, as shown in the following screenshot. In this, we can filter the load test results by types and TestSteps. We can either filter out log messages or status of the TestStep execution. You can right-click on each of the failed TestSteps and select the **Show Message Exchange** option to look at the request and response messages to debug the failures. If your load test includes multiple TestSteps, you can view the log of individual TestSteps at the right corner of **LoadTest Log** toolbar. You can do this by choosing the relevant step from the **Show Steps** drop-down menu.

By default, soapUI load tests generate two useful statistics graphs based on the test results included in the statistics table. A statistics graph is used to show the variations of statistics such as `tps` and `bps` of a load test as the test progresses. A statistics history graph shows the accumulated statistics of the load test. Let's run **getGuestDetailsLoadTest** with the thread strategy using 1 to 20 threads in 5 minutes and see the statistics graph. The result will be as follows:

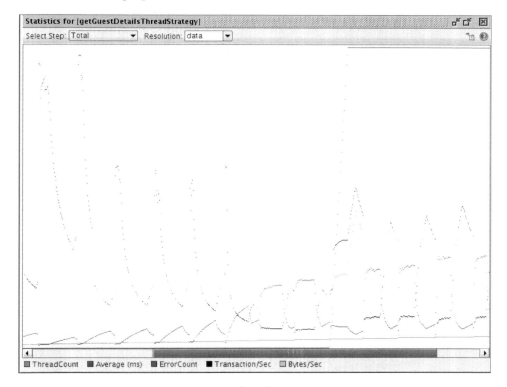

If you look at the statistics graph with the default options, you can clearly observe how the average response time and the TPS and BPS values change as the thread count increases. If your TestCase includes more than one TestStep, the statistics relevant to the particular TestStep can be filtered by the **Select Step** drop-down menu at the upper-left corner of the statistics toolbar.

The **Resolution** drop-down menu is used to set the frequency of updating the statistics graph. The default value, **data** updates the graph with same interval as the statistics table. You should also keep in mind that the statistics graphs show relative data and do not display the exact statistics related to the TestCase executions. Therefore, if you want to analyze the exact statistical figures, you should use the corresponding statistics table. The graph can be used to visualize the variations of service performance.

You can also export the statistics data into a file and refer to it later. In statistics toolbar of load test window, there is an option to export statistics to a file. This is available in the statistics table as well as both history and statistics graphs. If you export the data, it will be saved as a CSV file so that you can use any tool to manipulate the graphs or analyze results as you wish.

Using load test assertions in soapUI

Assertions are compulsory for automated tests regardless of the nature of the tests. As we used many assertions in functional testing, we must use the appropriate assertions for non-functional tests. soapUI allows you to configure assertions to verify the performance of web services under test. In this section, we are going to look at how different types of load test related assertions can be used.

soapUI provides us with five different assertions to use inside load/performance tests. These are as follows:

- **Max Errors**
- **Step Average**
- **Step TPS**
- **Step Maximum**
- **Step Status**

You can configure load test assertions using three different approaches:

- Select the **LoadTest Assertions** tab at the bottom of the load test editor. Then, you can add assertions by selecting the add assertion icon at the top left corner of the **LoadTest Assertions** tab.
- Right-click on the **LoadTest Assertions** tab and select **Add Assertion**.

- Right-click on the individual TestStep of the statistics table and select **Add Assertion**. You will see the **Add Assertion** window as follows:

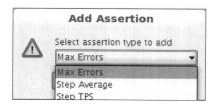

The Max Errors assertion

The Max Errors assertion can be used to verify whether the associated TestCase or TestStep does not exceed the given max absolute errors or max relative errors count. If you select the **Max Errors** assertion from the **Add Assertion** selection box, the corresponding assertion dialog will be opened where you can specify the options for the assertion. In the **Max Errors** assertion, you can specify a user-friendly name to uniquely identify the assertion. Max absolute errors can be used to define the maximum number of errors that the test can accept before failing.

Configure the options in the **Max Errors** assertion as follows for our sample **getGuestDetailsLoadTest**:

- **Max absolute errors = 30**
- **Max relative errors = 1**
- **TestStep = Any**

Start the test and after few seconds stop `Axis2Server.sh` so that some of the TestSteps will fail. When the error count exceeds 30, an error message will pop up:

```
LoadTest failed; Maximum number of errors [30] exceeded for step
[getGuestDetails]
```

Note that we have set the **Max relative errors** value to **1**, so that all absolute errors will be treated as relative errors. Max relative errors define the percentage of the absolute errors and if we want to take all errors into consideration, we can set **Max relative errors** to **1**.

The Step Average assertion

The Step Average assertion can be used to assert the average step time of a TestStep or TestCase in a load test. You need to specify the following options for the Step Average assertion:

- **Name**: This is any user-friendly name.
- **Minimum Requests**: Before applying the assertion, the number of requests that should be processed by soapUI must be specified here.
- **Max average**: This is the maximum allowed average step time value. If the average value exceeds this, an assertion error will be logged.
- **Max errors**: This defines the maximum number of errors allowed before failing the test. If we set **-1** as the max errors, the test will not fail on errors and the errors will be recorded in **LoadTest Log**.
- **Sample Interval**: Step Average cannot be measured by applying an assertion to each and every TestStep run. Instead, the assertion is applied at the intervals defined in the sample interval field. Suppose the sample interval is set to **10**, the assertion will be applied on each 10 second intervals to assert whether the actual average exceeds the Max average.

Configure the previous options in the Step Average assertion as follows for our sample **getGuestDetailsLoadTest**:

- **Minimum Requests**: 20
- **Max Average**: 1
- **Max errors**: 10
- **Sample Interval**: 10
- **TestStep**: getGuestDetails

When you run the load test, an error message will pop up after you get 10 errors as shown in the following screenshot:

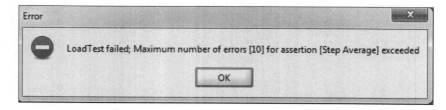

In the preceding assertion configuration, if you specify **-1** as **Max Errors**, the test will not fail. Instead, you will notice the messages similar to the following in **LoadTest Log**.

```
Average [15] exceeds limit [1] [thread index=4]
```

Step TPS assertion

The Step TPS assertion is similar to the Step Average assertion, however it checks that a TPS value of a TestStep does not go below a specified value. Let's add a Step TPS assertion to the sample **getGuestDetailsLoadTest** and look at how it works. We can specify the following values for the assertion options:

- **Name**: We can specify any user-friendly name.
- **Minimum Requests**: Before applying the assertion, the number of requests that should be processed by soapUI must be specified here. We will specify 10 as minimum requests.
- **Minimum TPS**: Minimum transactions per second value. If the actual TPS value of TestStep is lower than this value, an error is logged in **LoadTest Log**. We will set **10** as the minimum TPS value.
- **Max errors**: Maximum number of errors allowed before failing the test. We will set -1 as the max errors, so that the test will not fail on errors.
- **TestStep**: The target TestStep which needs to be asserted. We will specify "Any" as the value to apply the assertion for any TestStep in the load test.

Run the TestCase and check **LoadTest Log**. You will see error messages such as the following in **LoadTest Log**:

```
TPS[5] is less than limit[10][threadIndex=1]
```

The Step Maximum assertion

The **Step Maximum** assertion is another assertion included in soapUI load tests. It can be used to assert the maximum response time of TestStep or TestCase. As we did before, we will add this assertion into our sample test and look at the behavior. The following are the options associated with the Step Maximum assertion:

- **Name**: We can specify any user-friendly name.
- **Minimum Requests**: Before applying the assertion, this is the number of requests that should be processed by soapUI. We will specify **10** as minimum requests.

- **Max time**: This specifies the maximum response time allowed for the TestStep. If the maximum response time exceeds the given **Max time** value, an error is logged in the **LoadTest Log**. We will specify **5** as **Max time**.

- **Max errors**: This defines the maximum number of errors allowed before failing the test. We will set **-1** as the max errors, so that the test will not fail on errors.

- **TestStep**: This is the target TestStep which needs to be asserted. We will specify **Any** as the value to apply the assertion for any TestStep in the load test.

Run the TestCase and check **LoadTest Log**. You will see error messages similar to the following in the **LoadTest Log**.

```
Time[11] exceeds limit[5][threadIndex1]
```

The Step Status assertion

The last load test assertion which needs to be discussed is the **Step Status** assertion. The Step Status assertion is added to any load test by default. This assertion simply verifies the execution status of the associated TestCase or TestStep. You will find the following options associated with the Step Status assertion:

- **Name**: This is a user-friendly name to identify the assertion easily.

- **Minimum Requests**: The minimum requests option determines how many requests should be processed by soapUI before applying the assertion.

- **Max errors**: Maximum number of errors allowed before failing the test. We will set -1 as the max errors, so that the test will not fail on errors.

- **TestStep**: The target TestStep which needs to be asserted. We will specify "Any" as the value to apply the assertion for any TestStep in the load test.

Run the test and check **Load Test Log**. You can introduce a failure by shutting down Axis2Server or disconnecting the MySQL database connection.

 The **Minimum requests** option is applicable for most of the load test assertions. It is advised to specify an appropriate value for this in order to avoid assertion errors during the startup of a load test, and allow TestSteps or TestCase to run freely for some time before measuring up various figures.

LoadTest options

We can set some options, which are applicable for all TestSteps inside a particular load test regardless of the usage of different assertions. By clicking on the **LoadTest Options** icon in the toolbar of the **LoadTest** window, you can open the **LoadTest Options** dialog box. Some of the important settings included there are:

- **Thread Startup Delay**: We can introduce a delay in milliseconds before starting any thread. The default value is zero therefore there will not be a delay when starting threads.

- **Close connections between each request**: This is to set connections as keep-alive. By default, soapUI uses keep-alive connections.

- **Sample interval**: This is used to specify the time in milliseconds to set the interval to collect statistics during a test run. In order to preserve resources of the machine which runs soapUI, we need to set an optimum time for the sample interval.

We are not going to discuss all settings given in LoadTest options. You can hover the mouse pointer over any option and find out the purpose of these options.

Similar to the functional tests, soapUI allows you to specify setup and tear down scripts for load tests. Also, there is a set of load test related properties available for you to use in scripts.

Also, load tests can be invoked through command-line or shell, allowing you to integrate them into continuous integration systems or automated test frameworks. We will look into the command-line test runners in *Chapter 13, Automated Testing with soapUI*.

Summary

Non-functional testing is an extremely important activity in any service-oriented project. Performance, scalability, and usability are some of the key non-functional attributes expected from any application. In this chapter, we looked into the usage of soapUI to do performance tests of web services. First, we discussed why it is important to consider performance implications in an SOA. We proceeded with describing performance test planning of web services. Next, we looked at how soapUI can be used for various performance tests with our usual hotel reservation sample project. Finally, we discussed LoadTest-specific assertions provided by soapUI.

6
Web Service Simulation with soapUI

Simulation is not specific to the world of web services and SOA. It is coupled with most of the industrial scenarios. When manufacturing a new model of your favorite motor car, it usually goes through multiple simulations to mimic the representation and behavior of the final product. The massive and complex constructions are never done without simulations. Similarly, in large service-oriented projects, there are many situations where we need to mimic the behavior of web services and other entities that comprise the solution. Mock services or in simple terms, **mocking**, is a highly useful and important practice in the development and testing of web services. We will cover the following topics in this chapter which are related to the simulation of web services in soapUI:

- Mocking in web services testing
- Mock services with soapUI
- Dispatching styles of soapUI mock operations
- Using static and dynamic mock responses

Mocking in software testing

Before we delve into the details of web service simulation, it will be beneficial to discuss the basic use of mocking in software testing.

If you are familiar with unit testing, **mock objects** should not be a strange term. Specially, in **Test-driven Development (TDD)**, mock objects are used to test the functionality of a feature without actually calling the complex and real implementation classes. When the objects you are testing rely on other objects or are bound with complex environments, it is not always practical to instantiate them. Instead, a mock object, which conforms to the interface of the real object, can be used to mimic the behavior of the original. For example, when you are building an application, which uses a database, you do not want to wait till the database team implements the database-specific code. Instead, you would use mock objects to simulate the database modules.

 The complete explanation of mock objects and TDD is out of the scope of this book . You may find *Test-Driven Development: By Example* (http://www.amazon.com/Test-Driven-Development-Kent-Beck/dp/0321146530) by *Kent Beck,* a useful reference.

Mocking in web services testing

Mock services come in handy for web services testing in many ways. In simple terms, when you do not have access to the real web service, you have no option other than to simulate that service. Apart from that, what are the common situations where service mocking is highly desired?

Mock services and contract-first web service development

You may have remembered that we discussed two SOAP web services development approaches in *Chapter 1, Web Services Testing and soapUI*—**code first** and **contract first**. Though we followed the code-first methodology when implementing our sample web services project during *Chapter 2, The Sample Project*, the recommended web service development practice is contract first. In the contract-first methodology, you start from the web service's contract, in other words, the WSDL. Though there are many reasons for recommending contract first as the better choice over code first, the primary reason is its flexibility. When you start with the service implementation class, you cannot guarantee that the auto-generated WSDL remains intact when you change your SOAP engine (service container). Also, if you change a method signature of the service implementation class, the WSDL will also be changed accordingly, which directly affects the consumers of your service. However, if you start with WSDL, you can minimize such changes of consumers by introducing proper versions for schemas.

In contract-first methodology, the WSDL is written first by gathering the business requirements of the web service. Once the WSDL is defined, the service developers implement the business logic of the web service. Usually, the SOAP engine (or web service development framework) provides the developers with tools to generate the service skeleton so that the developers can focus on the business logic.

While the service is being implemented in a preferred programming language, deployed in the web service's container, what should the testers do? Do they just focus on designing the test cases?

In agile methodologies, we compete with time. There is no time for waiting or idling, but every second is spent effectively to be productive. In service-oriented solution testing, it is always important to begin the testing cycle as early as possible. Testers are not expected to wait till the web service implementation and deployment is over.

Mock services are a great way of getting testing early into the picture of a service-oriented project. Once the WSDL of the web service is ready, you can simulate the service implementation and start testing the consumer applications.

Simulating services that are not accessible

Regardless of the service development approach (contract-first or code-first), there are situations in which some of the web services are not in your control. Due to the heterogeneous and distributed nature of the components of SOA, some of your services may connect to services which are outside of your organization. Sometimes these services are blocked by firewalls. In some cases, these external services are not completed though the internal web services are ready for testing. Sometimes, your service-oriented solution may integrate with commercial pay-per-use web services. For testing, it is not cost effective to use such services. In these and many other cases, mock services help you to mimic the behavior of inaccessible, unavailable, or paid web services.

Dealing with test environmental restrictions

As we discussed before, early testing is highly desirable in agile testing, specially with service-oriented solutions. When building complex SOA-based solutions, which has multiple integrations, you cannot confirm the end-to-end functionality of your system till all services are deployed and integrated with various sub systems. For example, if you want to test a monitoring module of a solution, how do you test it if all services are not ready? Or else, if you want to test a message transformation rule at the **Enterprise Service Bus** (**ESB**) layer, how should you continue testing if the associated web service is not available? Mock services can be used to overcome these limitations by adding them instead of the real services in test setups.

In the following sections, we will look into how the MockService functionality of soapUI can be used to achieve the above objectives.

Mock services with soapUI

We briefly discussed service mocking in general and the purpose and objectives of service simulation. Now, it is time to apply the theory into practice. As we did in previous chapters, we will explore the soapUI service mocking features by simulating web services in our sample Hotel Reservation System.

soapUI allows you to create a simulation of the web service from its WSDL. This simulation is known in a soapUI project as a **MockService**. A consumer application can connect to the MockService as if it is the real web service.

Suppose one of the web services of our sample Hotel Reservation System are consumed by some other service-oriented solution. Let's call this solution **solution B** for simplicity. The solution B is almost done whereas the services of our Hotel Reservation System are still being implemented. The quality assurance team of solution B follows an agile testing approach and they do not wish to wait until all services of the Hotel Reservation System are ready. Instead, they are going to create mock services to mimic the functionality provided by hotel reservation services and continue the testing of solution B.

> In this example, we represent the testing team of solution B, so we do not have access to any of the web services that we created in the previous chapters. However, we do have the WSDLs of those web services. Therefore, I assume that you saved a copy of the WSDLs of **GuestManagementService**, **RoomManagementService**, and **ReservationService** in your filesystem during the previous chapters. If not, simply access `http://localhost:8080/axis2/services/ GuestManagementService?wsdl` through your browser, open the source view, and save the file as `GuestManagementService.wsdl`.

We are going to look into the details of how soapUI assists the testers of solution B in service simulation:

1. Create a new soapUI project. Name it `HotelReservationMockServices`. Browse for `GuestManagementService.wsdl` in your filesystem and enter it as the initial WSDL.

2. Accept the default settings and click on **OK**.

3. Once the project is created, remove the SOAP-1.2 binding as we did in the previous samples.

Now, we can create a mock service to simulate the **GuestManagementService**. Before that, we should discuss the MockService model used in a soapUI project so that we will have a better understanding when moving further with the examples.

The structure of soapUI MockService

We can identify three basic elements in the soapUI MockService model — MockService, MockOperations, and MockResponses.

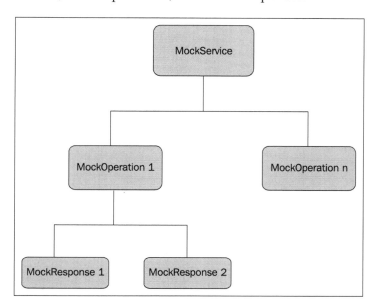

A MockService can include any number of MockOperations that in turn contain multiple MockResponses as shown in the preceding diagram. MockOperations represent operations of the WSDL that is imported in the soapUI project. MockResponses are the response messages that correspond to those operations. When you create a MockService and ask soapUI to run the service, it can act as the real web service simulation. As the MockService is created from the WSDL of a real web service, the MockOperations are automatically created from the <wsdl:operation> element under each binding of the WSDL. As the schema of the WSDL contains the definition of the SOAP responses, MockResponses are created by soapUI from the respective response elements corresponded to operations.

Let's create a MockService for **GuestManagementService** and continue our discussion:

1. Select the **HotelReservationMockServices** project that we created earlier and right-click on the **GuestManagementServiceSoap11Binding** interface. Next, select the **Generate MockService** option.

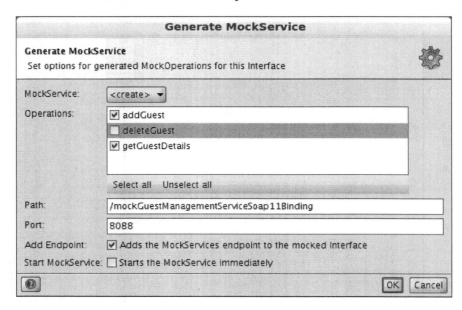

2. We do not expect to simulate all three operations in **GuestManagementService**. Hence, select the **addGuest** and **getGuestDetails** operations as shown in the preceding screenshot.

3. When generating the MockService, we can change the URL where the mock service is hosted. By default, the service is hosted in a path which is prefixed with the interface name. For example:

   `/mock<interfacename>`

4. soapUI hosts the generated mock service in the embedded Jetty server which runs on port 8088. We can change the default port as needed.

5. When you click on **OK**, as shown in the preceding screenshot, you will be asked to enter a name for the MockService. Enter `GuestManagementMockService`.

6. Once the MockService is created, soapUI will show the MockService details with the corresponding MockOperations as follows:

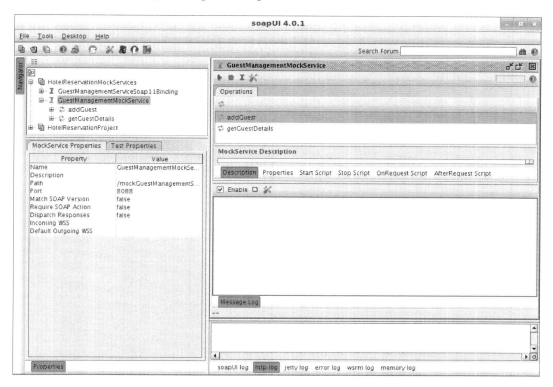

MockService details

The MockService **Properties** tab at the left-hand side pane can be used to edit the default properties of the MockService. For example, you can emulate WS-Security for your service through the **Default outgoing WSS** property. If you want to verify how your consumer applications react when sending a SOAP message without a SOAP Action HTTP header, you can set the **Require SOAP Action** property to **true**. In the same way, you can edit the default mock service properties and test the consumer applications.

In the right pane of the above screen, soapUI allows to do some pre- and post-processing for the MockService. **Start Script** can be used to call a Groovy script at the time of the mock service start. Usually, if we want to initialize some global resources such as database connections, we can call **Start Script**. **Stop Script** is called when the mock service is stopped. When the MockService receives a request, **OnRequest Script** can be called. For example, if you want to mediate the original request before dispatching to service, you can include a Groovy script as **OnRequest Script**. Similarly, **AfterRequest Script** is called after a request is processed by the MockService.

Once we check all properties and options associated with the MockService, we can start the mock service by clicking on the green arrow icon at the upper-left corner of the preceding screen. The status of the MockService can be found at the soapUI log at the bottom pane.

```
INFO:Started mockService [GuestManagementMockService] on port [8088] at
path [/mockGuestManagementServiceSoap11Binding]
```

MockOperation details

Double-clicking on one of the MockOperations in the preceding screen will bring up the MockOperation details window as shown in the following screenshot:

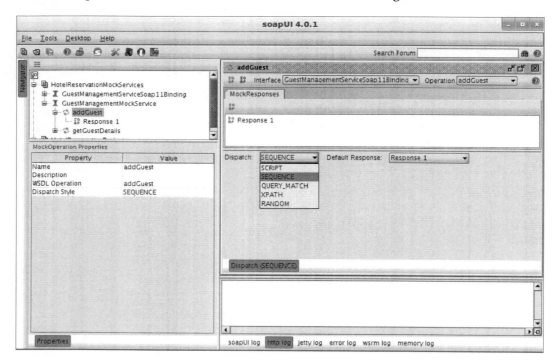

Out of the many properties given in MockOperation details window, we should clear ourselves about the **Dispatch** style property as it is utmost important in determining the mock response.

Dispatching styles of MockOperation

A MockOperation can include multiple MockResponses. Therefore, when we send a request to the MockService and subsequently dispatch to the MockOperation, there should be a way to determine to which MockResponse the request must be forwarded to. The dispatch style of the MockOperation is used to select the preferred dispatching mechanism for mock responses. The soapUI Mock Services model supports the following dispatch styles:

- **SEQUENCE**: This is the default dispatching style. With this style, when sending requests to the MockOperation, MockResponses are selected iteratively one after the other as they appear in the MockResponses list. For example, when we have two MockResponses, response1 and response2 under the MockOperation, if you send two requests to the MockService, the first request will be dispatched to response1 and the second will be dispatched to response2.

- **SCRIPT**: This dispatching style gives the ability to control responses based on Groovy scripting. The MockResponse is determined by the execution of the specified script.

- **RANDOM**: This style chooses the MockResponses randomly without any order.

- **QUERY_MATCH**: This style returns MockResponse by evaluating multiple XPath expressions. For example, you can specify multiple query matches that are basically XPath expressions applied on requests, the expected value of the XPath expression and the MockResponse to which the request must be dispatched to.

Suppose we need to dispatch requests to MockResponses based on the different values of the requests. In that case, we can define multiple XPath expressions to extract the desired values and forward requests to the corresponding MockResponses as shown in the following screenshot:

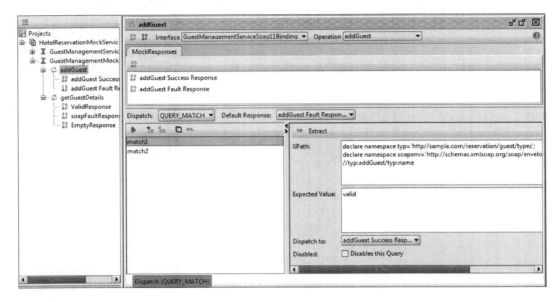

In the preceding example, there are two Mock Responses, **addGuest Success Response** and **addGuest Fault Response**. There are two XPath match queries, **match1** and **match2**; each of them act on the request and extract some value which is defined under the **Expected Value** field in XPath query editor. If the value returned by the XPath expression matches the expected value, the request is forwarded to the response which is defined under the **Dispatch to** drop-down list. Using this style, you can use different XPath queries to evaluate different types of requests and dispatch the requests to MockResponses appropriately.

- **XPATH**: This dispatching method is used to dispatch the request to a response based on the XPATH expression result of the request.

We will look into the use cases of some of the important MockResponse dispatching styles later in this chapter.

MockResponse details

Double-clicking on a MockResponse in the MockResponses list in a MockOperation detail window will bring up the MockResponse editor.

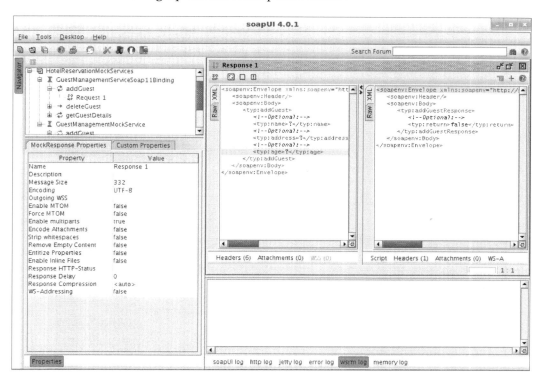

Similar to the MockService and MockOperation, we can configure the properties associated with the MockResponses from the left-hand side pane. We can configure the HTTP headers of the response from the **Headers** section in the right-hand side pane, under the mock response editor. Also, we can even insert an attachment for the response. A response-specific dynamic content can also be generated by specifying a script at the response level.

soapUI mock services in action

In the following sections, we will move forward with our sample MockService with trying out the various options which we discussed previously. First, we will look into the simplest use case, where we use a static MockResponse.

Static responses – the basic scenario

Creating a static MockResponse in soapUI is pretty straightforward. You may question whether the static responses are used in real-world scenarios. Though static MockResponses are simple they are of course very useful in a lot of enterprise integration test scenarios.

Service chaining

In a typical service-oriented solution, the messages can be transmitted through multiple hops before reaching the destination. We cannot always expect single client to service message exchange. **Service chaining** is a concept where the response of one service acts as an input for another service. When testing such a service chaining scenario, static MockResponses can be used if some of the services are not completely available at the time of testing.

Content-based routing

If an **Enterprise Service Bus** (**ESB**) is used as a broker in your SOA, you should test the various routing rules defined at the ESB level. In case the web services are not ready for testing, you can use a static MockResponse and test the routing rules. You can even set custom HTTP headers in MockResponses and test the HTTP header based routing mechanisms.

Message transformation

Static MockResponses can be used to test the message transformation rules usually defined at the ESB layer of your service-oriented solution. Suppose there is an XSLT transformation before sending back the web service response in your solution. If the web service is not available for testing, you can use a static MockResponse and test the XSLT transformation rules.

We will create a static MockResponse to simulate the **getGuestDetails** operation. To do this, follow these steps:

1. Double-click on the **getGuestDetails** operation of the operations list which appears under **GuestManagementMockService**. The **getGuestDetails** MockOperation details window will be opened and you will see one response (Response 1) in the list. Double-click on Response 1 to open the MockResponse editor.

2. Replace the ? values of the response as follows. As you can see, this is a static MockResponse with hard-coded data:

```
<typ:getGuestDetailsResponse>
    <typ:return>
    <typ:address>Colombo, Sri Lanka</typ:address>
    <typ:age>30</typ:age>
        <typ:name>Saman</typ:name>
    </typ:return>
</typ:getGuestDetailsResponse>
```

3. For any request which is received by **GuestManagementMockService**, this particular static response will be returned. Now, select the SOAP request of the **getGuestDetails** operation from the **GuestManagementServiceSoap11Binding** interface. Change the endpoint to `http://hostname:8088/mockGuestManagementServiceSoap11Binding` so that the request will be forwarded to the MockService and submit the request.

4. You will get the static response that we defined above.

As we discussed earlier, the static response are very useful for the test scenarios where the actual data of the response payload is not important.

Using dynamic responses

In our first example of the dynamic responses, we are going to simulate the behavior of the **getGuestDetails** MockOperation with multiple responses instead of a hard-coded static response. The response will be chosen according to the **guestName** value of the SOAP request:

1. Rename Response 1 of `getGuestDetails` MockOperation to something meaningful; for example, `ValidResponse`.

2. Add two more responses and name them `soapFaultResponse` and `EmptyResponse`.

3. Now, you will have three responses: `ValidResponse`, `soapFaultResponse`, `EmptyResponse`. Our objective is to see how our system reacts to these responses.

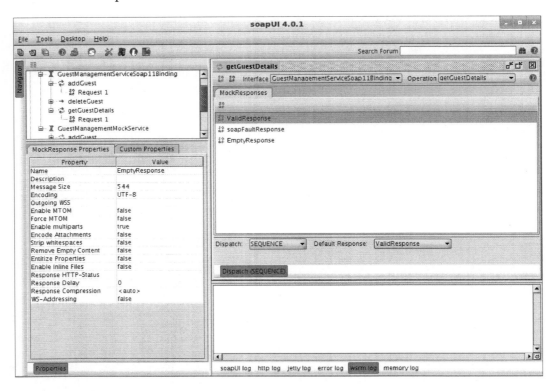

4. Double-click on **soapFaultResponse** and replace the content with the following soap Fault message:

```
<soapenv:Envelope xmlns:soapenv="http://schemas.xmlsoap.org/soap/
envelope/">
    <soapenv:Body>
        <soapenv:Fault>
            <faultcode>soapenv:Server</faultcode>
            <faultstring>Guest does not exist</faultstring>
            <detail>
                <ns:GuestManagementServiceGuestManagementException
xmlns:ns="http//sample.com/reservation/guest/types">
                    <GuestManagementException xsi:type="ax21:GuestM
anagementException" xmlns="http//sample.com/reservation/guest/
types" xmlns:ax21="http://exception.reservation.sample.com/xsd"
xmlns:xsi="http://www.w3.org/2001/XMLSchema-instance">
```

```
            <ax21:message>Guest does not exist</
ax21:message>
                </GuestManagementException>
            </ns:GuestManagementServiceGuestManagementException>
        </detail>
    </soapenv:Fault>
  </soapenv:Body>
</soapenv:Envelope>
```

5. EmptyResponse should be something like the following:

```
<soapenv:Envelope xmlns:soapenv="http://schemas.xmlsoap.org/soap/
envelope/" xmlns:typ="http//sample.com/reservation/guest/types">
    <soapenv:Header/>
    <soapenv:Body>
        <typ:getGuestDetailsResponse>
            <typ:return>
            <typ:address></typ:address>
            <typ:age></typ:age>
            <typ:name></typ:name>
        </typ:return>
        </typ:getGuestDetailsResponse>
    </soapenv:Body>
</soapenv:Envelope>
```

6. In this example, the response is chosen out of the above three
    MockResponses. The selection is based on the `<typ:guestName>` value in
    the SOAP request. If the value is "valid", we will dispatch the request to
    the **ValidResponse** MockResponse. If the value is "fault", the request will
    be dispatched to the **soapFaultResponse** MockResponse. Finally, if the
    guestName value is "empty", the **EmptyResponse** MockResponse will
    be returned.

7. To achieve this, we cannot use the default **SEQUENCE** dispatch style
    which simply iterates through the three response messages. We need to
    decide the response based on the content of the request. Therefore, we need
    to have some kind of a script to read the request and dispatch to the relevant
    MockResponse. We are going to use the **SCRIPT** style for dispatching.

8. In **getGuestDetails** MockOperation editor, select **SCRIPT** from the **Dispatch**
    drop-down list.

9. Add the following script:

```
def payload = new com.eviware.soapui.support.
XmlHolder(mockRequest.requestContent)
def guestname = payload["//typ:getGuestDetails/typ:guestName"]
def response = "";
```

```
if(guestname.equals("valid")){
  response="ValidResponse"
}else if(guestname.equals("fault")){
  response="soapFaultResponse"
}else if(guestname.equals("empty")){
  response="EmptyResponse"
}else {
  response="ValidResponse"
}
return response
```

Here, the requests are dispatched to the MockResponses based on the **guestName** value of the SOAP request message. The XmlHolder object is used to hold the current SOAP request message. An XPath expression is passed as an argument to the constructor of the XmlHolder object to extract the **guestName** value. Then the appropriate response is chosen evaluating the **guestName** value.

With the dispatching script, the **getGuestDetails** MockOperation editor will look similar to the following:

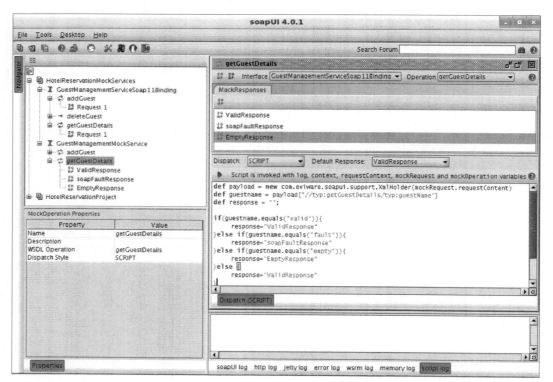

10. Now, open the **getGuestDetails** SOAP request editor and send a request with the **guestName** "fault":

```
<typ:guestName>fault</typ:guestName>
```

You will get the soapFaultResponse. Similarly, try with the other responses.

The above methodology is quite helpful if you need to verify the middleware-oriented operations of your solution such as message mediations, transformation rules, and so on, when the web services are not ready for testing.

We looked at the MockResponse dispatching at the MockOperations level. Without using multiple responses, we can dynamically generate the MockResponse by including a script at the MockResponse level. The following example will guide you through the steps of responding with a dynamic MockResponse based on the content of the SOAP request.

As we saw in *Chapter 2, The Sample Project*, the **GuestManagementService** consists of the service implementation class and the associated database operation handling class (in our example, it is `Storage.java`). Think about a scenario where this database handling class is not ready for testing, but you need to test some consumer applications. In that case, you cannot just use static MockResponses, as you need to make sure the data is correctly handled by the consumer application. In other words, the correctness of the data is important for testing.

We are going to retrieve the data from the database according to the content of the SOAP request message. When the **getGuestDetails** SOAP request is sent with the **guestName**, the GUEST_T table of the HOTEL_RESERVATION_DB database is queried to find out the associated record. Then the MockResponse is updated with the retrieved data and sent back to the client.

1. The MockService level is the most suitable location to initialize the database connection. When the MockService is started, the database connection is established. Open the **GuestManagementMockService** editor and click on **Start Script**. Add the following script in the script editor:

```
import groovy.sql.Sql
com.eviware.soapui.support.GroovyUtils.registerJdbcDriver("com.
mysql.jdbc.Driver")
def sql = Sql.newInstance("jdbc:mysql://localhost:3306/HOTEL_
RESERVATION_DB","root","root","com.mysql.jdbc.Driver")
log.info "Succesfully connected to database"
context.dbConnection = sql
```

By calling `registerdbDriver()` method, the MySQL JDBC driver is registered with soapUI so that we can issue calls to the MySQL database from the Groovy script. First, we need to set up the MySQL database instance using the `Sql.newInstance(dbpath, dbuser, dbpassword, dbdriver)` factory method. We will save this connection in the context (`context.dbConnection`) so that it will be available for all scripts under the MockService.

2. Establishing the connection to the database is not just enough. We should close the connection when our tasks with the database are over. We established the connection at MockService level; hence we can close the connection at the same level. Click on **Stop Script** and add the following script:

```
if( context.dbConnection != null )
{
log.info "Closing database connection"
context.dbConnection.close()
}
```

3. We can restart the MockService now. Before that, make sure to copy the MySQL JDBC driver (which we used in *Chapter 2, The Sample Project*) to `SOAPUI_HOME/bin/ext` and restart soapUI.

   Once soapUI is restarted, restart the MockService. You will see the following log if the database connection is successful. The logs related to the running scripts can be found at the **script log**, which is at the bottom of the MockService editor.

```
INFO:Succesfully connected to database
```

4. Now, we need to configure the MockResponse to retrieve the data from the database table based on the request content. For that, we can insert a Groovy script at the MockResponse level. Click on the **ValidResponse** MockResponse that appears in the **getGuestDetails** operation.

5. Click on **Script** in the MockResponse editor and add the following script:

```
def holder = new com.eviware.soapui.support.XmlHolder(mockRequest.
requestContent)

def name = holder["//typ:getGuestDetails/typ:guestName"]
def sql = context.dbConnection
def res = sql.firstRow("select address from GUEST_T where name =
?", [name])
context.address=res.address
```

Here, the database connection is obtained from the context. The first row entity of the ResultSet is obtained by passing a SQL query as the argument. In the SQL query, we pass the name value which we captured by executing the XPath statement on the request message. This SQL query returns the address value of the corresponding guest. Then we set the address value which we got from the GUEST_T table to the ${address} property which we set at the response (see the following screenshot):

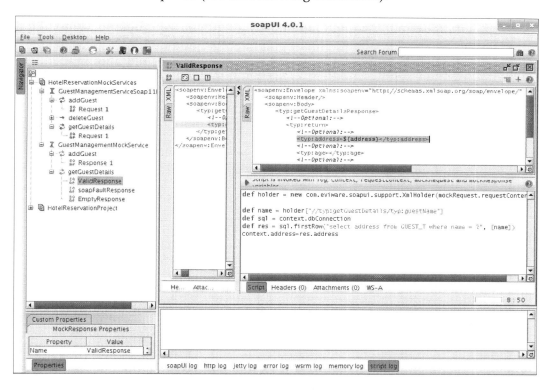

6. Now, populate the GUEST_T table of the HOTEL_RESERVATION_DB database with some guest records (see *Chapter 2, The Sample Project*).

7. Edit a **getGuestDetails** SOAP request message with a name of the user who is in the GUEST_T table:

```
<typ:guestName>Chanmira</typ:guestName>
```

8. Submit the request to **GuestManagementMockService**.

9. You will get the response with the corresponding address value which should be the address of the guest in GUEST_T table.

We extracted the address of the guest from the GUEST_T table in the database without actually calling the web service. We used the MockResponse generated by soapUI from the WSDL and did the simple Groovy scripting to query the database and set the data in the response.

Summary

This chapter guided you through one of the most important aspect of web services and SOA testing, **service simulation**. We have discussed the situations where the service mocking is required in general. Then we went through how soapUI facilitates you to create mock services. The MockService model of soapUI consists of three key elements known as MockService, MockOperation and MockResponse. We briefly discussed each of these elements using examples. We also looked into MockResponse dispatching methods and how one MockResponse can be chosen from multiple responses inside a MockOperation. With Groovy scripting facilities, soapUI allows us to do various manipulations on mock services, hence dynamic response generation is not a complex task for a soapUI user.

7
Advanced Functional Testing with soapUI

In SOA, many types of **Quality of Service (QoS)** requirements have to be fulfilled in order to provide the web service consumers with a satisfactory level of service. Especially in SOAP-based services, different kinds of mechanisms are used to assure guaranteed message delivery and secure communication among the participants of message routing chain. These mechanisms commonly referred to as web service extensions, provide the necessary QoS aspects expected from web services.

One of the greatest advantages of using soapUI for web service testing is that it can be used in testing web services that make use of various web service extensions. Although there are free and commercial tools which can be used to directly invoke web services, most of the tools are unable to continue the operations if the web services under testing are configured with different QoS aspects. This chapter is dedicated to discussing the capabilities of soapUI in testing various web service extensions such as WS-Addressing and WS-Security. These extensions are applicable for both sides of the web service equation. In other words, we should configure the extensions at the web service level as well as the client (soapUI) level. Because of that, first, we will look into enabling the necessary QoS features in our sample web services project. Then, we will make use of soapUI to test the sample web services which are configured with the web service extensions.

The following topics related to web services extensions and soapUI that we will be covering in this chapter are as follows:

- Introduction to web services extensions
- WS-Addressing
- WS-Security

- Configuring Apache Axis2 for WS-Addressing and WS-Security
- Testing WS-Addressing with soapUI
- Testing WS-Security with soapUI

Introduction to web services extensions

Web services extensions are used to provide additional capabilities to web services. For example, if we want to protect web services from unauthorized access, we can make use of the relevant web services extension. Web services extensions are usually governed by a set of specifications referred to as the WS-* standards. For example:

- WS-Addressing
- WS-Policy
- WS-Security
- WS-ReliableMessaging
- WS-Discovery
- WS-Transfer
- WS-AtomicTransaction

There are different types of specifications which address various aspects of web services in order to extend the core features. These specifications are governed by various standard bodies such as W3C (http://www.w3.org/) and OASIS standards (https://www.oasis-open.org/standards).

Web service frameworks adhere to most of these specifications in order to be interoperable with each other. For example, Apache Axis2 implemented WS-Security specification; so, we can communicate with any service that is deployed on Axis2 via a .NET service or client, that adheres to the same specification. Like-wise, it is the responsibility of the relevant SOAP engine providers to implement the WS-* specifications to work seamlessly with the other frameworks which support the WS-* standards.

The extensible nature of the SOAP messaging model allows us to plug in different web services extensions to raw SOAP messages. All these extensions are included inside the header element of SOAP messages. Thus, if you want to invoke a web service with WS-Security, you must send the request message with the necessary WS-Security headers adhering to the WS-Security specifications.

A SOAP Envelope structure is shown in the following diagram:

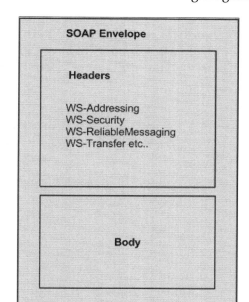

One or two chapters of this book are not sufficient to discuss all of these WS-*
specifications. Therefore, we will limit our discussion to WS-Addressing and WS-
Security specifications which are widely used by the SOAP web services community.

What is WS-Addressing

Web Service Addressing (WS-Addressing) provides mechanisms to address
web services in a transport neutral manner. In the SOAP world, without having
WS-Addressing, we make use of the facilities provided by the underlying transport
protocol (for example, HTTP, FTP or JMS) to route the messages between the SOAP
nodes. However, by using WS-Addressing, the messages can be routed in a generic
way independent of the transport protocol that is used. As WS-Addressing is used
by many of the other WS-* specifications, it is one of the preliminary building blocks
of WS-* standards. The W3C Web Services Addressing Working Group (`http://
www.w3.org/2002/ws/addr/`) made available version 1.0 of the WS-Addressing
recommendation (`http://www.w3.org/2002/ws/addr/`) in May 2006, and it is
considered as the mainstream specification.

There are two constructs that are defined by the WS-Addressing specification.

Endpoint references

An **endpoint** is an entity to which a message can be addressed. An endpoint reference is a collection of three abstract properties, address, reference parameters, and metadata. Out of these, address is a mandatory property, which must be available in any endpoint reference element. An example of an endpoint reference element is as follows:

```
<wsa:EndpointReference>
        <wsa:Address>http://localhost:8080/axis2/services/
GuestManagementService/</wsa:Address>
</wsa:EndpointReference>
```

Here, the `<wsa:Address>` element is used to define the endpoint location of `GuestManagementWebService`.

Message addressing properties

Message addressing properties are used to convey end-to-end message characteristics of source and destination endpoints. The following are the basic set of message addressing properties. Out of these, `wsa:Action` is the only mandatory property.

- `wsa:To`: This property specifies the destination URL. If not present, the destination will be considered as `http://www.w3.org/2005/08/addressing/anonymous`.

- `wsa:From`: This property specifies the source endpoint reference (that is, where the message comes from).

- `wsa:ReplyTo`: This property specifies the endpoint reference for the intended receiver (that is, to whom the reply of the message would be sent).

- `wsa:FaultTo`: This property specifies where to send the fault messages in case of a fault. If this is not present, the fault will be sent to the endpoint where the request came from.

- `wsa:Action`: This property specifies the action of message. In other words, this property is used to dispatch the message to the correct operation of web service upon receiving a request message.

- `wsa:MessageID`: This property specifies the ID which uniquely identifies the message.

- `wsa:RelatesTo`: This property specifies the message ID of the related message.

> According to the 3.4 *Formulating a Reply Message* section at `http://www.w3.org/TR/2006/REC-ws-addr-core-20060509/#formreplymsg` of the WS-Addressing specification, the `wsa:MessageID` property is mandatory for the request-response MEP. Therefore, if you invoke an operation expecting a response back, you should send the `messageID` with the request.

What is WS-Security

Traditionally, the communication between the SOAP nodes is secured using the mechanisms provided by the underlying transport protocol. For example, SSL is a widely used transport-level security mechanism. However, SOAP messages can be transmitted over various transport protocols such as SMTP and JMS. So the transport level security is never sufficient. In SOA, we cannot always expect messages are delivered from one source to destination. Messages can be routed through many hops using different transport protocols and different security domains. Transport level security mechanisms only address point-to-point security. However, in complex service-oriented solutions, we need to consider end-to-end security aspects. WS-Security facilitates this end-to-end security by maintaining integrity and confidentiality of messages.

Leveraging existing industry standards such as X.509 and Kerberos tokens for authentication, XML encryption, and XML signature to encrypt and digitally sign XML documents, WS-security extends those standards to be used with the SOAP messages. WS-Security is not a standalone specification, which solely manages security in web services. It is associated with many of the following specifications:

WS-Policy

The WS-Policy (`http://schemas.xmlsoap.org/ws/2004/09/policy/`) defines a framework for allowing web services to express their constraints and requirements as policy assertions.

WS-SecurityPolicy

As stated in WS-SecurityPolicy specification (`http://docs.oasis-open.org/ws-sx/ws-securitypolicy/v1.2/ws-securitypolicy.html`), WS-SecurityPolicy defines a set of security policy assertions that describe how messages are to be secured based on the WS-Policy framework.

WS-Trust

WS-Trust specification (`http://docs.oasis-open.org/ws-sx/ws-trust/v1.4/ws-trust.html`) provides extensions to WS-Security specification which defines methods for issuing, renewing, and validating security tokens. It also defines the ways to establish, assess the presence of, and to broker trust relationships.

WS-SecureConversation

WS-SecureConversation specification (`http://docs.oasis-open.org/ws-sx/ws-secureconversation/v1.4/ws-secureconversation.html`) provides secure communication between web services using session keys. It defines a mechanism to establish security contexts for multiple exchanges of a SOAP message.

Configuring Apache Axis2 for WS-Addressing and WS-Security

As we discussed early in the chapter, it is the responsibility of the service container (SOAP web services engine) to implement the necessary WS-* specifications and make sure that it is interoperable with the rest of the web service frameworks. Using the modular and pluggable architecture, Apache Axis2 extends its functionality over almost all types of WS-* standards. The following are some of the modules which implement various WS-* specifications on top of the Apache Axis2:

- **Addressing**: This module is an implementation of the WS-Addressing specification

- **Apache Rampart**: This module implements the WS-Security, WS-SecureConversation, and WS-SecurityPolicy specifications on Axis2

- **Sandesha2**: This module is an implementation of the WS-ReliableMessaging specification

- **Rahas**: This module is an implementation of the WS-Trust specification

In this section, we will look into enabling the WS-* extensions at the server side. Obviously, in order to enable WS-Security for web services hosted in Apache Axis2, we must configure the Apache Rampart module. First, we will look into the configurations for the WS-Addressing specification in Apache Axis2.

WS-Addressing in Apache Axis2

There is no configuration required in Axis2 to switch on WS-Addressing support for web services. By default, the addressing module is globally engaged for all services hosted in Axis2 by using the following parameter in the `axis2.xml` descriptor file located at `AXIS2_HOME/conf` as:

```
<module ref="addressing"/>
```

This implies that any service hosted in Apache Axis2 is capable of interpreting WS-Addressing headers. Therefore, if you send a request with WS-Addressing headers (for example, `wsa:Action`), Axis2 can process them and send back the response with the relevant headers.

WS-Security in Apache Axis2

Enabling WS-Security for services hosted in Axis2 is not as straightforward as configuring WS-Addressing. Apache Rampart module is used to secure the messages, which are processed by Axis2. We need to download and install Apache Rampart separately in order to integrate it with Axis2.

Follow these steps to integrate Apache Rampart with Apache Axis2:

1. Download Apache Rampart-1.6.1 binary from `http://axis.apache.org/axis2/java/rampart/download/1.6.1/download.cgi` that is compatible with Apache Axis2 v1.6.1 – the one used in this book.
2. Extract the downloaded binary distribution into a location in your filesystem. Let's refer to it as `RAMPART_HOME`.
3. Copy all JAR files included in `RAMPART_HOME/lib` to `AXIS2_HOME/lib`.
4. Copy all the module files (`.mar`) included in `RAMPART_HOME/modules` into `AXIS2_HOME/repository/modules`.
5. Restart Axis2 server.

We can simply engage the Rampart module globally, similar to the Addressing module, but it is not a common practice as we cannot expect that all services hosted in Axis2 are secured with the WS-Security policies. Therefore, we selectively configure security for the services, which need to be secured.

We will discuss the details of securing services in the following sections.

Testing the WS-Addressing with soapUI

When we communicate with a web service, which expects the WS-Addressing information in the requested SOAP messages, we can follow a programmatic approach to write a client program using the APIs provided by the underlying web services framework and insert WS-Addressing headers manually. Almost all SOAP web services stacks provide users with client APIs which facilitate such programmatic invocations with WS-* extensions. Instead of spending an unneccessarily long time writing client programs from scratch, you can use soapUI to submit messages with the WS-Addressing headers and validate the responses automatically. We are going to extend our sample **HotelReservation** soapUI project to test GuestManagementService with WS-Addressing. To test GuestManagementService, perform the following steps:

1. Select the **getGuestDetails** TestCase of the GuestManagementService TestSuite. Open the **getGuestDetails** SOAP request.

2. Click on the **WS-A** tab which is located at the bottom of the request editor window. This will open the WS-Addressing properties window as shown in the following screenshot:

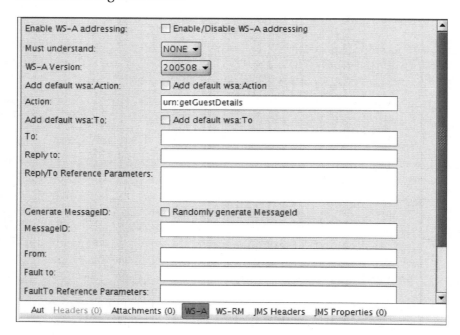

3. Select the following properties and submit the request:
    1. Check the checkbox in front of **Enable WS-A addressing**.
    2. Set **Must Understand** to **True** by selecting it from the drop-down list.
    3. Check the checkbox in front of **Add default wsa:Action**.
    4. Check the checkbox in front of **Add default wsa:To**.
    5. Check the checkbox for **Randomly generate MessageId**.

4. Have a look at the **Raw** view of the request. You will notice the following WS-A headers:

```
<soapenv:Header xmlns:wsa="http://www.w3.org/2005/08/addressing">
<wsa:Action soapenv:mustUnderstand="1">urn:getGuestDetails</
wsa:Action>
<wsa:MessageID soapenv:mustUnderstand="1">uuid:cb993b0b-041d-43ca-
810d-f57ca4544b68</wsa:MessageID>
<wsa:To soapenv:mustUnderstand="1">http://
localhost:8080/axis2/services/GuestManagementService.
GuestManagementServiceHttpSoap11Endpoint/</wsa:To>
</soapenv:Header>
```

In case you see an empty HTTP body in the **Raw** view, which prevents showing the SOAP message, the following steps will help you to configure the soapUI request editor appropriately:

- Open the **soapUI Preferences** window by selecting the **Sets Global soapUI Preferences** icon at the tool bar.
- Click on **UI Settings**. Increase the default value of **Size of Raw Request Message to Show**.

We have already discussed the usage of message addressing properties such as wsa:Action and wsa:To in the previous sections. In addition to the message addressing properties defined by the WS-Addressing specification, soapUI allows us to set the mustUnderstand property for request messages.

According to the SOAP 1.1 specification, the mustUnderstand attribute can be used to indicate whether a header entry is mandatory or optional for the recipient to process. The value of the mustUnderstand attribute is either 1 or 0. If a header element is tagged with the SOAP mustUnderstand attribute with a value of 1, the recipient of that header entry either must obey the semantics and process correctly to those semantics, or must fail processing the message.

To demonstrate the usage of the `mustUnderstand` property, you can simply set `mustUnderstand` to `true` in the soapUI addressing properties section, disable addressing at Axis2 level (comment out the line `<module ref="addressing"/>` from the `axis2.xml` file) and restart the Axis2 server. Then, resubmit the preceding SOAP request. You will get the following error:

```
<soapenv:Envelope xmlns:soapenv="http://schemas.xmlsoap.org/soap/
envelope/">
    <soapenv:Body>
        <soapenv:Fault xmlns:axis2ns1="http://schemas.xmlsoap.org/
soap/envelope/">
            <faultcode>axis2ns1:MustUnderstand</faultcode>
            <faultstring>Must Understand check failed for header
http://www.w3.org/2005/08/addressing : Action</faultstring>
            <detail/>
        </soapenv:Fault>
    </soapenv:Body>
</soapenv:Envelope>
```

In simple terms, we sent a request with the `mustUnderstand` property set to `true`, which implies that the server must process the header block or return a fault. As WS-Addressing is disabled at the server side, the web service could not interpret the header hence it threw the preceding fault.

The real advantage of using soapUI as a WS-Addressing client is that we can simply set the message addressing properties and test the functionality of the solution under test. By specifying an endpoint URL of another web service as the `wsa:ReplyTo` header, the response message can be directed to that particular service instead of sending it back to the client. We can also specify the `wsa:FaultTo` header to a different web service endpoint and forward the fault messages to it.

5. We looked at the WS-A headers of the request SOAP message. The response headers for the preceding request will be similar to the following:

```
<soapenv:Header xmlns:wsa="http://www.w3.org/2005/08/addressing">
        <wsa:Action>urn:getGuestDetailsResponse</wsa:Action>
        <wsa:RelatesTo>uuid:cb993b0b-041d-43ca-810d-f57ca4544b68</
wsa:RelatesTo>
    </soapenv:Header>
```

6. The web service responded with two addressing headers, `wsa:Action` and `wsa:RelatesTo`. The `wsa:RelatesTo` header represents the `messageID` of the related message, in other words the `messageID` of the request. It is obvious that `uuid:cb993b0b-041d-43ca-810d-f57ca4544b68` is the `messageID` of the SOAP request (as seen in the preceding SOAP request header).

Validating the WS-Addressing responses

SoapUI provides us with WS-Addressing specific assertions to automatically validate the headers of the response message. The WS-Addressing response assertion can be used to validate that the last received response contains valid WS-Addressing headers. To validate the WS-Addressing response, perform the following steps:

1. Click on the **Select Assertion** icon at the bottom of the TestStep window and select the **WS-Addressing Response** assertion.

2. The **WS-A properties to assert** dialog box will be opened as shown in the following figure:

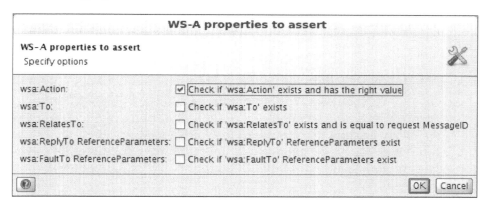

We can select which message-addressing properties of the response we need to assert from the preceding dialog box. In our sample, we can check whether the wsa:Action header exists in the response and wsa:RelatesTo header equal to the request's messageID. Setting the relevant property's assertion depends on the usage of WS-Addressing in your solution.

> Generally, WS-Addressing related issues can occur due to the misconfiguration of the service container or bugs in the particular version of the service container. Therefore, it is always advisable to assert the presence of at least the wsa:Action mandatory message addressing property.

3. Once you add the assertion with the relevant properties and submit a request, you will get the response results as follows:

```
WS-Addressing Response - VALID
```

Testing WS-Security with soapUI

soapUI makes use of the Apache WSS4J project for providing WS-Security support. More information about Apache WSS4J can be found at `http://ws.apache.org/wss4j/`.

We can discuss the usage of soapUI as a WS-Security client in two basic aspects:

- Authentication using transport binding assertions
- Signature using asymmetric binding assertions

We will look into these subtopics during the remainder of this chapter. We use our sample Hotel Reservation web services to demonstrate the preceding topics.

Web service authentication

Authentication is required to identify the entity or entities involved in the web service message transmission. WS-Security provides multiple ways in which one can authenticate a user when they need to access a service. UsernameToken authentication is one such mechanism which is used to pass around caller credentials through a username and password combination as shown in the following diagram:

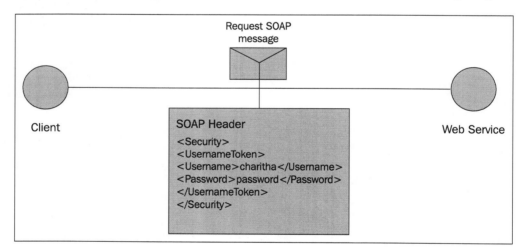

The preceding diagram shows how the user credentials are placed inside a SOAP message header block when UsernameToken authentication is used. There are two ways in which passwords can be passed between client and service when using UsernameToken authentication; clear text and digest. In the case of clear text type, the username token carries the actual password. In the digest type, the client creates a digest of the actual password and sends it to the service, this serves better protection as compared to a plain text password type.

In our first sample, we will use UsernameToken authentication to secure the GuestManagementService and use soapUI to pass credentials to the service. To do that, first we will configure WS-Security at the server side.

Securing GuestManagementService

As we discussed in the *WS-Security in Apache Axis2* section, the Apache Rampart module provides the necessary WS-Security constructs for the services deployed on Axis2. We need to carry out a set of steps to enable UsernameToken authentication for GuestManagementService to be deployed on Axis2.

We need to advertise to the rest of the world that our GuestManagementService is accessible only by submitting proper credentials. The WS-SecurityPolicy specification allows us to define a security policy for our service and expose it so that any consumer can look into the policy and find out how to talk to the service. Thus, our first task is to construct the relevant security policy as shown in the following XML document:

```
<wsp:Policy wsu:Id="UTOverTransport" xmlns:wsu="http://docs.oasis-
open.org/wss/2004/01/oasis-200401-wss-wssecurity-utility-1.0.xsd"
xmlns:wsp="http://schemas.xmlsoap.org/ws/2004/09/policy">
        <wsp:ExactlyOne>
          <wsp:All>
            <sp:TransportBinding xmlns:sp="http://schemas.xmlsoap.org/
ws/2005/07/securitypolicy">
              <wsp:Policy>
                <sp:TransportToken>
                  <wsp:Policy>
                    <sp:HttpsToken RequireClientCertificate="false"/>
                  </wsp:Policy>
                </sp:TransportToken>
                <sp:AlgorithmSuite>
                  <wsp:Policy>
                    <sp:Basic128/>
                  </wsp:Policy>
```

```
          </sp:AlgorithmSuite>
          <sp:Layout>
            <wsp:Policy>
              <sp:Lax/>
            </wsp:Policy>
          </sp:Layout>
          <sp:IncludeTimestamp/>
        </wsp:Policy>
      </sp:TransportBinding>

      <sp:SignedSupportingTokens xmlns:sp="http://schemas.
xmlsoap.org/ws/2005/07/securitypolicy">
          <wsp:Policy>
              <sp:UsernameToken sp:IncludeToken="http://schemas.
xmlsoap.org/ws/2005/07/securitypolicy/IncludeToken/AlwaysToRecipient"
/>
          </wsp:Policy>
      </sp:SignedSupportingTokens>
      <ramp:RampartConfig xmlns:ramp="http://ws.apache.org/
rampart/policy">
<ramp:passwordCallbackClass>com.sample.reservation.security.
PWCBHandler</ramp:passwordCallbackClass>
      </ramp:RampartConfig>
    </wsp:All>
  </wsp:ExactlyOne>
</wsp:Policy>
```

It is out of the scope of this book to explain each element of the preceding security policy. However, we can identify two main policy assertions in the above policy, a `sp:TransportBinding` assertion and a `SignedSupportingToken` assertion.

> A **policy** assertion is a way of defining a requirement, constraint or a property. The WS Security policy language introduces a set of security policy assertions to enable security requirements of web services to be able to be stated in a standard, interoperable manner.

In the preceding policy, the `TransportBinding` assertion is used for handing over the message protection to the underlying transport layer. The required transport is configured through the `<sp:TransportToken>` element.

Ideally, we should use HTTPS as the transport medium as we rely on the underlying transport for message protection. But for the simplicity in configurations at the server side, we use HTTP transport. Therefore, when we include the preceding security policy in the sample `GuestManagementService`, we will remove the `<sp:HttpsToken RequireClientCertificate= "false"/>` element. However, we need to keep in mind that it is not recommended to use HTTP transport when `UsernameToken` authentication is used with plain text passwords. I will leave it to you to try out the sample with HTTPS.

We also used `SignedSupportingToken` assertion in our policy. Supporting tokens are used to provide additional claims for the client. In case of `TransportBinding`, the message is signed outside the message's XML by the underlying transport protocol and the signature itself is not part of the message. Because of that, you will not find the signature in the SOAP request when `UsernameToken` authentication is used.

The last assertion, `RampartConfig` is used to provide Apache Rampart specific configuration details such as the `passwordCallbackClass` which is used to provide passwords that are needed to validate incoming username tokens.

We have defined `com.sample.reservation.security.PWCBHandler` as the callback handler class. Now, we need to implement this particular class and make it available at the web service's class path by performing the following steps:

1. Open the hotel reservation sample project which we worked on in *Chapter 2, The Sample Project* and add the following class inside a new package, `com.sample.reservation.security`, as follows:

```
package com.sample.reservation.security;

import org.apache.ws.security.WSPasswordCallback;

import javax.security.auth.callback.Callback;
import javax.security.auth.callback.CallbackHandler;
import javax.security.auth.callback.UnsupportedCallbackException;
import java.io.IOException;

public class PWCBHandler implements CallbackHandler {

    public void handle(Callback[] callbacks) throws IOException,

UnsupportedCallbackException {
```

```
         for (int i = 0; i < callbacks.length; i++) {


                 WSPasswordCallback pwcb = (WSPasswordCallback)
callbacks[i];
//Usage value is set to USERNAME_TOKEN_UNKNOWN when the Rampart
// engine
//wants the password callback handler to validate the username and
// password in the username token.
if (pwcb.getUsage() == WSPasswordCallback.USERNAME_TOKEN_UNKNOWN)
{
                 if (pwcb.getIdentifer().equals("charitha") &&
pwcb.getPassword().equals("charitha")) {
                         return;
                 } else {
                         throw new UnsupportedCallbackException(callbac
ks[i], "check failed");
                 }
         }


     }
   }
}
```

 The complete source code of the PWCBHandler.java class can be found at src\com\sample\reservation\security\ PWCBHandler.java in the code bundle of this chapter.

2. Now, we need to engage the Rampart module at the service level in order to enable WS-Security for GuestManagementService. Open the services. xml file which can be found inside the conf folder of the sample project. Add the following element under <service name="GuestManagementService"> as follows:

```
<module ref="rampart" />
```

3. Also, add the security policy which we discussed previously, at the same level in services.xml.

4. Finally, the GuestManagementService element in services.xml will be similar to the following XML document:

```
<service name="GuestManagementService">
        <description>
         <wsp:Policy wsu:Id="UTOverTransport">
            ..
```

```
      . .
      . .
      </wsp:Policy>
      <module ref="rampart" />
      <schema>
      <messageReceivers>
      <parameter name="ServiceClass">com.sample.reservation.
GuestManagementService</parameter>
          <operation name="addGuest" mep="http://www.w3.org/2006/01/
wsdl/in-out">
          -------
      </service>
```

The complete `services.xml` file with the security policy can be found in the `conf` folder within the chapter 7 folder of the code bundle.

5. Now, we should rebuild our sample hotel reservation service because we need to include a new class, `PWCBHandler.java` and we have also done some modifications in the `services.xml` file.

If you are using a Java IDE such as Eclipse or Intellij IDEA, you could easily compile the preceding `PWCBHandler.java` by including the `AXIS2_HOME/lib` folder in the class path. If not, you can use the ant build script given in the code bundle associated with this chapter. Make sure to follow the instructions in the `README.txt` file of the code bundle when building the service.

6. Once the service is built, redeploy `HotelReservation.aar` in the Apache Axis2 server. (You can simply remove the existing service archive and deploy the updated one).

7. Check the autogenerated WSDL of the `GuestManagementService` by accessing `http://localhost:8080/axis2/services/GuestManagementService?wsdl`. You will find the `UTOverTransport` policy element in there.

Testing the secured GuestManagementService with soapUI

So far, we have discussed securing `GuestManagementService`. Since we have done the necessary WS-Security configurations at the server side, let's proceed with invoking the service with soapUI. If we submit the SOAP request of the `getGuestDetails` TestStep in `GuestManagementServiceTestSuite` without any security-related configurations, we should get a SOAP Fault similar to the following:

```
<soapenv:Fault xmlns:wsse="http://docs.oasis-open.org/wss/2004/01/
oasis-200401-wss-wssecurity-secext-1.0.xsd">
<faultcode>wsse:InvalidSecurity</faultcode>
<faultstring>Missing wsse:Security header in request</faultstring>
<detail />
</soapenv:Fault>
```

We got this error because we did not instruct soapUI to insert the WS-Security headers to the request. The security policy which we configured previously at the server side looked for the headers and as those were not available in the request, it returned a SOAP Fault.

There are multiple ways to configure WS-Security for outgoing requests in soapUI. The simplest possible mechanism is to configure it at the SOAP request level using the **TestRequest** Properties. You will find the following WS-Security-related properties at the **TestRequest** Properties pane:

- **Username**: This property has the username of the user who invokes the service.

- **Password**: This property has the password of the user.

- **Domain**: This property has the domain to use if the request requires NTLM authentication (this is not applicable for our sample use case).

- **WSS-Password Type**: This property determines how the password is carried over a SOAP message, as clear text or digest.

- **WSS-TimeToLive**: This value specifies the time period in seconds during which the request is considered as valid. In simple terms we can consider this as the life time of the message. In secure communications, timelines of data is a very important factor so that the replay attacks can be avoided by making sure the request message is not an expired one.

- **SSL Keystore**: This specifies the path of the key store when using SSL (we do not use SSL in our example).

TestRequest Properties	Test Properties	
Property		**Value**
Interface		GuestManagementServiceSoap11Binding
Operation		getGuestDetails
Username		charitha
Password		**************
Domain		
WSS-Password Type		PasswordText
WSS TimeToLive		60
SSL Keystore		

Specify the values for the security-related properties as shown in the preceding screenshot. We have given 60 seconds as WSS TimeToLive assuming it will not take 60 seconds for a request message to reach the service.

Submit the request and look at the **Raw** view of the message, it will look as follows:

```
<Header>
    <wsse:Security xmlns:wsse="http://docs.oasis-open.org/wss/2004/01/
oasis-200401-wss-wssecurity-secext-1.0.xsd" mustUnderstand="1">
    <wsu:Timestamp xmlns:wsu="http://docs.oasis-open.org/wss/2004/01/
oasis-200401-wss-wssecurity-utility-1.0.xsd" wsu:Id="Timestamp-4">
    <wsu:Created>2012-05-01T12:58:55Z</wsu:Created>
    <wsu:Expires>2012-05-01T12:59:55Z</wsu:Expires>
</wsu:Timestamp>
<wsse:UsernameToken xmlns:wsu="http://docs.oasis-open.org/wss/2004/01/
oasis-200401-wss-wssecurity-utility-1.0.xsd" wsu:Id="UsernameToken-3">
<wsse:Username>charitha</wsse:Username>
<wsse:Password Type="http://docs.oasis-open.org/wss/2004/01/oasis-
200401-wss-username-token-profile-1.0#PasswordText">charitha</
wsse:Password>
<wsse:Nonce EncodingType="http://docs.oasis-open.org/
wss/2004/01/oasis-200401-wss-soap-message-security-
1.0#Base64Binary">KE00ltP/538A8Pco3w/Sew==</wsse:Nonce>
<wsu:Created>2012-05-01T12:58:55.362Z</wsu:Created>
</wsse:UsernameToken>
</wsse:Security>
</Header>
```

The header block of the request will be similar to the preceding XML document. Make a note of the `<wsu:Timestamp>` element which includes two child elements, `<wsu:Created>` and `<wsu:Expires>`. These elements are added because we have specified the **WSS TimetoLive** value as a `TestRequest` property. The difference between the `<wsu:Created>` value and the `<wsu:Expires>` value is exactly 60 seconds which matches with the **WSS TimetoLive** value we have specified in the request.

Also look at the `<wsse:Password Type="http://docs.oasis-open.org/wss/2004/01/oasis-200401-wss-username-token-profile-1.0#PasswordText">` element which defines that the password is a plain text value.

In addition to the WS-Security properties which we have been specified in the soapUI test request, we can identify the `<wsse:Nonce>` element in the preceding request which has been added by soapUI (Apache WSS4J rather) itself. A **nonce** is a random value that the sender creates to include in each `UsernameToken` that it sends. According to the `UsernameToken` profile, this specifies a cryptographically random nonce. Each message including a `<wsse:Nonce>` element must use a new nonce value in order for the web service producers to detect replay attacks.

 It should be well understood that the load testing with soapUI is not another form of message replay attacks. When you add the preceding **getGuestDetails** TestStep to a load test, soapUI generates a unique message with each run. Hence, each instance of the message will have its own TimeStamp value as well as nonce.

The response header, which is related to the preceding request message, will be similar to the following XML document:

```
<soapenv:Header>
    <wsse:Security soapenv:mustUnderstand="1" xmlns:wsse="http://
docs.oasis-open.org/wss/2004/01/oasis-200401-wss-wssecurity-secext-
1.0.xsd">
        <wsu:Timestamp wsu:Id="Timestamp-748" xmlns:wsu="http://
docs.oasis-open.org/wss/2004/01/oasis-200401-wss-wssecurity-utility-
1.0.xsd">
            <wsu:Created>2012-05-01T12:58:55Z</wsu:Created>
            <wsu:Expires>2012-05-01T13:03:55Z</wsu:Expires>
        </wsu:Timestamp>
    </wsse:Security>
</soapenv:Header>
```

According to the `<wsu:Timestamp>` element's value, the life time of the response is 5 minutes by default. We can configure this in the WS-Security policy of `GuestManagementService`.

Project level WS-Security configurations in soapUI

So far, we have discussed configuring WS-Security at the individual TestRequest levels. However, it is usually required to apply security configurations at the project level so that the WS-Security settings can be used in multiple levels in a soapUI project. For example, the project level WS-Security configurations can be shared by all TestSuites, thereby all outgoing requests and responses can make use of the security configurations.

Let's look at how we can repeat the preceding UsernameToken authentication test by configuring WS-Security at the soapUI project level. Before that, make sure to clear the TestRequest level WS-Security properties which we updated previously. To configure the WS-Security at the soapUI project level,perform the following steps:

1. Right-click on the **HotelReservationProject** and select **Show Project View**. Select the **WS-Security Configurations** tab. By default, the **outgoing WS-Security Configurations** tab is selected. Outgoing WS-Security configurations are used to apply security configurations for the messages, that go out of soapUI. When soapUI acts as the SOAP sender, the outgoing security configurations are used.

2. Click on the **Add new outgoing WSS configuration** icon. As we can have multiple outgoing WSS configurations, we should specify a unique name for the configuration. Specify UTConfig as the name.

3. Each WSS configuration can include many WSS entries which are used to provide encryption properties, Timestamp configurations, Signature properties, **SAML** configurations, or UsernameToken properties.

4. Enter the username and password, which we have specified in GuestManagementService in the previous example as the default username and password. These default values will be used in all the child WS entries associated with the WSS configuration.

5. Now, select the **UTConfig** WSS configuration and click on the **add a new WSS entry** icon which is at the bottom pane of the window.

6. Select the **Username** option from the combo box in the **Add WSS Entry** dialog box, that is prompted as shown in the following screenshot:

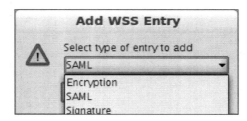

7. The WSS **Username** entry will be opened in a new tab where you can specify `UsernameToken` specific properties such as **Username**, **Password**, **Nonce**, and **WSS Password Type**. These are the same settings which we have entered when configuring `UsernameToken` authentication at the individual TestRequest level.

8. As we added a default username and password, it is not necessary to repeat the credentials again inside the WSS **Username** entry. However, we can override the default username/password values which have been specified in the WSS configuration.

9. Select the **Adds a nonce** option which will include the nonce value for each request, and select the **Adds a created** option which will add `<wsu:Created>` value. Also, select the **Password Type** as **PasswordText**.

10. According to the WS-Security policy that we have added for `GuestManagementService`, it is not sufficient to have the preceding values when interacting with the service. We should include a **Timestamp** value in each request. Therefore, click on the **Adds a new WSS entry** icon and select **Timestamp**. This will add a Timestamp WSS entry. Specify a valid **Time to Live** value (for example, 60 seconds).

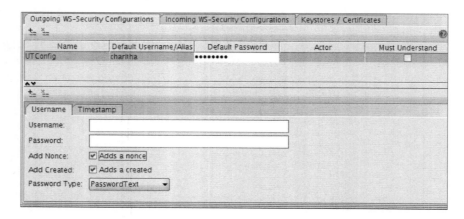

11. We have completed the WSS configuration of `UsernameToken` authentication. Now, we need to apply these configurations into the SOAP requests that need to be authenticated. Open the **getGuestDetails** TestRequest, which is under **GuestManagementServiceTestSuite**, and click on the **Aut** tab which is at the bottom corner. Locate the **Outgoing WSS** drop-down list and select the **UTConfig** WSS configuration where we have configured the necessary `UsernameToken` properties.

12. Submit the request and observe the request and response headers.

Testing asymmetric binding policy with soapUI

In the previous section, we looked into two approaches of testing a service secured with transport binding assertion. In this section, we will secure a different service in our sample project using an asymmetric binding policy.

Asymmetric binding

In web services communication, when both the service requestor and provider possess their own key pairs, it can be considered as an asymmetric binding use case.

 According to WS-Security policy specification (`http://docs.oasis-open.org/ws-sx/ws-securitypolicy/200702/ws-securitypolicy-1.2-spec-os.html#_Toc161826560`), the asymmetric binding assertion is used in scenarios in which message protection is provided by means in WSS:SOAP Message security using the asymmetric key (public key) technology.

In asymmetric binding, the sender derives a shared key and encrypts the message using the shared key. Then the sender encrypts the shared key using the public key of the recipient and signs the message using his/her private key. The recipient decrypts the shared key using his/her private key and decrypts the message using the decrypted shared key. Then, the recipient can verify the signature of the message using the public key of the sender.

We are not going to discuss all topics such as XML encryption, XML signature, and public key infrastructure, which are related to the scenario we are going to demonstrate. These topics cannot be covered as part of a chapter in this book. So I would assume you possess basic knowledge about the cryptographical concepts which we will use in this section. You can find more information about these topics from the Internet. For example:

- http://en.wikipedia.org/wiki/Public-key_cryptograpy
- http://msdn.microsoft.com/en-us/library/ms229749.aspx

Signing SOAP messages

We will demonstrate the use of asymmetric binding with soapUI by sending a signed message to **RoomManagementService**. Signing a SOAP message ensures the integrity of the message, where the message is not tampered with during transit between the sender and reciever. This also ensures non-repudiation of messages which guarantees that the sender of a message cannot later deny having sent the message and the recipient cannot deny having received the message. Signing a message involves the following preliminary steps:

1. Create a digest value of the message – a **Digest** is a hash value which is computed through a cryptographic hashing algorithm. Generally, altering the message will change the corresponding hash value, so it is used in digital signatures to ensure the integrity of messages.

2. Encrypt the digest value using the private key of sender (in our case, the sender is soapUI).

3. Sender submits the message along with the encrypted digest value.

4. Decrypt the encrypted digest value using the public key of sender. This returns the pure hash value of the message.

5. The receiver creates a digest value of the received message using the same hashing algorithm (as it is the first task of receiver to validate the signature) and ensures that the generated hash value equals the decrypted digest value.

In order to digitally sign the SOAP messages through soapUI, we need to have a set of resources in hand. The key stores are the first prerequisite to have for signing a message. A **key store** is a file which contains the key and certificate entries in an encrypted form. A key store is protected by a password. Also, the private keys stored in key stores are separately protected using passwords.

1. First, we need to create key stores for both web service and client to store their respective public/private keys. Generating keys can be done using the Java key tool which is a key and certificate management utility. keytool is a part of the standard java development kit (JDK).

2. Let's first create a key store for the client (soapUI). Open a command window or shell and enter the following command to create the client key store:

```
keytool -genkey -alias clientks -keyalg RSA -keystore clientks.jks
-storepass clientks
```

   This will prompt the following questions. Make sure to provide answers as per your environment:

```
What is your first and last name?
  [Unknown]:  Charitha Kankanamge
What is the name of your organizational unit?
  [Unknown]:  QA
What is the name of your organization?
  [Unknown]:  Test
What is the name of your City or Locality?
  [Unknown]:  Colombo
What is the name of your State or Province?
  [Unknown]:  Western
What is the two-letter country code for this unit?
  [Unknown]:  LK
Is CN=Charitha Kankanamge, OU=QA, O=Test, L=Colombo, ST=Western,
C=LK correct?
  [no]:  yes
Enter key password for <clientks>
  (RETURN if same as keystore password):
```

   You will find the client key store, `clientks.jks` at the location where you launched the preceding command. Make a note of the key store password and private key password (both are `clientks` in our example).

3. Similarly, create a server key store for `RoomManagementService` as follows :

```
keytool -genkey -alias serviceks -keyalg RSA -keystore serviceks.
jks -storepass serviceks
```

4. Note that, the key store password of the service key store, `serviceks.jks` is `serviceks` and the private key password is also the same.

5. Next, we need to export the public certificate of the client to the service key store. In order to do that, the public certificate of the client must be taken out from the client key store, which is explained as follows:

    ```
    keytool -export -alias clientks -keystore clientks.jks -file
    client.cert
    ```

    This will prompt for the keystore password and enter 'clientks'. Then, the certificate will be stored in a file called client.cert.

6. Now, this certificate can be imported into the service key store as follows:

    ```
    keytool -import -file client.cert -keystore serviceks.jks
    -storepass serviceks -alias clientks
    ```

7. Entering the preceding command will result in the following:

    ```
    Owner: CN=Charitha Kankanamge, OU=QA, O=Test, L=Colombo,
    ST=Western, C=LK

    Issuer: CN=Charitha Kankanamge, OU=QA, O=Test, L=Colombo,
    ST=Western, C=LK

    Serial number: 4fa1477c

    Valid from: Wed May 02 20:11:00 IST 2012 until: Tue Jul 31
    20:11:00 IST 2012

    Certificate fingerprints:
          MD5:  1D:4B:FF:8A:24:D5:F9:58:D8:C3:FD:71:7F:7C:70:71
          SHA1: D6:88:1A:06:7A:5B:4B:34:56:7B:48:A1:9B:C5:AA:B1:B8:91:7
    2:1C
          Signature algorithm name: SHA1withRSA
          Version: 3

    Trust this certificate? [no]:  yes
    Certificate was added to keystore
    ```

8. Similarly, we can import the public certificate of the service into the client key store as follows:

    ```
    keytool -export -alias serviceks -keystore serviceks.jks -file
    service.cert

    keytool -import -file service.cert -keystore clientks.jks
    -storepass clientks -alias serviceks
    ```

9. Now, we possess both client and service key stores. We can proceed with securing the web service.

Both serviceks.jks and clientks.jks keystore files can be found in the keystores folder within the chapter 7 folder of the code bundle.

Securing RoomManagementService

I hope you remember how we secured the `GuestManagementService` in the previous section using the `UsernameToken` WS-Security policy. Similarly, now we are going to secure `RoomManagementService` using an asymmetric binding security policy by performing the following steps:

1. Open the `services.xml` file, which can be found inside the `conf` folder of the sample hotel reservation project and add the following policy as a child of the `<service name="RoomManagementService">` element:

```
<wsp:Policy wsu:Id="SigOnly"
            xmlns:wsu="http://docs.oasis-open.org/wss/2004/01/
oasis-200401-wss-wssecurity-utility-1.0.xsd"
            xmlns:wsp="http://schemas.xmlsoap.org/ws/2004/09/
policy">
    <wsp:ExactlyOne>
        <wsp:All>
            <sp:AsymmetricBinding xmlns:sp="http://schemas.
xmlsoap.org/ws/2005/07/securitypolicy">
                <wsp:Policy>
                    <sp:InitiatorToken>
                        <wsp:Policy>
                            <sp:X509Token
                                sp:IncludeToken="http://
schemas.xmlsoap.org/ws/2005/07/securitypolicy/IncludeToken/
AlwaysToRecipient">
                                <wsp:Policy>
                                    <sp:RequireThumbprintRefer
ence/>
                                    <sp:WssX509V3Token10/>
                                </wsp:Policy>
                            </sp:X509Token>
                        </wsp:Policy>
                    </sp:InitiatorToken>
                    <sp:RecipientToken>
                        <wsp:Policy>
                            <sp:X509Token
                                sp:IncludeToken="http://
schemas.xmlsoap.org/ws/2005/07/securitypolicy/IncludeToken/Never">
```

```
                                                  <wsp:Policy>
                                                      <sp:RequireThumbprintRefer
ence/>

                                                      <sp:WssX509V3Token10/>
                                                  </wsp:Policy>
                                              </sp:X509Token>
                                          </wsp:Policy>
                                      </sp:RecipientToken>
                                      <sp:AlgorithmSuite>
                                          <wsp:Policy>
                                              <sp:TripleDesRsa15/>
                                          </wsp:Policy>
                                      </sp:AlgorithmSuite>
                                      <sp:Layout>
                                          <wsp:Policy>
                                              <sp:Strict/>
                                          </wsp:Policy>
                                      </sp:Layout>
                                      <sp:IncludeTimestamp/>
                                      <sp:OnlySignEntireHeadersAndBody/>
                                  </wsp:Policy>
                              </sp:AsymmetricBinding>
                              <sp:Wss10 xmlns:sp="http://schemas.xmlsoap.org/
ws/2005/07/securitypolicy">
                                  <wsp:Policy>
                                      <sp:MustSupportRefKeyIdentifier/>
                                      <sp:MustSupportRefIssuerSerial/>
                                  </wsp:Policy>
                              </sp:Wss10>
                              <sp:SignedParts xmlns:sp="http://schemas.xmlsoap.
org/ws/2005/07/securitypolicy">
                                  <sp:Body/>
                              </sp:SignedParts>
                              <ramp:RampartConfig xmlns:ramp="http://ws.apache.
org/rampart/policy">
                                  <ramp:user>serviceks</ramp:user>
                                  <ramp:passwordCallbackClass>com.
sample.reservation.security.PWCBSignatureHandler</
ramp:passwordCallbackClass>
                                  <ramp:signatureCrypto>
                                      <ramp:crypto provider="org.apache.
ws.security.components.crypto.Merlin">
```

```
                              <ramp:property name="org.apache.
ws.security.crypto.merlin.keystore.type">JKS</ramp:property>
 <ramp:property name="org.apache.ws.security.crypto.merlin.
file">serviceks.jks</ramp:property>
                              <ramp:property name="org.apache.
ws.security.crypto.merlin.keystore.password">serviceks</
ramp:property>
                    </ramp:crypto>
                 </ramp:signatureCrypto>
              </ramp:RampartConfig>
           </wsp:All>
        </wsp:ExactlyOne>
     </wsp:Policy>
```

You will be interested to see the asymmetric binding policy assertion in the preceding policy which specifies the keys used for signing and verification of signatures. The `<sp:InitiatorToken>` and `<sp:RecipientToken>` are the two main elements inside the asymmetric binding assertion. The InitiatorToken element specifies the token used by the client (sender) for signing whereas the RecipientToken defines the tokens used by the service for signing.

We already saw the usage of the `RampartConfig` assertion in the `UsernameToken` policy. In this policy, the `RampartConfig` assertion is used to refer to the key stores and certificates used for signing and verifying the signatures of the messages. Here, the value of `<ramp:user>` element is the username used to retrieve the password of the corresponding private key from the CallbackHandler.

2. The `<ramp:passwordCallbackClass>` element is used to retrieve the password of the private key that is used for signing. We will write a new password callback handler class, `com.sample.reservation.security.PWCBSignatureHandler.java`, as follows:

```
package com.sample.reservation.security;

import org.apache.ws.security.WSPasswordCallback;
import javax.security.auth.callback.Callback;
import javax.security.auth.callback.CallbackHandler;
import javax.security.auth.callback.UnsupportedCallbackException;
import java.io.IOException;

public class PWCBSignatureHandler implements CallbackHandler {
```

```
public void handle(Callback[] callbacks) throws IOException,

UnsupportedCallbackException {
        WSPasswordCallback pwcb = (WSPasswordCallback)
callbacks[0];

        String id = pwcb.getIdentifer();
        int usage = pwcb.getUsage();
//Usage value is SIGNATURE when rampart wants to get the pass
// phrase of the private key of the keypair when it wants to
// create a signature in an outgoing message
        if (usage == WSPasswordCallback.SIGNATURE) {
            // Logic to get the private key password for given
// alias
            if ("serviceks".equals(id)) {
                pwcb.setPassword("serviceks");
            } else if ("clientks".equals(id)) {
                pwcb.setPassword("clientks");
            }
        }
    }
}
```

The complete source code of the PWCBSignatureHandler.java class can be found at src\com\sample\reservation\security\ PWCBSignatureHandler.java in the the chapter 7 folder of the code bundle..

3. Engage the Rampart module by adding the following element in the services.xml file in order to enable WS-Security for RoomManagementService:

```
<module ref="rampart" />
```

The complete services.xml file with the security policy can be found at conf folder within the chapter 7 folder of the code bundle.

4. Now, we can rebuild our sample service by including the libraries in AXIS2_ HOME/lib in the class path. We must also make sure to copy the service key store (serviceks.jks) into the root of the service archive.

You can use the ant build script given in the code bundle associated with this chapter to build the service with all of the preceding configurations.

5. Deploy the `HotelReservation.aar` file again. When you access the WSDL URL of RoomManagementService (`http://localhost:8080/axis2/services/RoomManagementService?wsdl`), you will see that the auto-generated WSDL is updated with the signature policy.

Testing secured RoomManagementService with soapUI

We completed the configurations at the web service side which are required for securing the service with an asymmetric binding policy. Our next objective is to invoke this secured service using soapUI. In order to do that we need to construct the corresponding asymmetric binding security policy in soapUI project configuration. We have already witnessed that enabling asymmetric binding policy for a web service requires a lot more configurations than the `UsernameToken` scenario. This is true for the client side as well. In soapUI, we need to complete the following tasks in order to submit a digitally signed message to the preceding web service:

1. Specify the key pairs used to create the signature and passwords to access the key store and private key.

2. Specify the set of algorithms used for digest generation, signature, and signature canonicalization.

3. Specify the parts of the message which need to be signed.

In this section, we will go through the detailed configurations of the soapUI project to fulfill the preceding work items

1. Open **Project** view of the **HotelReservationProject**.

2. First, we will specify the key stores which are required for our scenario. In asymmetric binding, the client (soapUI) signs the request using its private key. The private key is stored in the `clientks.jks` file. Also, the client decrypts the encrypted digest value of the response using the service's public key which is also stored inside `clientks.jks`.

3. Click on the **Keystores/Certificates** tab and select the + icon to add a new key store. Browse for the `clientks.jks` file in your filesystem and specify its password as `clientks`.

4. Enter `clientks` as the **Default Alias** and **Alias Password.** We will point to the private key which is used to sign the request using the default alias and use the alias password as the private key password.

5. The new key store will be listed in the **Keystores/Certificates** windows as shown in the following screenshot:

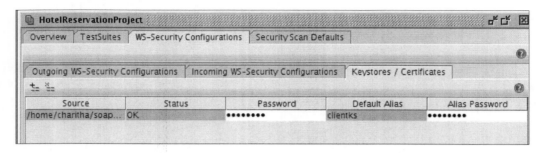

6. The **Status** column shows the loading status of the given key store. This will report an error if the key store location is invalid.

Outgoing WS-Security configurations

Now, we will add an Outgoing WS-Security configuration for our project as follows:

1. Click on the **Outgoing WS-Security Configurations** tab and click on the + icon to add a new outgoing WSS configuration. Specify SignOutgoingConfig as the unique name of outgoing WSS configuration. We will keep the **Default Username/Alias**, **Default Password**, **Actor**, and **Must Understand** fields blank as we do not want to use the default values for child WSS entries.

2. As we did in UTConfig WSS configuration previously, we can add multiple WSS entries for a WSS configuration. Select the newly added **SignOutgoingConfig** and click on the + icon at the bottom of the pane to add a new WSS entry. Select **Signature** as the entry and click on **OK**.

3. You will notice the following properties of the Signature WSS entry:

   ○ **Keystore**: It is the key store which holds the private key used to sign the message. For example, clientks.jks

   ○ **Alias**: It is the alias of the private key, for example, clientks

   ○ **Password** : It is the private key password, for example, clientks

   ○ **Key Identifier Type**: It defines which key identifier type to use for signature. For example, Binary Security Token or X509 certificate

   ○ **Signature Algorithm**: This is the algorithm used for generating a signature using an asymmetric key. WS-SecurityPolicy specification recommends to use RsaSha1 algorithm which is identified by the URI; http://www.w3.org/2000/09/xmldsig#rsa-sha1. In our example, we can select that or use the **default** as the signature algorithm.

- ° **Signature Canonicalization**: The XML canonicalization (`www.w3.org/TR/xml-exc-c14n/`) is part of the XML digital signature. There are various canonicalization algorithms and each represents using their identifier in soapUI WSS entry properties. In our example, we will leave the default signature canonicalization as it is.

- ° **Digest Algorithm**: This specifies the algorithm used for generating a message digest value. Once selected, this will include in `<ds:DigestMethod>` element in SOAP header of the request. You can use the default or whatever algorithm is preferred. We will select `http://www.w3.org/2000/09/xmldsig#sha1`.

 Selecting **default** as the digest algorithm returns an error, **XMLSignatureException**, in soapUI v4.0.1.

4. Check the **Use Single Certificate** checkbox, this instructs soapUI to use a single certificate for signing.

5. **Parts** defines what parts of the SOAP message should be signed. We can specify multiple parts by clicking on **Add new part +** icon. The **Parts** table consists of four columns:
   - ° **ID:** This column is used to specify a unique ID of the XML element to be signed
   - ° **Name**: This column is for specifying the name of the XML element (for example, Body)
   - ° **Namespace**: This column has the associated namespace of the XML element
   - ° **Encode**: This column states how the signing should be done related to an XML element

     There are two possible values, content and element. Element encoding can be used if we want to sign the whole XML element. Content encoding can be used to sign inner parts of XML elements.

6. In our example, we will use the following values in the **Parts** table:
   - ° ID: empty
   - ° Name: Body
   - ° Namespace: `http://schemas.xmlsoap.org/soap/envelope/`
   - ° Encode : Content

 If we leave the Parts table empty, soapUI signs the SOAP body of the request by default

7. Once completed, the **Signature** properties of the **SignOutgoingConfig** outgoing WSS configuration will be similar to the following screenshot:

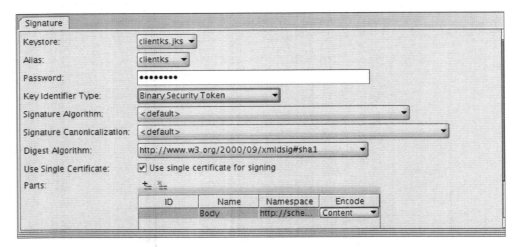

8. Now, if you just associate this configuration with a SOAP request and submit, you will get a SOAP Fault with the **Missing Timestamp** fault string. You should be able to explain the reason for that by looking at the security policy of `RoomManagementService`.

   In the WS-Security policy of the service, `<sp:IncludeTimestamp/>` tells the requestor to always send a timestamp with a request.

9. In order to send the **Timestamp** with the request, we need to add **Timestamp** WSS entry as we did in `UsernameToken` scenario. Click on the **+** icon in the bottom pane of the **SignOutgoingConfig** outgoing WSS configuration and select **Timestamp** from the Add WSS Entry drop-down menu. Specify the sufficient **TimeToLive** value in seconds (for example 60 seconds).

Incoming WS-Security configurations

Now, we are done with the outgoing security configurations of the soapUI project. However, the responses we get from the service are also secured by the service in the same manner. Therefore, we should configure soapUI to interpret and process the responses. Incoming WS-Security configurations provide us with the necessary settings required to process the responses as follows:

1. Click on the **Incoming WS-Security Configurations** tab. Click on the **+** icon at the top-left corner of the configuration tab to add a new incoming WSS configuration.

2. Enter `SignIncomingConfig` as the name of the configuration. Once we get the secured response, soapUI needs to verify the signature of the message using the public key of the service which can be found at the client key store. Therefore, select `clientks.jks` as the **Signature** key store.

3. Finally, make sure to specify the password (clientks) of the **Signature** key store. This is shown in the following screenshot:

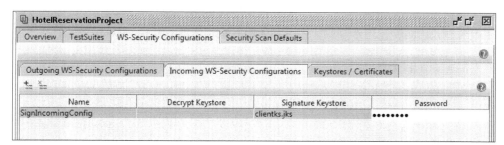

Applying WS-Security configurations to the SOAP request

We are ready to apply the Outgoing and Incoming WSS configurations into a SOAP request which invokes RoomManagementService as follows:

1. Select the **getRoomDetails** TestStep of **RoomManagementServiceTestSuite**. Select the **Aut** (authentication and security related settings) tab which is at the bottom corner of the request window.

2. Select Outgoing WSS and Incoming WSS which we have been just configured. This will associate the out-flow and in-flow security to the SOAP request.

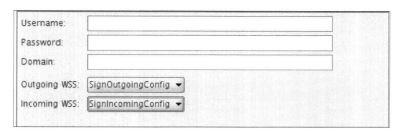

3. Run the test. You will see the following security headers of the request in the **Raw** view of the message. Analyze these header values with the Outgoing WSS configuration properties which we have specified in the soapUI project:

```
<soapenv:Header><wsse:Security xmlns:wsse="http://docs.oasis-
open.org/wss/2004/01/oasis-200401-wss-wssecurity-secext-
1.0.xsd"><wsu:Timestamp wsu:Id="Timestamp-37" xmlns:wsu="http://
docs.oasis-open.org/wss/2004/01/oasis-200401-wss-wssecurity-
utility-1.0.xsd"><wsu:Created>2012-05-03T03:19:08.667Z</
wsu:Created><wsu:Expires>2012-05-03T03:20:08.667Z</wsu:Expires></
wsu:Timestamp><wsse:BinarySecurityToken EncodingType="http://
docs.oasis-open.org/wss/2004/01/oasis-200401-wss-soap-message-
security-1.0#Base64Binary" ValueType="http://docs.oasis-
open.org/wss/2004/01/oasis-200401-wss-x509-token-profile-
1.0#X509v3" wsu:Id="CertId-602C22F25E72EF3491133601514866237"
xmlns:wsu="http://docs.oasis-open.org/wss/2004/01/oasis-200401-
wss-wssecurity-utility-1.0.xsd">MIICTTCCAbagAwIBAgIET6FHfDANBgk
qhkiG9w0BAQUFADBrMQswCQYDVQQGEwJMSzEQMA4GA1UECBMHV2VzdGVybjEQMA
4GA1UEBxMnHwsnYPKT006UgCLAGr5XkeII/7qH4yr4MHmvMu6qURLSFm8afrgvY
aic=</wsse:BinarySecurityToken><ds:Signature Id="Signature-35"
xmlns:ds="http://www.w3.org/2000/09/xmldsig#">
<ds:SignedInfo>
<ds:CanonicalizationMethod Algorithm="http://www.w3.org/2001/10/
xml-exc-c14n#"/>
<ds:SignatureMethod Algorithm="http://www.w3.org/2000/09/
xmldsig#rsa-sha1"/>
<ds:Reference URI="#id-36">
<ds:Transforms>
<ds:Transform Algorithm="http://www.w3.org/2001/10/xml-exc-
c14n#"/>
</ds:Transforms>
<ds:DigestMethod Algorithm="http://www.w3.org/2000/09/
xmldsig#sha1"/>
<ds:DigestValue>eICjYxx0xAb/lFPCuO50NLJLGRo=</ds:DigestValue>
</ds:Reference>
</ds:SignedInfo>
<ds:SignatureValue>
a6RMP79BpjunwwUn6b9vupaUU91iza42QTAnxRhg9MZfXO3Nnc
M4xdbxxkpjVzp6ukDIheGFn95q
osUzeRfYXYM40WqWpOrCJErmWopbLeuOoqRIMyP0Q411SdRTqLYyD/
rBvPFnivut78eb8rBm2b4M
Kq722BVCyRYcpSlTGhA=
</ds:SignatureValue>
```

```
<ds:KeyInfo Id="KeyId-602C22F25E72EF3491133601514866238">
<wsse:SecurityTokenReference wsu:Id="STRId-602C22F25E72
EF3491133601514866239" xmlns:wsu="http://docs.oasis-open.
org/wss/2004/01/oasis-200401-wss-wssecurity-utility-
1.0.xsd"><wsse:Reference URI="#CertId-602C22F25E72
EF3491133601514866237" ValueType="http://docs.oasis-open.org/
wss/2004/01/oasis-200401-wss-x509-token-profile-1.0#X509v3"/></
wsse:SecurityTokenReference>
</ds:KeyInfo>
</ds:Signature></wsse:Security></soapenv:Header>
```

Validating WS-Security responses

Similar to the WS-Addressing specific assertion, soapUI provides us with an assertion to automatically validate secured responses. WS-Security Status assertion can be used to validate that the last received message contained valid WS-Security headers as follows:

Click on **Adds an assertion to this item** icon at the bottom of the **getRoomDetails** SOAP request editor and select the **WS-Security Status** assertion as shown in the following screenshot:

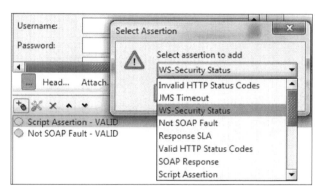

This assertion validates the WS-Security headers in the last response message and reports as **VALID** when the WS-Security headers are present.

Summary

Web service extensions play a key role in service-oriented architecture. WS-Addressing and WS-Security are two such standards which are commonly used in service oriented solutions. Although most of the web service testing tools are capable of directly invoking the services, if the services are configured with various Quality of Service features such as the WS-Security, it is complex or impossible to use tools in testing. This is not the case with soapUI. soapUI provides users with simple and UI based utilities to quickly configure web services extensions and submit the requests including various WS-* headers.

In this chapter, we looked into the details of using secure SOAP message transmissions in soapUI. We discussed two security-binding mechanisms, TransportBinding through UsernameToken and asymmetric binding using an XML signature. WS-Security is a relatively complex subject, so the reader should refer to the relevant specifications when trying out the samples given in this chapter.

8
Getting Started with REST Testing

There are various technologies that can be used to implement interoperability between heterogeneous applications. As we discussed in previous chapters, web services technology can be considered as the de facto standard for enterprise integration. We can identify two distinguished mechanisms in implementing web services, namely, SOAP based web services and RESTful web services. So far, we looked into the various aspects of SOAP-based web services and how soapUI facilitates the testing of SOAP web services. Our sample hotel reservation application has also been completely based on SOAP based web services where we used the SOAP messaging model. The WSDL is used to describe web services as well as SOAP web service extensions such as WS-Addressing, WS-Security, and so on. (*Chapter 7, Advanced Functional Testing with soapUI*)

SOAP versus REST has been a debatable topic over the last few years. Due to the simplicity and extensive use of popular web-based technologies such as HTTP, REST has become popular among developers. However, some people argue that the true advantages of web services such as extensibility, message-level security, and addressing cannot be achieved through RESTful services, thus SOAP can still be considered as the standard way of implementing web services. In this chapter, we will explore the world of testing RESTful web services using soapUI with the help of the following topics:

- Introduction to REST
- Testing RESTful APIs using soapUI
- REST services in soapUI
- REST parameters
- Functional testing of REST services using soapUI
- WADL

Introduction to REST

In his doctoral dissertation (`http://www.ics.uci.edu/~fielding/pubs/dissertation/rest_arch_style.htm`), Roy Fielding introduced the term "REST". **Representational State Transfer (REST)** can be defined as an architectural style for designing software systems. REST is not a specification or W3C standard such as SOAP or WS-* stack. Because of that, working with RESTful services is relatively easier and you do not usually need to use specific middleware frameworks. Most often, the standard libraries included in programming languages can be used directly.

The key principles of REST are as follows:

- Represent everything with a unique ID; a URI
- Make use of standard HTTP methods such as GET, POST, DELETE, and PUT
- Link resources together
- Resources can have multiple representations
- Stateless communication

Let's discuss each of these concepts briefly to get a preliminary understanding about RESTful services.

Represent everything with URIs

In REST, any named information is considered as a resource. Therefore, an image, person, or a document can be considered as examples of resources. Each resource can distinguishably be identified using a unique ID; a URI. The following represent two distinct resources:

- `http://test.com/products/0020`: Represents the product with ID 0020
- `http://test.com/orders/2012/01`: Represents all orders placed in 2012 January

With this approach, any resource can be identified by its URI. When designing RESTful services, it is best practice to map all the resources which are exposed to the outside world through proper directory-structure like URIs.

Using standard HTTP methods

REST is built based on the proper use of HTTP methods. Because of the sole HTTP based interactions, in a way, the **World Wide Web (WWW)** can be viewed as a complete representation of a REST-based architecture. As HTTP is the standard and widely adopted transport protocol in web, it can be used to access any resource including HTML pages, images, and videos. For clients to interact with resources exposed by our services, we should implement the HTTP methods correctly. We can access resources through HTTP by specifying two elements:

- **HTTP verb**: This is the action to be performed on the resource
- **Resource Identifier**: This is the URI of the resource which needs to be accessed

For example, we can retrieve details about the product with product ID 0020 using the following pattern:

```
GET http://test.com/products/0020
```

The HTTP specification defines a set of verbs and their purpose. We can summarize the commonly used HTTP methods as shown in the following table:

HTTP Verb	Description
GET	Retrieves a resource identified by the URI. Can be compared to READ operation.
POST	Creates a new resource. Can be compared to the CREATE operation.
PUT	Updates resource with the provided data or creates the resource if it does not exist. Can be compared to the UPDATE operation.
DELETE	Deletes the resource identified by the URI. Can be compared to the DELETE operation.

The HTTP verbs provide a uniform interface to interact with resources. In order to build truly RESTful applications, we should make sure we use the appropriate HTTP verbs for the correct purposes. For instance, we should not use HTTP GET to trigger something transactional on the server which violates the intended use of the GET method.

Linking resources together

Resources can be related to each other. For example, one document can be linked to another document. It is always a good RESTful design practice to not include too much information in a single resource. Rather, a resource should contain links to additional information similar to how HTML pages are linked. As links are URIs, they can point to resources which are managed outside your application.

Multiple representations of resources

With REST, multiple representations of resources can be provided for different needs. As REST is purely HTTP oriented, the content negotiation (`http://en.wikipedia.org/wiki/Content_negotiation`) principle can be used to achieve different representations of the same resource. With this, a client can request the preferred response format using the Accept HTTP header and the server responds with a representation of the resource in the requested format. Having multiple representations of the same resource will help in many ways. Information about your application can be accessed by various types of clients who consume different representations such as HTML and XML.

Stateless communication

REST mandates that a server should not retain communication state of the clients beyond a single request. This is very important to achieve loose coupling among RESTful services and client applications. When a client communicates with a server, the request should contain all the necessary information that must be present in order to access and use the server. It should not assume that the server holds information about the state of the client. With stateless communication, the server does not require to maintain information about the client's state, thus it does not get overwhelmed by multiple clients accessing the server simultaneously.

We looked into the key principles of REST. It is time for us to use soapUI to invoke a RESTful service as we started discussion on SOAP services testing in *Chapter 3, First Steps with soapUI and Projects*.

Testing RESTful APIs using soapUI

You may be wondering why I introduced a new term "API" instead of "services" to start off the topic. Be it REST or SOAP, web services can be considered as another form of APIs. With the widespread adoption of mobile devices and service-oriented computing, business organizations have begun to expose applications and services to external parties. These third party developers have built applications to integrate with the systems of API providers allowing the providers to extend the capabilities of their businesses as well as helping the third party developers to earn their own livelihood.

Today, there are enormous applications built by the third party developers based on the APIs exposed by many vendors. For example, big names such as Twitter, Facebook, Google, and Amazon expose their key features as APIs to the outside world allowing developers to build various applications.

Due to the easy-usage and lightweight nature of REST, most of those popular APIs are offered as purely RESTful interfaces. The testing of REST APIs can be done either using the utilities provided by the API provider or by an external tool such as soapUI. Usually, when APIs are provided through an API management solution such as Apigee, Mashery, or WSO2, the API management solution provides you with facilities to test the APIs. However, merely sending messages to APIs is not sufficient if you are an API provider or a consumer who wants to build third party applications. soapUI brings with it RESTful services/API testing facilities which allows us to use various functional and performance testing capabilities.

Without further discussion, let's start using soapUI for RESTful service testing. We can find a large number of APIs such as Google+ and Google Maps at the Google Developers portal (`https://developers.google.com/`) which can freely be tried out. As these Google APIs are truly RESTful in nature and readily available for use, we are not going to spend time on writing our own RESTful service for demonstration purposes. To use any Google API, you must first create a Google account (if you do not have one) and then request an API key. We can do so by performing the following steps:

1. Create a Google account if you do not already have one.

2. Access the Google Developers portal at `https://developers.google.com/`.

3. Click on the API Console which can be found under the Developer Tools.

4. Log into the API console (`https://code.google.com/apis/console/`) using your Google account.

5. Click on **Create project** to start using Google APIs.

6. You will find the list of Google API offerings such as Analytics API, Blogger API, Places API, and so on. For our demonstration, we will use Google Places API. Locate the Places API in the services list and click on the on/off icon to make it active.

7. You will be prompted to register your organization and website URL. Enter something valid and click on **Submit**. This will direct you to the terms of services page. Accept the terms and conditions.

8. Now, go to the API Access page by clicking on **API Access** in left menu. You will find your API key at the bottom of the page under the **Simple API Access** section.

9. Now, we possess an API key to try out the Google Places API.

> The Google Places API gives information about various places. According to the API documentation (`https://developers.google.com/maps/documentation/places/`), place requests specify locations such as latitude/longitude coordinates and the following basic searches are exposed through the API:
> - Place Searches: This returns a list of nearby places based on a user's location
> - Place Details requests: This returns a detailed information about a specific place
> - Place check-ins: This allows to report that a user has checked into a place
> - Place reports: This allows to add new places and delete places
>
> Make sure to carefully read the API documentation before you try out the sample, which we will try out in the next section.

REST Services in soapUI

All REST testing capabilities of soapUI are based on a logical representation known as REST service. We should not confuse this with the term "service" here since it is not a service implementation but a mapping of the RESTful service that is being invoked. We can add as many REST Services as we can in a soapUI project; each represents a particular RESTful service. The REST service model in soapUI can be represented as shown in the following diagram:

Each REST service consists of a number of resources. As we discussed at the beginning of the chapter, resources represent any named information that is identified as URIs. So, each resource can be addressed through a specific URI. For example, the guests' resource can be accessed through URI path /guests whereas guest resource is found at the /guest/{guestName} URI.

A resource may have child resources. The complete URI of the child resource is a concatenation of the parent resource URI with its own.

Resources can have multiple methods. As we just discussed, a fundamental principle of RESTful services is the existence of multiple representations of resources. Therefore, the same resource can be manipulated through multiple HTTP methods. Thus, the same resource URI can be made accessible via HTTP GET and POST, depending on the requirements.

Requests are the leaf nodes of the soapUI REST service hierarchy, which represents the actual request message based on the HTTP method.

We will look into each of the above entities with a sample REST service by performing the following steps:

1. Create a new soapUI project and name it GooglePlaces. We can select the **Add REST Service** option in the **New soapUI project** dialog box and click on **OK** to create the service on-the-fly. Note that we do not want to mix things by including the REST service inside the same hotel reservation project which we used to demonstrate the SOAP web services.

2. The **New REST Service** dialog box will be opened as shown in the following screenshot:

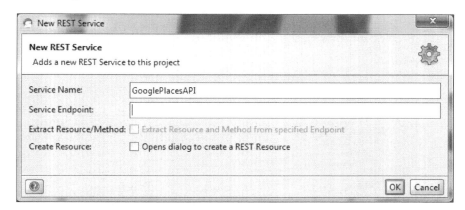

Enter `GooglePlacesAPI` as the service name. The endpoint is the base URL of the API which we are going to invoke. In our case, the base URL is `https://maps.googleapis.com`.

> soapUI provides us with a very useful option to extract the resource and the associated method automatically from the endpoint URL. Otherwise, we can manually create the REST resource in the next dialog box. For soapUI to extract the resources and methods, the endpoint URL should contain the query strings and URL parameters. Usually, the request URL format of an API is given in the corresponding API documentation. In the Google Places API document, we can find the general format of the request URL for the place search request as:
>
> ```
> https://maps.googleapis.com/maps/api/place/search/
> output?parameters
> ```
>
> You will find the details about the parameters which must be included in a place search request in the same section of the API documentation. According to it, a complete URL for a place search request will be similar to the following:
>
> ```
> https://maps.googleapis.com/maps/api/place/search/
> json?location=-33.8670522,151.1957362&radius=500&types
> =food&name=harbour&sensor=false&key=AddYourOwnKeyHere
> ```
>
> This is the exact same request given as an example in the API documentation. This URL shows the search request for places of type `food` within `500` m radius of a point in Sydney Australia.

3. As we have an example of the complete URL of a particular place search, enter it as the endpoint URL and select the **Extract Resource and Method from specified endpoint** option as shown in the following screenshot:

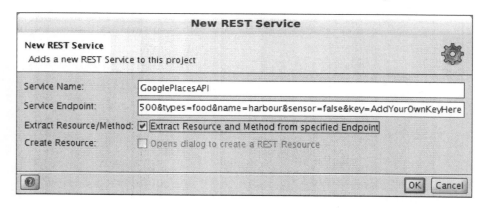

4. Once you click on **OK** in the preceding dialog, the **New Rest Resource** dialog will be displayed. Enter a valid resource name (for example, "places") and click on **OK** as shown in the following screenshot:

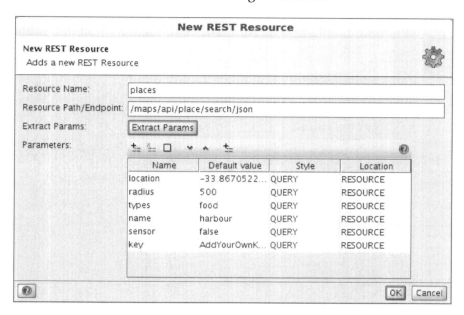

Here, you can see that the all query parameters have been extracted from the endpoint URL which we specified in the previous step. If there are any additional parameters that need to be captured, we can use the **Extract Params** button. Also, we can add new parameters or remove existing parameters using the **Parameters** tool bar which is on top of the parameters table.

 Note that the parameters which are defined at the resource level are visible to all child entities in a REST service. This means these parameters can be accessed from REST methods as well as requests.

5. Now, we can add a REST method to access our **places** resource. Apparently, the request should be an HTTP GET because we just do a search on places and do not want to add, update, or delete a resource. Therefore, specify GET as the HTTP method. Enter **searchPlaces** as the method name as shown in the following screenshot:

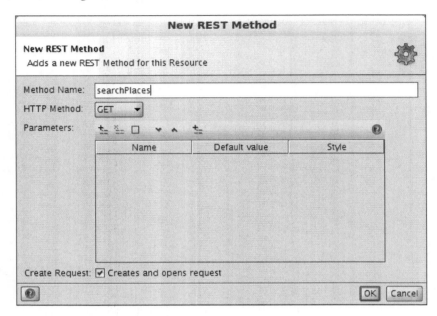

We can add HTTP method specific parameters in the **Parameters** table. Parameters defined at the method level are available for all requests defined under the method. In our example, we do not have any method specific parameters since we have defined everything at the resource level. By selecting the **Creates and opens request** option, we can proceed to creating a request for this HTTP method in the next window.

6. Finally, the REST request editor will be displayed as shown in the following screenshot:

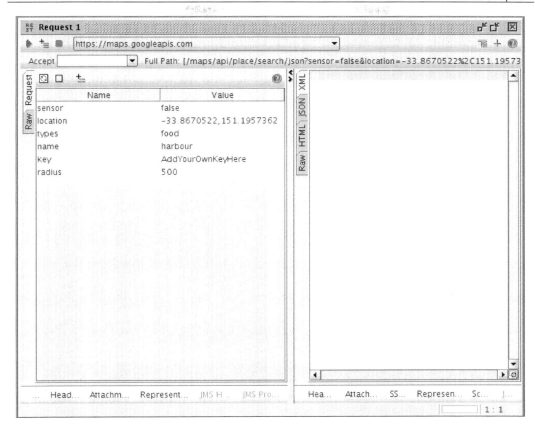

You can observe that the parameters which were extracted and defined at the resource level are shown in request editor. Regardless of the level of the REST service in which the parameters are defined, all parameters should be part of the request and are accessible from the request level. Therefore, the **Parameters** table in the request editor can be considered as an aggregation of all parameters.

At the top of the request editor, the endpoint is shown as `https://maps.googleapis.com`.

Under that, you can find the full path of the request. Actually, the complete path of the request will be a concatenation of the endpoint and the full path [endpoint+full path]. If we want to update the existing parameter list with a new URL, we can click on the **Updates this Requests params from a specified URL** icon, which can be found at the top of the request editor.

Now, we can send the request. Before that, make sure to replace the **key** parameter value with your API key, which you created at the time of registration at the Google developers website.

7. Click on the green arrow icon at the top-left corner to submit the HTTP GET request. You will get a response and it will be shown in XML format by default. Click on the **JSON** tab to view the response in JSON format.

You will find some elements which we have not seen with the SOAP request editor but are specific to the REST requests and responses. Two of such are the request and response representation tabs.

Request and response representation

As we discussed earlier, the fundamental feature of RESTful services is the ability of resources to provide multiple representations. This is achieved basically using the HTTP content-negotiation mechanism. Each method in a resource can have multiple request and response representations.

Right-click on the searchPlaces method and select **Show Method viewer**. Open the **Representations** tab. Once you send the first request of a particular method, a default response representation is added automatically based on the received response (the automatic creation of representations from the response messages can be turned off by deselecting the **Auto-Create** option at the bottom of the response editor). Therefore, we can see a response representation is already added in the table as shown in the following screenshot:

Type	Media-Type	Status Codes	QName
RESPONSE	application/xml	200	defect
FAULT	text/xml	404	html
REQUEST		n/a	

Depending on the REST service which you consume, you can add as many response representations as you wish. You can specify different media types or status codes for the responses in **Representations** table. When sending the request, you can specify the required media type in the **Accept** drop-down box which can be found at the top-left corner of the request editor. The **Accept** drop-down box of the request editor is auto-populated with the response representations which were specified in the **Representations** table as shown in the following screenshot:

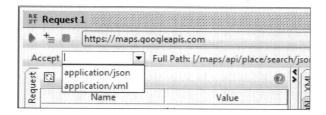

Using this response representation approach, you can achieve content negotiation of REST resources.

Representations are not limited to the responses. You can specify representations for requests as well as fault messages. By clicking on the + icon in the **Representations** tab, you can select the representation type for a method. As with responses, a representation of the fault type will also be populated automatically once you get a fault response.

The representations which you added at the method level will be available at the request level hence the request and response editors also show the corresponding representations.

I'm not planning to take you through all methods exposed by the Google Places API. You can try them on your own and become more familiar with the REST service model in soapUI. However, we will discuss the Place Check-Ins API in detail as it makes use of the HTTP POST requests.

Using POST or PUT requests in soapUI REST services

We will use the Place Check-Ins API (`https://developers.google.com/places/ documentation/actions#PlaceCheckinRequests`) of the Google Places API to demonstrate the POST method handling in soapUI REST services. As per the API documentation, once we have a reference parameter from the response of Place Search (you can find the response message in the soapUI response editor in the preceding Google Place Search API method invocation), we can use it to indicate that a user has checked into that place. A place check-in request is of the following form:

```
POST https://maps.googleapis.com/maps/api/place/check-in/
xml?sensor=true_or_false&key=AddYourOwnKeyHere
```

As this URL represents another resource based on the endpoint, `https://maps.googleapis.com`, we can include place check-in resources under the same REST service which we created previously.

Let's add an HTTP POST method to the REST service by performing the following steps:

1. Right-click on the Google PlacesAPI REST service and select **New Resource.** Enter `placecheckins` as the resource name. Enter the preceding place checkin request URL (`https://maps.googleapis.com/maps/api/place/check-in/xml?sensor=true&key=AddYourOwnKeyHere`) as the resource path.

2. Click on the **Extract Params** to extract the parameters from the preceding URL and click on **OK.**

3. Add a new REST Method for this resource. Give `placeCheckin` as the method name. Make sure to select **POST** as the HTTP method. Click on **OK** to add the new HTTP method.

4. The request editor will be displayed for the POST request. You will notice a specific text area in the request pane to add the POST request body. Enter the following XML element in the POST request body and submit the request. Make sure to replace **AddYourOwnKeyHere** string with your API key which you used in the previous example.

```
<CheckInRequest>
<reference>CnRsAAAAgiDEO99XwaV8DrfbOuYzNloCFVSOg-
eB6nfHVnqic56Tbf1-RMvwfOr4Y7c1zwJzHGJ6BNXG_1zztACgHs5_LN0REaOtuMh
5dsjU8VsaLc9vkbpwc9jfS-V32FddVCLxMNEo6doD60f-17R1nhaC_xIQOUQ9G0sW-
uKGpc7F4dYdNxoUJya-FxUMqpqtWEp_tCk3QP6uXzg</reference>
</CheckInRequest>
```

Note that the reference value has been captured from the response of the previous place search request. This is shown in the following screenshot:

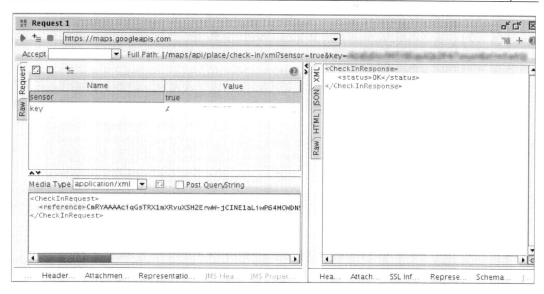

You will notice the **Media Type** drop down box in the POST message content editor which can be used to select a media type for the request from a pre-populated list of standard media types or add any other value. In our case, we can either use **application/xml** or **application/json** media types. When you select different media types and submit the request, the corresponding request **representation** is added to the representations tab in the request editor.

Reading POST message content from a file

Let's see how we can read the content of a POST request from a file without specifying it in the POST message content editor:

1. First, we need to clear the message content in the POST message editor and leave it blank.

2. Copy the request message content into a file in your file system. Name the file `request.xml`.

3. Click on the **Attachments** tab which can be found at the bottom of the request editor.

4. Click on the **+** icon to add an attachment. Browse for the `request.xml` in your filesystem and click on **Open**. You will be asked if you wish to cache the attachment in request. Click on **Yes**.

5. The file will be listed as an attachment with the content type as **text/xml**. Now, if you just submit the request with these details, you will receive the response as **HTTP 400 bad request**. The reason being that the media type of the request has been set to **application/xml** but the content type of the attachment is **text/xml**. Therefore, make sure to change the content type of the attachment into the media type value of the POST request, in our case, **application/xml**.

6. Now, submit the request again. You will get a successful response. Look at the **Raw** view of the request. You will notice that the content of the file has been inserted into the message body.

In the POST request message content editor, you will see an option to select the Post QueryString. This can be used to put a query string of the request into the POST body. Once you select this option, you will notice that the query strings (the parameters preceded by ? in the request URL) are appended to the POST body and the content type is changed to application/x-www-form-urlencoded as shown in the following message:

```
POST https://maps.googleapis.com/maps/api/place/check-in/xml HTTP/1.1

Accept-Encoding: gzip,deflate

Content-Type: application/x-www-form-urlencoded

User-Agent: Jakarta Commons-HttpClient/3.1

Host: maps.googleapis.com

Content-Length: 55


sensor=true&key=dummykeyvalue
```

We looked into how soapUI REST services handle HTTP POST requests. The same options can be applied to HTTP PUT requests as well. If the HTTP method is PUT, the associated request includes a request content editor similar to POST requests.

Inserting the HTTP Basic Authentication header to requests

The **Aut** tab at the bottom of the request editor allows us to configure security settings for the requests. As WS-Security is not applicable in the context of RESTful services, a possible alternative is to use HTTP(S) basic authentication. Let's look at how we can insert basic authentication into the requests by performing the following steps:

1. Click on the **Aut** tab at the bottom of the request pane. Enter a valid username and password according to your RESTful service (in our example, we are accessing Google Places API which does not expect Basic Auth headers. So we can just use any credential).

2. Usually the servers secured with basic authentication challenge the authentication headers, so you can just submit the request. If we want soapUI to send credentials, if there is no challenge from the server side, continue with the following steps.

3. Click on the **Global soapUI Preferences** icon in the main tool bar. Then click on the **HTTP settings** tab.

4. Locate the **Authenticate Preemptively** parameter and select **Adds authentication information to outgoing request**.

5. With these settings, resubmit the previous POST request. You will see the basic authentication headers in the Raw view of the message as follows:

```
POST https://maps.googleapis.com/maps/api/place/check-in/
xml?sensor=true&key=dummykey HTTP/1.1

Accept-Encoding: gzip,deflate

Content-Type: application/x-www-form-urlencoded

Authorization: Basic c3NhZGFzOnNhYXNhc2E=

User-Agent: Jarta Commons-HttpClient/3.1

Host: maps.googleapis.com

Content-Length: 250

<CheckInRequest>
  <reference>CmRYAAAAciqGsTRX1mXRvuXSH2ErwW-jCINE1
aLiwP64MCWDN5vkXvXoQGPKldMfmdGyqWSpm7BEYCgDm-iv7Kc
2PF7QA7brMAwBbAcqMr5i1f4PwTpaovIZjysCEZTry8Ez30wpE-
hCNCXpynextCld2EBsDkRKsGhSLayuRyFsex6JA6NPh9dyupoTH3g</reference>
</CheckInRequest>
```

REST parameters

We have already worked with some REST parameters in the previous examples. However, we have not yet looked into all the possible parameter types included in a soapUI REST service.

Parameters are used to include additional information in a request. For example, our initial place search request URL (`https://maps.googleapis.com/maps/api/place/search/json?location=-33.8670522,151.1957362&radius=500&types=food&name=harbour&sensor=false&key=dummykey`) includes multiple parameters. Let's go through the common REST parameters included in soapUI.

Query parameters

Query parameters are the most commonly used parameter type in request URLs. A query string is appended to the request URL with a leading "?" followed by name/value pairs.

If you look at the resource viewer of the **places** resource, you can identify the extracted parameters; each of them is in the **QUERY** style as shown in the following screenshot:

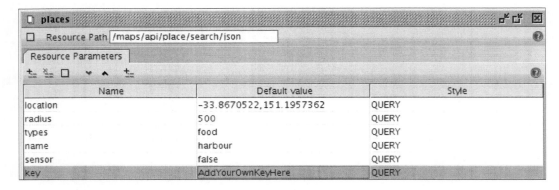

Template parameters

Template parameters can be used to parameterize request URL paths. This can be better explained using an example, which we will explore in the following scenario.

Suppose we are invoking a RESTful service which implements a defect (bug) management solution. This application allows you to submit new defects, retrieve all defects, or get information about a specific defect.

We will use a sample SimpleDefects application which is part of the Apache Wink distribution. You can download the Apache Wink binary from `http://incubator.apache.org/wink/downloads.html` and find the sample in the `/examples/apps/SimpleDefects` folder.

Assume the URL to get details of a particular defect (say the defect with ID 2) is `http://localhost:8080/SimpleDefects/rest/defects/2`.

Now, we may have a corresponding resource in a soapUI REST service as shown in the following screenshot:

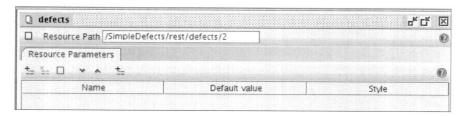

We can add an HTTP GET method and the associated request for this particular resource. However, for each invocation, we will get the details of the defect ID 2. How can we request different defects without changing the URL?

Template parameters help us in these types of situations. Click on the + icon of the resource viewer and add a new parameter (name it `defectid`). Specify a default value and select **TEMPLATE** as the style of the parameter.

Now, in the resource path, parameterize the defect ID as {defectid}.

For example: `/SimpleDefects/rest/defects/{defectid}` as shown in the following screenshot:

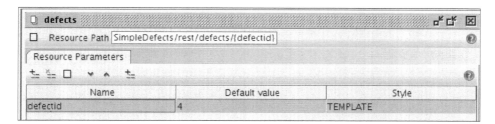

Submit the request associated with the GET method of this particular resource. You will notice that the `defectid` is replaced with the default value of the parameter.

Matrix parameters

Matrix parameters are another type of request parameter used in a URL. However, this is not widely used today. In a way, matrix parameters closely resemble query parameters. However, the most notable difference is that the matrix parameters can appear anywhere in the path.

For example: `http://server/products;order=random;color=red/2012/location`.

You can learn more about matrix parameters at `http://www.w3.org/DesignIssues/MatrixURIs.html`.

If we add a matrix parameter called `matrixparam` to the `places` resource of the GooglePlacesAPI REST service, the request message will be similar to the following HTTP headers:

```
GET https://maps.googleapis.com/maps/api/place/search/json;matrixparam
=matrixparamvalue?sensor=true&location=-33.8670522%2C151.1957362&types
=food&name=harbour&key=dummykey&radius=500 HTTP/1.1
```

Header parameters

Header parameters are different from the preceding set of parameters because they are added to the HTTP header of the request instead of the request URL. Suppose we need to add a header parameter in the **searchPlaces** HTTP GET method of the `GooglePlacesAPI` REST service. Then, we can add a new method parameter and select **HEADER** as the **style** as shown in the following screenshot:

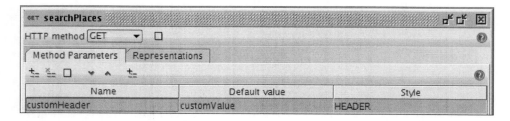

When you submit the corresponding request of the searchPlaces HTTP GET method, you will notice the preceding header parameter is added as a custom HTTP header. This can be observed in the raw view of the HTTP GET message, shown as follows:

```
GET https://maps.googleapis.com/maps/api/place/search/
json?sensor=true&location=-33.8670522%2C151.1957362&types=food&name=ha
rbour&key=dummykey&radius=500 HTTP/1.1
```

```
Accept-Encoding: gzip,deflate

customHeader: customValue

Accept: application/xml

User-Agent: Jakarta Commons-HttpClient/3.1

Host: maps.googleapis.com
```

Functional testing of REST services

We came across several features provided by soapUI to invoke RESTful services. The true advantage of using soapUI to test RESTful services is that we can get the comprehensive functional testing support provided by soapUI out-of-the-box with REST services as well. In this section, we will look into the integration of REST requests into TestCases so that they can be managed through TestSuites and validate the responses using various assertions.

Let's insert a REST test request (Request 1) of the searchPlaces HTTP GET method of the GooglePlaces project into a soapUI TestSuite by performing the following steps:

1. Right-click on the **GooglePlaces** project and select **New TestSuite**. Name it `GooglePlacesTestSuite`.

2. Once `GooglePlacesTestSuite` is added to the project, right-click on it and select **New TestCase**. Name it `searchPlaceTestCase`.

3. Now, right-click on **searchPlaceTestCase** and select **Add Step | REST Test Request**. Enter a name for the test step.

4. A pop-up menu appears with a drop-down list to select the REST methods and the corresponding REST requests which are included in the soapUI project. The list contains all the REST methods and REST requests in your soapUI project as shown in the following screenshot:

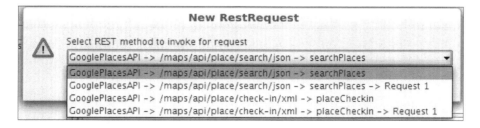

5. **Select the searchPlaces** method from the drop-down list and click on **OK**. The new REST request will be added to the TestCase. Now, this can be used for the usual functional tests which we have already looked at in the previous chapters. As the REST test request is just another TestStep, we can include it in a load test and carry out the performance tests of RESTful services too.

6. **Click on the Assertions** tab at the bottom of the REST test request editor. If you click on the **Add an assertion to this item** icon, you will see a list of allowed assertions which support REST requests. There is no REST-specific assertion but we can use the assertions such as XPath Match or script to validate the response as required.

In the preceding procedure, we started with the TestSuite and added the REST test request into the TestCase. This can be considered as a Top-down approach. Instead of that, we can also follow a Bottom-up approach where we can directly add a given REST request to a TestCase by clicking on **Add this REST request to a TestCase icon** which is at the top left corner of the request editor.

We covered a considerable level of detail about RESTful services testing in the previous sections. We will conclude this chapter by discussing a bit about the Web Application Description Language (WADL).

WADL

WADL is designed to provide a machine process-able description of HTTP-based web applications. We can find more information about WADL in the latest version of the W3C submission of the WADL specification at `http://www.w3.org/Submission/wadl/`.

We discussed WSDL when we first looked into the SOAP based web services. Though WSDL can be used to describe SOAP-based web services in a comprehensive manner, it has limitations with HTTP operations such as PUT and DELETE, among others. As REST services often deal with HTTP methods, WSDL is not a good option for documenting RESTful services. More precisely, WSDL 1.1 is not a good choice for RESTful services. Later on, WSDL 2.0 specification was launched to address the concerns encountered with WSDL 1.1, and it provides better support for RESTful services over WSDL 1.1.

WADL can be considered as an alternative to WSDL 2.0. WADL is lightweight and easier to understand than the WSDL specification. Hence, it is much appropriate for documenting RESTful services.

However, in the REST world, the services are usually documented by textual description (for example, Google API documentation) and WADL is still not a widely adopted concept.

When we create a REST service from an endpoint , the WADL of the service is automatically generated for us by soapUI. We can access the generated WADL by performing the following steps:

1. Right-click on the **GooglePlacesAPI** service of the **GooglePlaces** project and select **Show Service Viewer.**

2. In the service viewer, click on the **WADL Content** tab to open the WADL of the service as shown in the following screenshot:

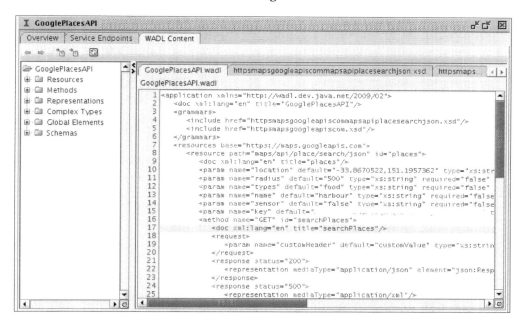

As with SOAP based services, we can create a REST service from an initial WADL and generate a TestSuite for the imported WADL automatically. Let's see how we can create a TestSuite from an imported WADL.

1. In the preceding WADL content window of the **GooglePlacesAPI** service viewer, click on the **Exports the entire WADL and included/imported files to a local directory** icon. This will export the WADL into your filesystem.

2. Now, we have a complete WADL to start with. Click on **File | New soapUI Project** and use GooglePlaces-WADLFirst as the name of the project. Browse for the WADL which has been saved in your filesystem in the previous step and specify it as the initial WADL.

3. Select the **Create TestSuite** option and click on **OK**. This will open the **Generate TestSuite** dialog box as shown in the following screenshot:

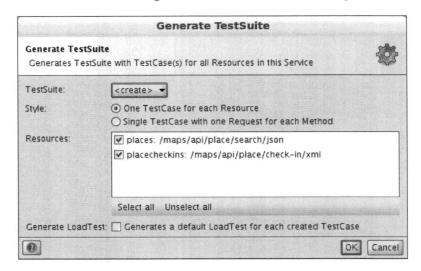

Here, you can see the resources were extracted and listed from the given WADL definition. Click on **OK** and leave the default options intact.

4. Enter a name for the TestSuite and continue. You will see a new project is created with a REST service and two resources. Also, a TestSuite is created with two TestCases for each resource in the REST service.

Now, submit the REST requests which are included in each HTTP method and observe the results.

Summary

RESTful web services are a lightweight alternative to SOAP-based services. Due to popularity and high demand of public API offerings such as Twitter and Google, the RESTful services have become a key ingredient in web application development. In this chapter, we looked into the testing aspects of RESTful web services using soapUI. Deviating from our sample hotel reservation application, which is purely SOAP based web service implementation, we used a public API offering hosted at the Google developers portal as the sample RESTful service. We went through some fundamentals of REST theory and proceeded with discussing various REST testing features provided by soapUI.

9
Testing Databases with soapUI

Data handling is a key requirement expected from any software regardless of the architectural style used to build them. In SOA, there can be various heterogeneous application integrations. An application that runs on the Oracle database can be communicated with a data processing web service which connects to an MS SQL database. The brokering middleware solutions such as **Enterprise Service Buses (ESB)** facilitate the necessary data format transformations, which need to be happening when communicating incompatible systems. Before the web services take part in such integrations, it is always recommended to verify the data-related operations in isolation. In other words, when your database schemas are ready, testers can start testing the integrity of the databases used in your solution. By testing the database schema in advance without waiting to access data through web service interfaces, testers can utilize time effectively and explore potential test failure scenarios.

soapUI provides users with a data interface which can be used to interact with any DBMS. We will discuss the following topics in this chapter, which are related to database testing aspects of soapUI:

- Testing data in isolation
- JDBC Request TestStep in soapUI
- JDBC test assertions

Testing data in isolation

There can be several reasons for testing data separately from other applications. In web services testing, you may need to read data from multiple tables and analyze them before actually consuming data through services. Sometimes, it is important to isolate the bugs in a system by calling databases directly. Let's look at the following example:

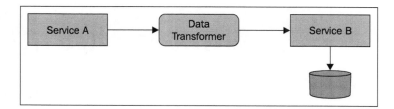

Service A needs to go through a brokering middleware (data transformer) in order to be compatible with the data formats accepted by Service B. The data transformer is used to transform the data into the format that conforms to the schema of Service B. Suppose a bug that is related to the data handling is uncovered when performing integration testing of services. Such a defect can occur due to an issue at individual services, issue of the logic in data transformer, or data in the database itself. In this type of situation, the testers usually try to isolate the bugs by calling databases through separate SQL client applications. Without moving into separate SQL applications, if the tool that we use for service testing is able to directly call database and assert data, we can effectively carry out testing.

soapUI brings JDBC testing capabilities to the web services testing to help testers to incorporate JDBC-level verifications as part of services testing.

> This chapter is not for general data testing. We are exploring the capabilities of soapUI in the context of databases. You can use JDBC API within unit tests to test most of the data-related operations in an application. The advantage of bringing JDBC tests to soapUI is to have database verifications inside the same soapUI project to manage all service testing from a central location.

Setting up soapUI to connect to the database

We will use our sample HOTEL_RESERVATION_DB MySQL database in the examples of this chapter. To make soapUI aware of our MySQL database, we need to include the MySQL JDBC driver inside soapUI binary distribution. We have already configured soapUI to connect to the MySQL database in *Chapter 6, Web Service Simulation with soapUI*. There, we have performed the following two steps to configure soapUI with MySQL:

1. Downloading MySQL JDBC driver from http://dev.mysql.com/ downloads/connector/j/.

2. Copying the driver JAR file to soapUI_HOME/bin/ext and restart soapUI.

JDBC Request TestStep

soapUI allows you to manage database operations using a TestStep called **JDBC Request**. You can add JDBC Request TestStep to an existing TestCase by right-clicking on TestCase level and selecting **Add Step | JDBC Request**. This will ask you to specify a name for the TestStep. Once a name is given for the TestStep, the JDBC Request TestStep editor will be opened as shown in the following screenshot:

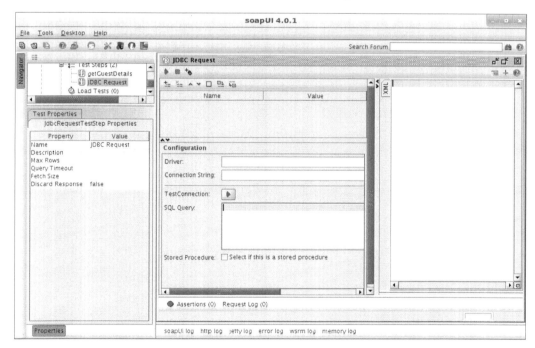

JDBC Request TestStep can be used to send JDBC calls to a database table. The request editor consists of a request pane where you can define database specific configurations and soapUI project-related properties. The response pane shows the data retrieved from a database table in XML format. Also in the lower-right pane, you can find some JDBC Request-specific properties such as Query Timeout and Fetch Size.

Now, we are going to make use of JDBC Request TestStep inside our sample Hotel Reservation soapUI project. As we did in the previous chapters, let's go through the simplest scenario first.

1. Let's add a JDBC Request to the **addGuest** TestCase which is under **GuestManagemetnServiceTestSuite**:

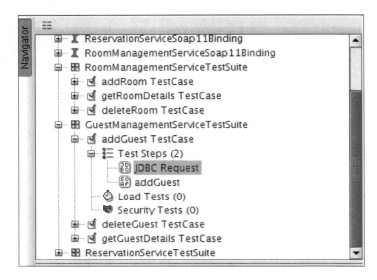

2. Rename **JDBC Request** to something meaningful (for example, `selectGuests JDBC Request`) by right-clicking on TestStep and selecting **Rename**.

3. Now, we must configure the JDBC Request. As we are connecting to a MySQL database, specify `com.mysql.jdbc.Driver` as the driver.

4. Enter the following as the **Connection String**:

   ```
   jdbc:mysql://localhost:3306/HOTEL_RESERVATION_
   DB?user=root&password=root
   ```

The connection string value depends on the JDBC driver used to connect to the database. As we have used MySQL Connector/J driver, the connection string should be in the following format:

```
jdbc:mysql://[host]:[port]/[database]?[property]
[=value]
```

5. Click on the **TestConnection** button to check whether you can connect to the database using the given driver and connection string. If successful, you will get a confirmation.

6. Now, we can specify a SQL expression to do one of the CRUD (create, read, update, or delete) operations on a table in HOTEL_RESERVATION_DB. Let's select all rows from the GUEST_T table first:

```
select * from GUEST_T
```

7. Submit the JDBC Request by clicking on the green arrow icon at the upper-left corner of the request editor. You will get the response in XML format as shown in the following screenshot:

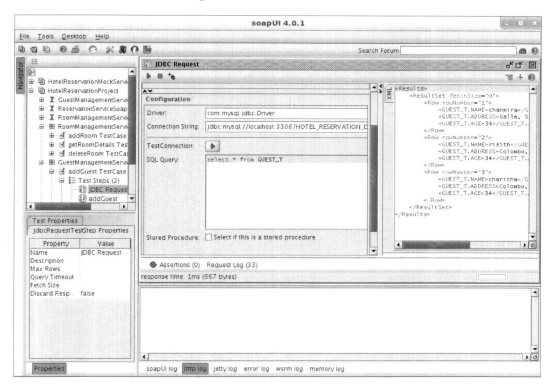

The JDBC Request TestStep is dependent on the underlying JDBC driver on SQL query execution. Therefore, it supports all SQL statements supported by the JDBC driver. If you send an in-only query such as `insert`, `update`, or `delete`, you will get an XML response as follows to indicate the status of the query execution:

```
<Results>
    <UpdateCount>1</UpdateCount>
</Results>
```

JDBC Request properties

You will observe a default set of properties at the lower-right pane of JDBC Request TestStep:

Property	Value
JdbcRequestTestStep Properties	Test Properties
Name	JDBC Request
Description	
Max Rows	
Query Timeout	2
Fetch Size	
Discard Response	false

Let's look at each of these default **JdbcRequestTestStep** properties. Similar to the other TestSteps in soapUI, **Name** and **Description** can be used to specify a meaningful name and description as needed for your test. The other properties are explained as follows:

* **Max Rows**: This property defines the maximum number of rows that should be included in the JDBC response. For example, if we set the **Max Rows** value to 2, the `ResultSet` element of the response will include only 2-row elements.

* **Query Timeout**: This property can be used to set the maximum time for executing a given SQL query specified in a JDBC Request. The timeout value should be specified in milliseconds. The default is `0 ms`, which means there is no limit for the timeout. If **Query Timeout** is set to 1, the JDBC call will get timed out if it takes more than 1 millisecond for SQL query execution.

- **Fetch Size**: This is the number of rows retrieved by the JDBC driver from the database at a time as scrolling through `ResultSet`. In other words, if the **Fetch Size** property is set to `100` and if you want to retrieve 1000 rows from the database, there will be 10 round trips between the database and soapUI. As it implies, the **Max Rows** value should be greater than or equal fetch size. The default fetch size is specific to the database and JDBC driver. In MySQL, `ResultSets` are completely retrieved and stored in memory by default.

JDBC test assertions

As we used various assertions with SOAP request TestStep, JDBC Request can also make use of most of those assertions. In soapUI, most of the assertions are independent from the TestSteps. Hence, the assertions such as `contains` and `Xpath match` can be used with JDBC Request TestStep as they are. By clicking on the **Adds an assertion to this item** icon at the top menu of JDBC Request TestStep, you can find out what assertions are supported by the TestStep. In addition to the generic assertions, you will find two JDBC Request TestStep-specific assertions there:

- **JDBC Timeout**: This assertion can be used to verify whether the current SQL query is executed within the specified **Query Timeout** property value
- **JDBC Status**: In order to check whether the SQL statement is executed successfully, we can use the **JDBC Status** assertion

Let's add a JDBC assertion to our sample **selectGuests JDBC Request** in **GuestManagementServiceTestSuite**:

1. Select **selectGuests JDBC Request** and click on add assertion icon which is at the top menu of the JDBC request editor.
2. Select the **JDBC Timeout** assertion from the **Select Assertion** drop-down menu.
3. Now, submit the JDBC request. The assertion status will be shown as **VALID**.
4. Specify `1 ms` as **Query Timeout** property so that the request will get timed out.

5. Run the test again. This time, you will see an assertion failure as shown in the following screenshot:

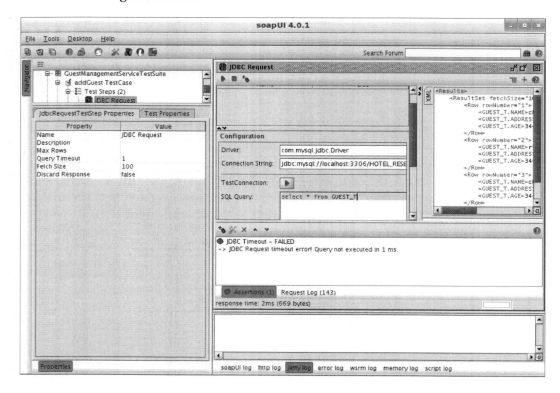

Stored procedures with JDBC Request TestStep

soapUI allows us to call existing stored procedures included in databases. If you want to invoke a stored procedure through JDBC Request TestStep, there is an option in SQL Query to denote it as a stored procedure. As shown in the following screenshot, you can check the **Select if this is a stored procedure** checkbox:

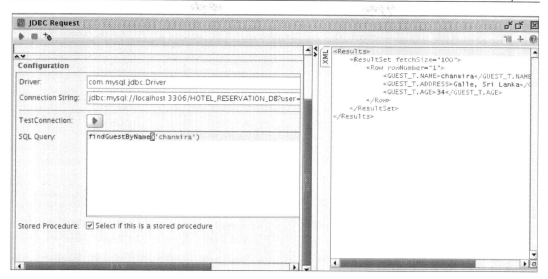

Accessing soapUI properties from SQL query

I hope you remember how we used properties to transfer values in between TestSuites, TestCases, and TestSteps in *Chapter 4, Working with Your First TestSuite*. Similarly, we can set properties at various levels in a soapUI project and read their values inside SQL queries in JDBC Request TestStep. Let's look at our sample TestSuite again. Suppose we need to set a property common to all TestSteps inside **addGuest TestCase**. For the sake of simplicity, let's set the name of a guest as a TestCase-level property. In the SQL query of **selectGuests JDBC Request**, we can read this property value (name of the guest) without hard-coding the guest name in the SQL statement. Let's look at how we can read properties inside SQL statements:

1. Suppose we modify the SQL query of **selectGuests JDBC Request** to read details of a specific guest record:

   ```
   select * from GUEST_T where name = 'charitha'
   ```

2. We are going to read the name of the guest from a TestCase-level property. Therefore, add a `GuestName` property at **addGuest TestCase** level, as shown in the following screenshot:

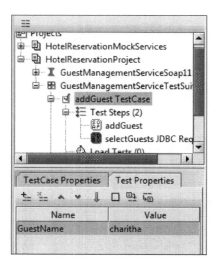

3. Set the **GuestName** property. Here, it is set to `charitha`.

4. Now, select the SQL query text area and move the mouse pointer to the = part of the `select` statement. Then right-click and select **Get Data**. You can select properties from multiple levels. In this example, we will select the **GuestName** property from **addGuest TestCase**, as shown in the following screenshot:

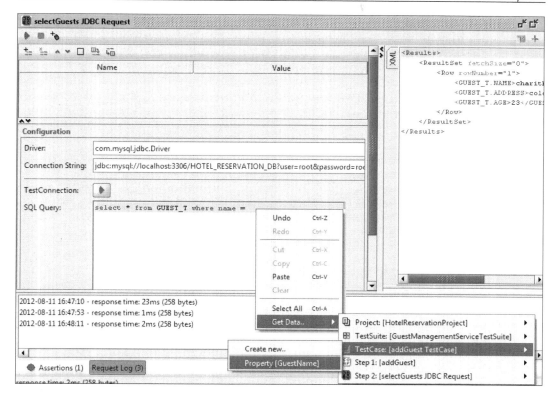

5. Once you select the property, the SQL statement will be similar to the following:

```
select * from GUEST_T where name='${#TestCase#GuestName}
```

6. Submit the request. The row that corresponds to the given **GuestName** property will be retrieved and shown in the results pane.

soapUI provides you with another very useful property that is specific to the JDBC Request TestStep. It is the **ResponseAsXml** property that can be used to manipulate the result of a SQL query.

Let's look at how we can use the **ResponseAsXml** property using an example. We are going to submit the **selectGuests** request first and get the response. Then we will extract the name of a guest from the first row of the result set and submit another JDBC Request to delete the particular guest.

1. Add a JDBC Request TestStep as a child in **addGuest TestCase**. Name the TestStep as **deleteGuest**.

2. Modify the SQL query of **selectGuests JDBC Request** to retrieve all rows from GUEST_T table and submit the request:

   ```
   select * from GUEST_T
   ```

3. Now, select the **deleteGuest** request and locate the SQL query. We want to delete an existing guest from the table. We are going to extract the guest name from the result of the **selectGuests JDBC Request** using **ResponseAsXML** property.

4. Enter SQL query as delete from GUEST_T where name='' and right-click at the end of the statement. Then select **Get Data | [Step 1: selectGuests] | Property[ResponseAsXML]**.

5. This will open up a dialog box, as shown in the following screenshot, where you can specify an XPath expression to extract the required element(s) from the response of the **selectGuests** request:

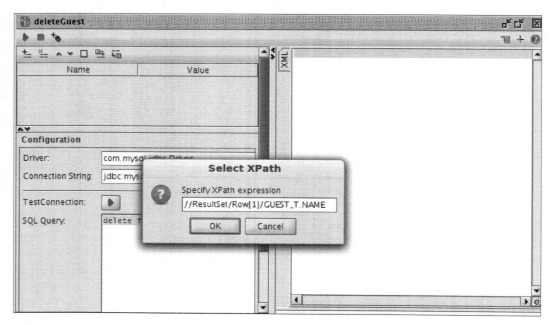

We need to extract the guest name from the first row of the result set. Therefore, the XPath expression will be:

```
//ResultSet/Row[1]/GUEST_T.NAME
```

6. Once you add the XPath expression, the SQL query will be similar to the following:

```
delete from GUEST_T where name='${selectGuests#ResponseAsXml#//
ResultSet/Row[1]/GUEST_T.NAME}'
```

7. Submit the **deleteGuest JDBC Request**. If you run the **selectGuests** request again, you will find that a guest record will be deleted from the table.

Summary

Data is a vital resource of any software. In SOA projects, data is subjected to go through various transformations and conversions when transmitting from a source to destination. Due to the complex integrations of service-oriented solutions, isolating data-related issues is usually a tedious activity. Therefore, it is important to include a sufficient amount of tests which directly communicate with the databases of your SOA instead of testing through web service interfaces. soapUI allows us to directly call database tables using JDBC Request TestStep. In this chapter, we looked at how soapUI can be used to test databases. We discussed about the properties associated with JDBC requests and how assertions can be used to validate database transactions.

10
JMS Testing with soapUI

It is a common practice to use different transport protocols in SOA. Usually, when integrating heterogeneous systems, we need to make use of various transports as well as messaging systems. So far, all our discussions on soapUI have been based on HTTP and HTTPS transports, which are the most common transport mediums used in SOA. In this chapter, we are going to explore the world of JMS with soapUI.

soapUI allows us to send SOAP messages to web services which are exposed over JMS transport. soapUI is integrated with an open source JMS management application, **HermesJMS**, which can be used to communicate with various JMS providers such as JbossMQ, IBM WebSphere MQ, ActiveMQ, and so on. We will be using Apache ActiveMQ as the JMS broker (provider) in this chapter.

We are planning to cover the following topics in this chapter:

- Introduction to JMS
- Configuring the Apache ActiveMQ JMS provider
- Integrating JMS in soapUI
- Working with JMS messaging in soapUI
- Validating JMS responses
- Verifying end-to-end JMS message delivery using the sample project

Introduction to JMS

The **Java Message Service (JMS)** is used to develop business applications that asynchronously send and receive messages. It has been defined under the JSR 914 specification (http://jcp.org/aboutJava/communityprocess/final/jsr914/index.html). In simpler terms, JMS is a set of interfaces and associated semantics that define how a JMS client accesses the facilities of an enterprise messaging product. JMS guarantees the reliable delivery of messages between heterogeneous systems and maximizes the loose-coupling nature of components.

There are two message delivery models used by JMS.

- **Point-to-point or queuing model**:

  In this model, the messages are delivered to a destination known as a queue and then one of the consumers registered for the queue reads the message. In other words, there can be multiple senders of messages but only a single receiver can exist.

- **Publish and subscribe model**:

  This is analogous to a news bulletin board. In this model, zero or more subscribers may register their interest in receiving messages on a particular message topic. Multiple publishers send messages to the topic. Then, all the subscribers of the topic receive the message sent to that particular topic.

JMS consists of the following key elements:

- **JMS provider**: This is an implementation of JMS specification. For example, Jboss MQ, Apache ActiveMQ

- **JMS consumer**: This is a JMS client that receives the message

- **JMS producer**: This is a JMS client that creates and sends the message

- **JMS message**: This is an object that is used to communicate information between JMS clients

In order to use JMS, we should have a JMS provider, which can manage the sessions, queues, and topics. We will use Apache ActiveMQ as the provider (JMS broker) in the context of this book.

Setting up Apache ActiveMQ

Though soapUI can be used with any JMS provider which is supported by HermesJMS, we will use Apache ActiveMQ, one of the most powerful, enterprise grade open source JMS brokers. Let's set it up first before using it with soapUI.

1. Download the latest stable version of Apache ActiveMQ from `http://activemq.apache.org/download.html`.

 At the time of writing, Apache ActiveMQ-5.3.0 was the latest stable version. Hence it has been used in all the samples and demonstrations.

2. Extract the binary distribution to a directory in your file system. Let it be `ACTIVE_MQ_HOME`. Now, go to `ACTIVE_MQ_HOME/bin` and start the broker.

    ° In Windows:

      Type `activemq` and hit *Enter*

    ° In Linux:

      Type `sh activemq` or `./activemq`

   If the startup is successful, you will see a log message similar to the following:

   ```
   INFO | ActiveMQ JMS Message Broker (localhost, ID:HO
   ST1-59724-1334377142200-0:0) started
   ```

3. Once the server is started, you can access the ActiveMQ management console through `http://localhost:8161/admin/`. Also make a note of the listener port used by the broker. It will be **61616** by default.

Now, we have the Apache ActiveMQ JMS provider configured and running. Our objective is to use soapUI to communicate with this particular JMS provider. In order to do that, we cannot directly use soapUI to submit a message to a queue or topic defined in ActiveMQ. soapUI uses an intermediary tool to facilitate the delivery of messages in between soapUI and JMS provider. HermesJMS acts as the intermediary between soapUI and JMS providers.

JMS integration in soapUI

HermesJMS is included as part of the soapUI installer. If you followed the steps of soapUI installation through the installer in *Chapter1, Web Services Testing and soapUI*, you may have already set up soapUI with HermesJMS.

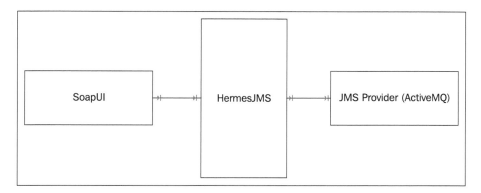

If you installed soapUI using a binary installer or excluded HermesJMS at the time of the installation, make sure to set it up with soapUI as explained in the following steps:

1. Download the latest version of HermesJMS from `http://sourceforge.net/projects/hermesjms/files/hermesjms/1.14/`.

2. Run the installer as follows:

    ```
    -java -jar hermes-installer-X.XX.jar
    ```

3. Follow the instructions given in the installation wizard and complete the installation. Once installed, HermesJMS management console will be shown as follows:

Regardless of having soapUI, now you can manage JMS sessions, queues, and topics of your preferred JMS provider using the HermesJMS management console shown in the previous screenshot. However, we are not planning to spend much time on the standalone HermesJMS application since our goal is to embed it with in soapUI. Therefore, let's integrate HermesJMS with soapUI.

1. Start soapUI and open the **soapUI preferences** window by selecting **File | Preferences**.

2. Locate the **Tools** tab and set the path of HermesJMS installation.

3. Now, we can open HermesJMS through soapUI. If you have already started the standalone HermesJMS application, make sure to close it first. Select **Tools | HermesJMS** from the soapUI main menu to open the HermesJMS management console.

   When HermesJMS is integrated with soapUI, we can simply add any JMS provider (broker) supported by HermesJMS and let soapUI submit the SOAP requests to that particular broker. Let's add the Apache ActiveMQ instance which we have configured previously as the JMS provider.

4. In order to access a JMS provider, HermesJMS wants us to create a new session with adequate information. Access the HermesJMS console and click on the **Create new JMS session** icon in the configuration tool bar. The **Preferences** dialog box will be opened.

5. In order for HermesJMS to access the JMS providers, we must make the relevant provider libraries available in the HermesJMS classpath. HermesJMS uses classpath groups to manage the libraries required for providers. Select the **Providers** tab at the bottom of the **Preferences** dialog box to manage classpath groups. We can add as many classpath groups as needed depending on the JMS providers which will be used. In our samples, we will use Apache ActiveMQ as the provider. Hence, we will add one classpath group which contains the ActiveMQ libraries which are essential for HermesJMS to communicate with the ActiveMQ broker.

6. Right-click on the **Classpath Groups** tab, select **Add Group**, and enter a name for the group (For example `ActiveMQGroup`).

7. Right-click on the **Library** tab associated with **ActiveMQGroup** and select **Add JAR(s)**. Browse for the following two jars inside the `lib` subdirectory of your ActiveMQ installation (`ACTIVE_MQ_HOME/lib`):

   ° `activemq-core-5.3.0.jar`
   ° `geronimo-j2ee-management_1.0_spec-1.0.jar`

 When adding the libraries, HermesJMS will prompt an option to scan the JAR(s) for JMS connection factories. Make sure to scan in order to avoid Connection Factory class loading problems in next configuration steps.

Make sure to apply the changes in the classpath groups by clicking on the **Apply** button at the bottom of the **Preferences** dialog box.

8. Once completed, the **ClasspathGroups** dialog box will appear similar to the following screenshot:

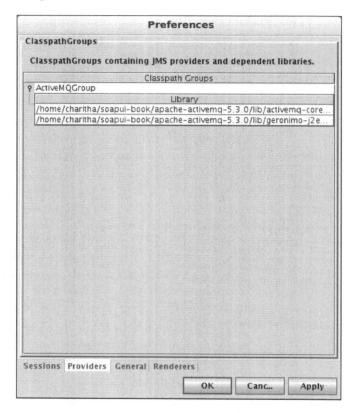

9. Now, we can configure the new session with the ActiveMQ provider. Select the **Sessions** tab in the **Preferences** dialog box. Specify a name for the session in the **Session** combo box. (For example, `ActiveMQSession`). Click on the **Apply** button to save the changes.

10. Next, we need to configure the connection factory so that HermesJMS can connect to ActiveMQ. Select ActiveMQGroup which we have created previously from the **Loader** combo box in the **Preferences** window. If you cannot see **ActiveMQGroup** there, close the **Preferences** dialog box and open it again. Once you select **ActiveMQGroup** as the loader, the associated Connection Factory classes will get loaded in the **Class** drop-down menu.

11. Select **org.apache.activemq.ActiveMQConnectionFactory** as the Connection Factory class. Add the following property by right-clicking on the **Connection Factory** table and selecting the **Add property**:

```
BrokerURL = tcp://localhost:61616
```

12. We also need to configure the JMS provider plugin so that HermesJMS can effectively perform tasks such as queue watching. The plugin configuration specifies more details than what we provide under the **Connection Factory** settings. Select **ActiveMQ** from the **Plug In** drop-down and add the following two properties:

```
BrokerName = localhost
serviceURL = service:jmx:rmi:///jndi/rmi://localhost:1099/jmxrmi
```

13. Click on **Apply** to save the changes.

14. Next, we can configure queues and/or topics. Right-click on the **Destinations** pane in the **Preferences** dialog box and click on **Add** to add a new destination. The **Destination properties** dialog box will be opened. Specify the following values in it:

    - **Name**: Q1 (this name will be used to locate the destination)
    - **Short Name**: Q1
    - **Domain**: Queue

15. Click on **Apply** to save everything. Finally, our HermesJMS session will look like the following:

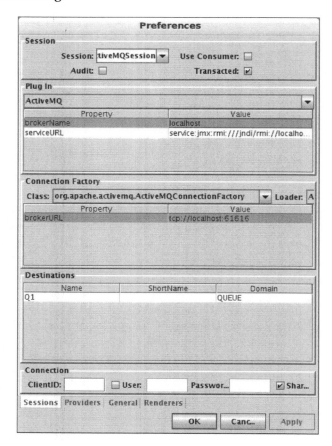

Working with JMS messaging in soapUI

We have integrated HermesJMS into soapUI and configured with a destination (queue) in the Apache ActiveMQ provider. Let's look at how a usual SOAP request can be forwarded to a JMS queue using soapUI. Obviously, if we want to use a different transport other than HTTP or HTTPs, we need to add the corresponding endpoint into the soapUI request editor. We could find the JNDI name of the JMS queue and edit an existing HTTP(s) endpoint to change it to a JMS endpoint. However, we cannot do this straightaway without configuring the relevant JNDI look-up mechanisms. Because of that reason, we used HermesJMS to configure the provider connections, the Connection Factory settings, and so on. Now, with all these in hand, we can use soapUI to submit messages to JMS destinations.

Let's start with our sample Hotel Reservation soapUI project. In this example, we will just place one of the SOAP requests into a queue in ActiveMQ and browse the message through HermesJMS.

1. Select `GuestManagementServiceSoap11Binding` in `HotelReservationProject` from the soapUI project navigator.

2. Right-click and select **Add JMS endpoint**.

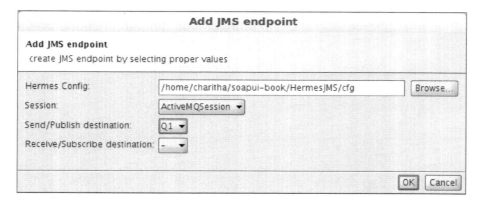

3. Browse for the HermesJMS configuration directory. By default, this can be found in the root directory of the HermesJMS installation. (`HermesJMS_HOME/cfg`). Next, we can select one of the available HermesJMS sessions. In our example, we have created only one session called **ActiveMQSession**.

4. Once you select the session, the destinations defined under the session configuration will be populated in the **Send/publish destination** and **Receive/Subscribe destination** drop-down lists. For this example, let's select **Q1** queue as the **Send/Publish destination** and leave **Receive/Subscribe destination** blank. This implies that we are going to submit the request to a queue and do not expect to receive/read the response message.

5. After adding the JMS endpoint, look at the endpoints list by selecting one of the SOAP requests in the request editor. You will find an endpoint similar to the following:

   `jms://ActiveMQSession::queue_Q1`

6. Select the SOAP request of the `getGuestDetails` operation in `GuestManagementServiceSoap11Binding`, change the endpoint to the previously mentioned jms endpoint and submit the request.

7. Now, open the HermesJMS console and browse for the queue, **Q1**, in **ActiveMQSession**. You will find the `<getGuestDetails>` SOAP request is placed in the queue.

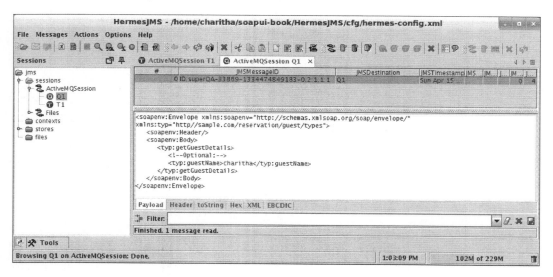

8. You can also look at the content of the message by browsing the queue, Q1, in the ActiveMQ management console. Just access `http://localhost:8161/admin/browse.jsp?JMSDestination=Q1` and check the messages.

9. Let's add another JMS endpoint to the same binding. This time, we will specify the same queue, Q1, as both **Send/Publish destination** and **Receive/Subscribe destinations**. So, when a message is placed in Q1, it will instantly be picked up by consumers from the same queue. Once the JMS endpoint is added, you will find a new endpoint which looks like the following:

   `jms://ActiveMQSession::queue_Q1::queue_Q1`

10. Change the endpoint as previously mentioned and submit the same `getGuestDetails` SOAP request. Since we sent and received a message from the same queue, the response pane of soapUI will show the message which has been delivered to the consumers.

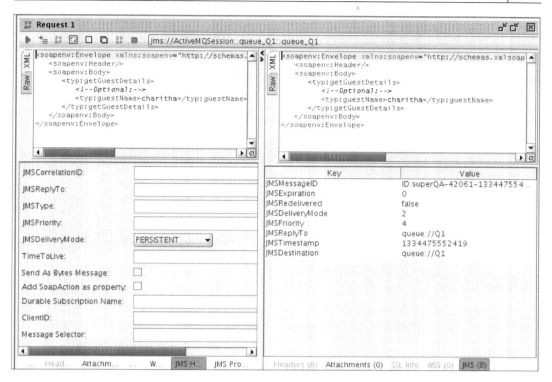

But, you will not find the corresponding message if you browse Q1 in the HermesJMS console. It is because the message is enqueued and dequeued instantly as we specified the **Receive/Subscribe destination** field when sending the message. However, you can find out that the **Messages Dequeued** column associated with Q1 is updated in the ActiveMQ management console as you send messages.

You can see in the previous image that soapUI shows the headers of the JMS message as key-value pairs in the bottom pane of the SOAP response editor. We can also set various JMS headers such as **JMSPriority**, **TimeToLive** when submitting the message. These JMS request headers can be set in the **JMS Headers** tab of the soapUI request editor. We can also create and set properties for messages if we need values in addition to those provided by the header fields. These additional properties can be set in the **JMS Property** section in the soapUI SOAP request editor.

The JMS API defines a set of message types (also known as body formats) to send and receive data in many different forms. With soapUI, we can use three major message types:

1. **Text Message**:

   This message type carries a `java.lang.String` object. This can be used to transport plain-text and XML messages.

2. **Bytes Message**:

   The payload is stored as an array of bytes. This can be used to transmit data when the data format is native to the application and the JMS client does not know the message payload type.

3. **Map Message**:

   Message payload is stored as a set of name-value pairs. This message type is useful for transmitting keyed data that can change from one message to the next.

By default, the message body format is set to text and this can be changed by selecting the **Send As Bytes Message** option.

Validating JMS responses

Regardless of the transport protocol used in communication, we can use most of the general SOAP assertions to validate the response messages used in web services. However, in addition to the generic assertions, soapUI provides us with two assertions which are specific to JMS transport:

- JMS Status
- JMS Timeout

- **JMS Status**:

  The JMS Status assertion can be used to validate the status of the communication. For example, it can be used to check whether there are any JMS specific errors in the response.

- **JMS Timeout**:

  The JMS Timeout assertion can be used to verify whether the message is received within the configured timeout period.

Let's use these assertions in our sample project and discuss further.

1. Select `GuestManagementServiceTestSuite` in our sample `HotelReservationProject` and locate the `getGuestDetails` TestCase.

2. Select the `getGuestDetails` SOAP request and select `jms://ActiveMQSession::queue_Q1::queue_Q1` as the endpoint (assuming this JMS endpoint has already been configured in a previous step).

3. Click on **Adds an assertion to this item** icon and select the **JMS Status** assertion.

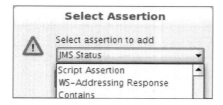

4. Shut down the ActiveMQ broker and submit the request. You will get an assertion failure with the message as follows:

    `JMS Status - FAILED.`

    In this case, the JMS status has been given as failed because soapUI could not connect to the broker. Therefore, if we want to validate the communication errors between soapUI and the JMS provider, the **JMS Status** assertion can be used quite easily.

Now, let's look at the usage of the JMS Timeout assertion. To do that, we should specify a non-zero time-out value as a SOAP test request property.

1. Select the `getGuestDetails` TestStep. In the **TestRequest properties** tab at the right-hand side pane, specify `1` in the **Timeout** (the timeout value should be specified in milliseconds) field.

2. In the `getGuestDetails` SOAP request editor, click on the **Add an assertion to this item** icon and select the **JMS Timeout** assertion.

3. Submit the request. You will get an assertion failure with the following message:

    `JMS Timeout - FAILED`

    `JMS Message timeout error! Message is not received within 1ms.`

    Due to the various application level changes as well as configuration settings of the JMS provider, messages can be timed out. In order to validate those cases, we can define an optimum time-out value for the requests and use the JMS Timeout assertion to validate them.

So far, we have discussed about JMS transport, the Apache ActiveMQ JMS provider, and the use of JMS inside soapUI. However, we did not go beyond just placing a message to a JMS destination (queue or topic) through soapUI. We cannot conclude our discussion without exposing one of the web services of our sample hotel reservation system over JMS and verifying an end-to-end message flow using soapUI. In the next section, we will look into configuring our sample project on JMS transport and using soapUI to test end-to-end message delivery.

Verifying end-to-end JMS message delivery using the sample project

In previous examples, we use the sample HotelReservation soapUI project just to submit requests to a queue in ActiveMQ. Though we have placed those messages in a queue, those were not consumed by our sample hotel reservation web services. In order to test the end-to-end functionality, we need to configure the web services so that they are aware of the messaging queues and consume the messages. For that, we will go through the following steps:

1. Enable JMS transport in Apache Axis2, so that all web services hosted in Axis2 will be exposed over JMS.

2. Configure a new session in HermesJMS to use a new ActiveMQ destination.

3. Add a new JMS endpoint in the soapUI project and test the message flow.

Configuring JMS in Apache Axis2

By default, all web services hosted in Apache Axis2 are exposed over HTTP transport. Therefore, all our web services, namely GuestManagementService, RoomManagementService, and ReservationService, include HTTP endpoints only. We can find this out by looking at the auto-generated WSDLs of these web services.

Axis2 uses two constructs, TransportReceiver and TransportSender to handle messages which comes in and goes out from the Axis2 engine. Any message which comes into Axis2 goes through the transport receiver and the messages which are sent out, go through the transport sender. Based on the transports used, we can have multiple transport receivers and senders in the Axis2 engine. Therefore, in order to enable JMS transport, we should configure the JMS specific transport receiver and sender. We can configure these in axis2.xml configuration file which can be found at the AXIS2_HOME/conf directory. Add the following element into axis2.xml in order to specify the transport receiver for JMS.

You can configure new transport receivers under the following section in `axis2.xml`:

```
<!-- This is where you'd put custom transports.  See the transports
project -->
    <!-- for more.  http://ws.apache.org/commons/transport
-->
<transportReceiver name="jms" class="org.apache.axis2.transport.jms.
JMSListener">

        <parameter name="myTopicConnectionFactory">

            <parameter name="java.naming.factory.initial">org.apache.
activemq.jndi.ActiveMQInitialContextFactory</parameter>

            <parameter name="java.naming.provider.url">tcp://
localhost:61616</parameter>

            <parameter name="transport.jms.ConnectionFactoryJNDIName">To
picConnectionFactory</parameter>

        </parameter>



        <parameter name="myQueueConnectionFactory">

            <parameter name="java.naming.factory.initial">org.apache.
activemq.jndi.ActiveMQInitialContextFactory</parameter>

            <parameter name="java.naming.provider.url">tcp://
localhost:61616</parameter>

            <parameter name="transport.jms.ConnectionFactoryJNDIName">Qu
eueConnectionFactory</parameter>

        </parameter>



        <parameter name="default">

            <parameter name="java.naming.factory.initial">org.apache.
activemq.jndi.ActiveMQInitialContextFactory</parameter>

            <parameter name="java.naming.provider.url">tcp://
localhost:61616</parameter>
```

```
            <parameter name="transport.jms.ConnectionFactoryJNDIName">Qu
eueConnectionFactory</parameter>

        </parameter>

    </transportReceiver>
```

In this configuration, three connection factories are defined. One for a queue, one for a topic, and a default Connection Factory. As we have discussed before, connection factories are essential to make connections with a JMS provider, such as Apache ActiveMQ.

Note that the default Connection Factory will be used by our sample web services. If we do not explicitly specify the Connection Factory and the associated destination to be used in `services.xml` of each of the web services, a JMS queue will automatically be created with the service name. So, we will have queues for all our web services with the names, `GuestManagementService`, `RoomManagementService`, and `ReservationService`.

Similar to the transport receiver configuration, add the following element under the **Transport Outs** section of `axis2.xml` to specify the JMS transport sender:

```
<transportSender name="jms"

                    class="org.apache.axis2.transport.jms.
JMSSender"/>
```

Now, we have configured both transport receiver and sender in `axis2.xml`. We need to make the relevant JMS provider libraries available in Axis2 classpath as we did with HermesJMS. Copy `activemq-core-5.3.0.jar`, `geronimo-j2ee-management_1.0_spec-1.0.jar` and `geronimo-jms_1.1_spec-1.1.1.jar` from `ACTIVE_MQ_HOME/lib` to the `AXIS2_HOME/lib` directory. In addition to that, due to a change in Axis2-kernal in Axis2-1.6.1 distribution, you need to copy the following two libraries to `AXIS2_HOME/lib`:

- `axis2-transport-jms-1.0.0.jar`
- `axis2-transport-base-1.0.0.jar`

You can download these two jar files from `http://axis.apache.org/axis2/java/transports/download.cgi`.

After copying all these libraries, restart the Axis2 server. You will notice log messages similar to the following at the server startup:

```
[INFO] JMS Transport Receiver (Listener) initialized...
```

Since we have enabled JMS transport globally at `axis2.xml` configuration file, all web services hosted in Axis2 will include a new JMS endpoint. Open the auto-generated WSDL of `GuestManagementService` by accessing `http://localhost:8080/axis2/services/GuestManagementService?wsdl`. You will notice the JMS endpoints there shown as follows:

```
<wsdl:port name="GuestManagementServiceJmsSoap11Endpoint" bind
ing="axis2:GuestManagementServiceSoap11Binding"><soap:address
location="jms:/GuestManagementService?transport.jms.ConnectionFact
oryJNDIName=QueueConnectionFactory&java.naming.provider.url=tcp://
localhost:61616&java.naming.factory.initial=org.apache.activemq.jndi.
ActiveMQInitialContextFactory"/></wsdl:port>
```

According to this, if we want to send a request to `GuestManagementService` through JMS, we must use the previous endpoint location URL. With this endpoint URL, the message will be placed in a queue, named as `GuestManagementService`, inside ActiveMQ. Since we have configured `axis2.xml` with the default **Connection Factory** settings, Axis2 will pick up the message from the queue and dispatch to the relevant service operation.

Configuring a session in HermesJMS

We are going to use soapUI to submit the SOAP request to the JMS queue, which is used by `GuestManagementService`. Therefore, we should create a new session and destination in HermesJMS as we did in previous examples.

1. Start by creating a new HermesJMS session. We can use the same provider, which we used previously. Therefore, use `ActiveMQGroup` as the classpath group. Give `Axis2Session` as the name of the session.

2. In **Connection Factory** configuration in HermesJMS preferences dialog box, select `ActiveMQGroup` as the loader. Select `org.apache.activemq.ActiveMQConnectionFactory` as the connection factory class and add the following property:

    `BrokerURL = tcp://localhost:61616`

3. In the **Plug In** configuration, select **ActiveMQ** and add the following two properties:

    `BrokerName = localhost`

    `serviceURL = service:jmx:rmi:///jndi/rmi://localhost:1099/jmxrmi`

4. Click on **Apply** and add a new destination by right-clicking on the **Destinations** pane. Specify the following properties:

- ○ **Name:**GuestManagementService
- ○ **ShortName:** GuestManagementService
- ○ **Domain:** Queue

As we discussed previously, Apache ActiveMQ creates queues for each of the three web services with their names. Therefore, name of the queue corresponding to the GuestManagementService is GuestManagementService. After all that, our new HermesJMS session will look like the following:

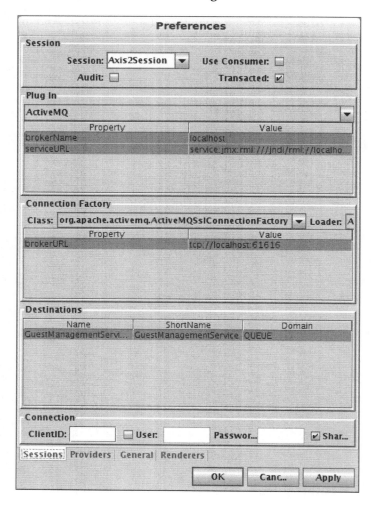

Adding a JMS endpoint in soapUI

Since we have configured the JMS destination through HermesJMS, we can add a new JMS endpoint in soapUI.

1. Select `GuestManagementServiceSoap11Binding` in `HotelReservationProject` from the soapUI project navigator.

2. Right-click and select **Add JMS endpoint**. Select **Axis2Session** as the session. Select `GuestManagementService` as the **Send/Publish destination field**. Leave **Receive/Subscribe destination** empty.

> We are going to invoke a `deleteGuest` one-way operation through JMS. Because of that, we do not expect a response message and leave **Receive/Subscribe destination** empty.

3. Finally, you will find the JMS endpoint similar to the following in the endpoint list of our soapUI project:

   `jms://Axis2Session::queue_GuestManagementService`

4. Next, select `GuestManagementServiceTestSuite` and locate the `deleteGuest` TestStep. We will invoke the `deleteGuest` operation by submitting a SOAP request through JMS transport.

5. Select the above JMS endpoint in `deleteGuest` SOAP request editor. Add an existing `Guestname` for `<typ:guestName>` in the payload of the SOAP message.

6. Submit the request. Since the `deleteGuest` is a one-way operation, you will not get a response. Check the `GUEST_T` table in `HOTEL_RESERVATION_DB`. You will notice that the corresponding guest record has been removed from the table.

Summary

The integration of heterogeneous systems is one of the objectives of adopting SOA in enterprise software development. In such systems, we usually have to deal with multiple transport protocols. soapUI as the complete SOA testing platform, allows users to extend test cases to deliver messages through JMS transport. By integrating HermesJMS, an open source JMS management application, soapUI facilitates submitting and receiving SOAP messages to JMS destinations. In this chapter, we looked at JMS integration in soapUI using multiple examples. We demonstrated the use of JMS in soapUI with our sample Hotel Reservation project and tested an end-to-end work flow.

11
Extending soapUI
with Scripting

The default features and utilities provided by soapUI are more than enough for us to explore the world of web services testing and build flexible test suites. When we become more and more familiar with the standard features of soapUI, we naturally tend to think about the extension possibilities. We need to extend the default functionalities provided by soapUI due to various reasons. For example:

- To minimize overhead maintenance of soapUI tests.

- Automated or manual execution of tests becomes a pain if we are supposed to do dramatic changes of tests when moving between various environments such as development, staging, and production, or when upgrading the services.

- To reduce complexities of building tests.

- To look for possibilities of avoiding repetitive manual tasks when writing tests. If we want to add the same assertion for hundreds of test suites again and again, we need to think about ways of extending the existing soapUI assertion features to facilitate that.

soapUI provides us with options to extend the default behavior of tests using various scripting mechanisms. soapUI allows us to use either Groovy or JavaScript as the possible scripting choices. In this chapter, we will look into the scripting capabilities given by soapUI using Groovy scripting language. Though JavaScript can also be used in scripting, Groovy is the natural choice for extending soapUI as there are optimizations added to Groovy libraries by soapUI developers in order to facilitate seamless integration with soapUI as well as it is widely used by the soapUI community.

We will look into the following topics in this chapter:

- Introduction to Groovy scripting
- Groovy scripting in soapUI
- soapUI ModelItems
- Request and response handling using scripts
- soapUI script assertion

Introduction to Groovy scripting language

As we are going to use Groovy scripts throughout this chapter, we should prepare in advance by familiarizing ourselves with the basics of Groovy. If you possess some knowledge about Groovy or have experience of working with it, you can skip reading this section.

What is Groovy?

Groovy is a dynamic programming language in which most of the program execution processes are done at runtime instead of compile time. Groovy can be categorized into the same family of scripting languages such as Ruby, Perl, or JavaScript. As we already know, learning a new language is a tedious activity because we need to learn the syntax, control structures, declarations, and so on for the new language. However, this is not true for Groovy if you already know the fundamentals of Java. Groovy uses Java-like bracket syntax and most Java code is syntactically valid in Groovy. Groovy scripts run on JVM similar to Java programs, hence we do not need to install and configure additional libraries. Groovy is a **loosely-typed language**, which means there is no need to define the data types for the variables and for the return types of the methods.

Let's go through some basic principles of Groovy with examples. In order to try out the simple Groovy examples that we are going to try out, you can use the following two approaches:

- Download the latest version of Groovy binary distribution from `http://groovy.codehaus.org/Download` (at the time of writing, the latest stable version was Groovy 1.8). Install Groovy on your machine as per the instructions given in the official Groovy installation guide (`http://groovy.codehaus.org/Installing+Groovy`). Then, you can use the interactive Groovy shell to write and run the example Groovy scripts.

- Use soapUI Groovy Script TestStep to test the sample scripts.

We will use the second approach as it minimizes the setup time and we can quickly try out some basic principles of the Groovy scripting language.

We will use a new workspace and a project in soapUI for Groovy examples as these are not a part of our sample hotel reservation project. Go to **File | New workspace** and add a new workspace in soapUI. Name it `GroovyExamplesWorkspace`. Once the new workspace is created, right-click on it and add a new soapUI project. Name the project `GroovyExamplesProject`. We do not add an initial WSDL for the project as we are not going to test any web services using this project. Now, add a new TestSuite and a TestCase in the project. Add a new **Groovy Script** Test Step by right-clicking on the TestCase and selecting **Add Step**, then selecting **Groovy Script** out of the steps available in the list. Finally, we will get a Groovy Script editor, as shown in the following screenshot, where we can try out the example scripts.

As we use **Groovy Script** Test Step in soapUI as an editor to write Groovy scripts, we will synonymously call it **Groovy editor** within this section of the book.

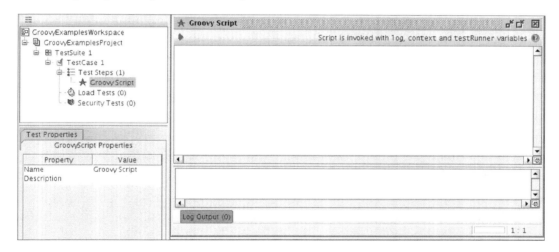

HelloWorld with Groovy

Let's begin with the usual HelloWorld script. Write the following script in the soapUI Groovy Script editor:

```
//Print "Hello soapUI" string in console
print "Hello soapUI\n"
```

Run the script by clicking on the green arrow icon which is at the upper-left corner of the script editor. You will observe the output in the soapUI startup console.

Variable and object declaration in Groovy

As with any programming language, variables or objects must be declared before they are referenced by somewhere else. The variables can be declared with the keyword def, as shown in the following script:

```
def name = "soapui" //declare variable name and assign value soapui
```

 We can even declare variables without the def keyword. You can assign any object to variables defined with def, and return any kind of object if a method is declared returning def. Remember, if you declare the variable with def, there is no need to specify a type. Therefore, the following declaration is unnecessary:

```
def String name ="soapui"
```

To read the value of a variable, you can just prefix the variable name with $ as in Case 1 or append it as in Java (Case 2).

- Case 1:

```
def name = "soapui"
print "Hello $name \n"
```

- Case 2:

```
def name ="soapui"
print "Hello " +name
```

By default the standard Java packages such as java.lang.*, java.util.*, java.io.*, and so on, are included by Groovy interpreter. Thus, the objects in Groovy can be declared in the same way as we do with Java. The following code will instantiate String object.

```
def strObject = new String("soapui")
```

Groovy has support for two collection data types:

- **Lists**: These are used to store ordered collections of data. A list can be declared as follows:

```
myList = [0, 32, -90, 45, 89923]
```

The above statement declares a list object, which holds integer values. We can access a value stored in list with myList[n], where *n* is the index of list.

- **Maps**: These store different types of data in key-value pairs. For example, consider the following script:

```
myMap = ["key1":"soapui", "key2":100, "key3":30.05] //different
// types of data are stored in a map
println myMap["key2"] //access the value assigned to "key2"
println myMap.key2 //another way of accessing value assigned to
// key2
```

Control structures in Groovy

The syntax of control structures such as "if-else", "for", and "while" are very similar to what we have in Java. Look at the following code snippet:

```
status = true
strObject = new String("Hello")
myList = ["1","2", "3"]

if (status && strObject && myList) { //All will evaluate to true
    println "Condition is true"
}else{
    println "Condition is false"
}
```

Run the code snippet and you will get `Condition is true` as the output. Here, `strObject` (String object) and `myList` (Collection object) will return `false` only if either of the two or both are null or empty. The syntax of the for loop is similar to the following:

```
for(Object in IterableObject){
    // Set of Statements.
}
```

`IterableObject` is a composite object which has multiple child entries so that it can be iterated. In order to understand the behavior of loops in Groovy, run the following code and check the output:

```
def names = ["Saman", "Nethul", "Risith", "Charitha"] // A List
// object holdingnames
for(name in names){//Iterate over the elements in names list
    println name
}
```

Class and method declarations in Groovy

Declaration of classes in Groovy is almost the same as it is in Java. Let's figure it out with an example:

```groovy
class Employee{

    private def id
    private def name
    def address

    public Employee(){
    }

    Employee(id, name, address){
        this.id = id
        this.name = name
        this.address = address
    }

    public String getId(){
        return id
    }

    def setId(id){
        this.id = id
    }

    public String getName(){
        return name
    }

    def setName(name){
        this.name = name
    }

    static main(arguments){

        def emp1 = new Employee("100", "Charitha", "Colombo")
        println("Employee name is "+emp1.getName())

    }
}
```

The output of the above code will be as follows:

```
Employee name is Charitha
```

You may notice that in the variable declarations section, we did not explicitly mention the data types of `id`, `name`, and `address` variables. We also did not specify what the access modifiers were. As Groovy is a loosely-typed language, we do not want to specify the data types and access modifiers. The default access modifier of Groovy is public.

We discussed the fundamentals which are required to proceed with the rest of the sections in this chapter. It is out of the scope of this book to cover large amount of concepts about Groovy programming. Therefore, it is recommended for you to read the resources available on the official Groovy website (`http://groovy.codehaus.org`).

Groovy scripting in soapUI

There are many reasons for using Groovy scripts in a soapUI project:

- To dynamically generate Mock Responses when simulating web services
- To add arbitrary functionality to TestCases using Groovy Script TestStep
- To use as Setup/TearDown scripts to initialize, and cleanup TestSuites and TestCases
- To use as Start/Stop scripts in initializing/cleaning up mock services
- To dynamically generate TestRequests and assertions based on database contents
- The OnRequest and AfterRequest scripts in Mock Services
- To perform arbitrary functionality during property expansion

We have discussed some of the scripting possibilities during *Chapter 6, Web Service Simulation with soapUI*, where we looked into the usage of scripts in Mock Services. We will see the other widely used patterns associated with Groovy scripting and soapUI during this chapter.

The Groovy scripts inside soapUI have access to the following context-related variables:

- `context`
- `testRunner`

In addition to the previous context-related properties, soapUI also provides us with a standard log4j Logger object—**log**—that can be used in scripts at any level in a soapUI project.

The context object

The `context` object holds information about a particular test run session. It can be used to read and write/update context-specific variables. There are different contexts available in a soapUI project, for example:

- `LoadTestRunContext`: This holds context information about the loadtest run session
- `MockRunContext`: This context is available for the duration of a Mock Services' execution
- `SubmitContext`: This is available during one submit of a request
- `TestRunContext`: This is available during a TestCase execution and all scripts in a TestCase run have access to the TestRunContext

Without digging into details, let's look at the usage of the `context` object using a simple example:

1. Open the **HotelReservation** project in soapUI and add a Groovy Script TestStep into **getRoomDetails** TestCase. Name the test step `GroovyTestScript1`.

2. Add the following script in script editor and run the test step by clicking on the green arrow icon which is in the upper-left corner of the Groovy Script editor:

```
//Get the name of current TestStep
log.info(context.getCurrentStep().getLabel())
//Get the name of parent TestCase
log.info(context.getTestCase().getLabel())
//Get the name of TestSuite
log.info(context.getTestCase().getTestSuite().getLabel())
log.info(context.getTestCase().getTestSuite().getProject().
getName()) //Get the name of the soapUI project
```

You will find the output of test run at the Log Output window which appears right below the script editor. It will look similar to the following.

```
Fri May 04 22:13:43 IST 2012:INFO:GroovyTestScript

Fri May 04 22:13:43 IST 2012:INFO:getRoomDetails TestCase

Fri May 04 22:13:43 IST 2012:INFO:RoomManagementServiceTestSuite

Fri May 04 22:13:43 IST 2012:INFO:HotelReservationProject
```

The statements of the script and the output are self explanatory. We just witnessed the usage of the `context` object at an individual TestStep run of a project. In other words, we made use of in implementation of the `SubmitContext` interface.

Script Logs are used to show the log messages dumped by scripts invoked from various levels of the project. There are two instances of script logs provided by soapUI. Groovy Script TestStep includes a Log Output pane at the bottom of the editor which shows the log output if you run the Groovy Script individually. There is also a **script log** tab at the bottom of the log toolbar, which displays the log messages dumped by execution of Groovy Scripts from the TestCase and TestSuite levels of the soapUI project. These two logs are shown in the following image.

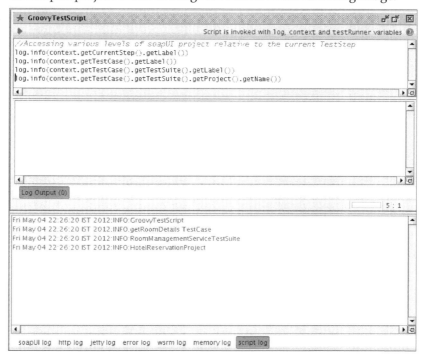

The `context` object is useful in situations where you want to read the property values of TestStep. For example, we have a property, **Endpoint**, defined at **getRoomDetails** SOAP Request TestStep. We can simply read the value of this property using a context object, as shown in the following script:

```
EndPointProp = context.getProperty("getRoomDetails","Endpoint")
```

Note that you cannot read the property value from a TestStep of a different TestCase using this method. The following will return null as `deleteRoom` TestStep is in a different TestCase:

```
EndPointProp2 = context.getProperty("deleteRoom","Endpoint")
log.info(EndPointProp2)
```

Now, let's do another test to find out what properties are available during a single run of a TestStep. Add the following script in the editor of Groovy Script TestStep and run the test step:

```
String[] props= context.getPropertyNames()
for (prop in props){
log.info(prop)
}
```

Here, we read all property names of the current context into a string array and iterate over the values. You will see the following output. There are three built-in properties associated with the context of request submission — RunCount, log, and ThreadIndex:

```
Sat May 05 09:59:10 IST 2012:INFO:RunCount

Sat May 05 09:59:10 IST 2012:INFO:log

Sat May 05 09:59:10 IST 2012:INFO:ThreadIndex
```

Double-click on the **getRoomDetails** TestCase to open the **getRoomDetails** TestCase editor. Now, you will have the **getRoomDetails** SOAP Test request and **GroovyTestScript1** TestSteps under the TestCase. Run the **getRoomDetails** TestCase by selecting the green arrow icon at the top of the **getRoomDetails** TestCase and look at the output. This time you will see 19 properties such as **httpMethod**, **requestUri**, and **postMethod**, which are available at the TestCase context of the run session.

In addition to the built-in properties, we can set the properties and retrieve them later during a particular test run.

```
PropertyVal=new String("This is a property value")
//Setting a value to property1
context.setProperty("property1", PropertyVal)
//Reading property1's value
readPropval1 = context.getProperty("property1")
```

The context.expand (<String>) method is a useful method, which is inherited from the com.eviware.soapui.model.support.AbstractAdminContext base class. This can be used in multiple situations and the simplest usage is for accessing a custom property at a different level of a test. If we have a custom property at project level (for example, Test), then we can use the expand method to read the property value from a script which runs from the TestStep level:

```
log.info(context.expand( '${#Project#Test}'))
```

The `context` object is very useful if we want to store some value in one TestStep and use it in subsequent script test steps:

1. Add another GrovyScript TestStep in the **getRoomDetails** TestCase. Let's name it **GroovyTestScript2**:

2. Add the following into GroovyTestScript1 to define a new property, `holder` in `context`:

   ```
   context.holder="testing"
   ```

3. Now, add the following in GroovyTestScript2 to read the property value:

   ```
   holderValue = context.getProperty("holder")
   log.info(holderValue)
   ```

Once you run the **getRoomDetails** TestCase, you will see the log output of GroovyTestScript2 run which prints **testing** as the result. In this example, context represented an instance of **TestCaseRunContext** where the context is visible inside TestCase.

The testRunner variable

The `testRunner` variables are used to execute tests in a soapUI project. The sub interfaces of the `com.eviware.soapui.model.testsuite.TestRunner` interface (`http://www.soapui.org/apidocs/com/eviware/soapui/model/testsuite/TestRunner.html`) are used to execute various elements of a soapUI Project. For example, the `com.eviware.soapui.model.testsuite.TestCaseRunner` interface, that extends `com.eviware.soapui.model.testsuite.TestRunner`, defines a set of methods to manipulate soapUI TestCases. In this section, we will look into the usage of `testRunner` inside a soapUI project.

The `testRunner` interfaces provide methods such as `start`, `cancel`, and `fail` to control the test execution. Follow these steps to see how testRunner can be used to control test execution flow:

1. Add the following statement in GroovyTestScript1 and run the **getRoomDetails** TestCase from the **getRoomDetails** TestCase editor:

   ```
   testRunner.cancel("CANCELLED THE TEST")
   ```

2. You will see that the further executions of TestCase immediately stop when they reach the preceding statement and the CANCELLED THE TEST message is logged at the TestCase log. This is useful if you want to cancel the test run, based on evaluation of certain conditions.

Let's look at how we can invoke a different TestCase in a different TestSuite using `testRunner`.

Suppose in our sample **HotelReservation** project, the **addReservation** TestCase should fail if the corresponding room does not exist in the system (note that, in the ReservationService implementation, we have not added a validation to check the availability of rooms). Thus, before invoking the **addReservation** TestCase, we may need to check the existence of the room which is going to be reserved. In this case, of course we can directly use the Run TestCase TestStep. However, let's try to use a GroovyScript TestStep as a child of **addReservation** TestCase to invoke **getRoomDetails** TestCase so that we can look in to the possibilities of using the `testRunner` object:

1. Select **ReservationServiceTestSuite** and add Groovy Script TestStep as an immediate child of **addReservation** TestCase. Name it `findRoomScript`.

2. Add the following script:

```
import com.eviware.soapui.model.testsuite.TestRunner.Status

//Get hold of the getRoomDetails TestCase which is at a different
// TestSuite than the current Suite
def getRoomDetailsTestCase = testRunner.testCase.testSuite.
project.testSuites["RoomManagementServiceTestSuite"].
testCases["getRoomDetails TestCase"]
//Run the getRoomDetails TestCase synchronously
def testcaserunner = getRoomDetailsTestCase.run(null, false)

//Fail if getRoomDetails TestCase fail
assert testcaserunner.status == Status.FINISHED
```

Here, we first got a reference to **getRoomDetails** TestCase. Then, we invoked the `run(stringToObjectMap properties, boolean async)` method of the `WsdlTestCase` class (`com.eviware.soapui.impl.wsdl.testcase.WsdlTestCase`) that implemented the TestCase interface (`http://www.soapui.org/apidocs/com/eviware/soapui/impl/wsdl/testcase/WsdlTestCase.html`). Finally, we used assert statement to check the status of the TestCase execution.

3. Give an existing room number as value in `<typ:roomNumber>` in **getRoomDetails** SOAP request. Also, specify the same room number in the **addReservation** SOAP request. Run **ReservationTestSuite**. Make sure to disable GroovyTestScript2 TestStep, which has been added previously to cancel the execution of **getRoomDetails** TestCase:

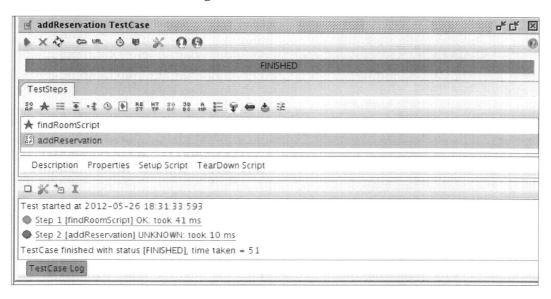

The TestCase log will be updated with the results, where you can find the **findRoomScript** is marked in green, denoting the success of execution of the **getRoomDetails** TestCase.

4. Now, submit the **getRoomDetails** TestStep of **RoomManagementService** TestSuite with a non-existing room number. We should add an assertion to denote that the **getRoomDetails** TestStep of the **getRoomDetails** TestCase fails if we submit the getRoomDetails SOAP request with a non-existing room. Thus, add the **Not SOAP Fault** assertion to getRoomDetails SOAP Request TestStep.

5. Run the **addReservation** TestCase of **ReservationTestSuite** again. You will get a test failure, as shown in the following screenshot:

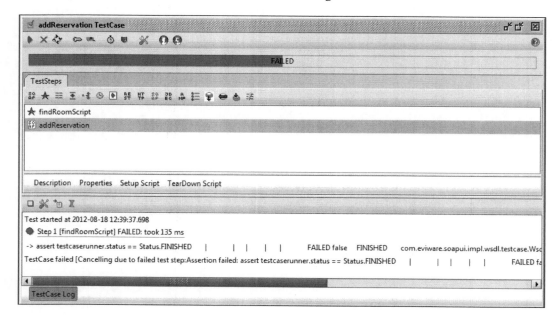

soapUI ModelItems

ModelItems are the preliminary building blocks of a soapUI project. The elements such as projects, test suites, test cases, test steps, mock services, mock responses, and assertions are all implemented as ModelItems. The `com.eviware.soapui.model.ModelItem` interface (`http://www.soapui.org/apidocs/com/eviware/soapui/model/ModelItem.html`) is the super interface which defines the general behavior of all soapUI model items.

When you get hold of a ModelItem in your script, you can use the corresponding getters to retrieve values such as `id`, `name`, and `description` of a ModelItem.

```
getRoomDetailsTestCase.name
```

Also, ModelItems provide us with various methods to access parent and child entities.

Let's look at some methods in TestCase ModelItem that are frequently used to retrieve TestSteps in a TestCase:

- `getTestStepByName(String stepName)`: To retrieve a specific test step inside a TestCase

- `getTestStepCount()`: To get the TestStep count of a TestCase
- `getTestStepList()`: To get list of TestSteps included in a TestCase

Add the following script as a Groovy Script TestStep in any of the TestSuites in the **HotelReservation** sample project and run the TestStep:

```
def getGuestDetailsTestCase = testRunner.testCase.testSuite.project.te
stSuites["GuestManagementServiceTestSuite"].testCases["getGuestDetails
TestCase"]

//To get specific test step
getGuestDetailssoapStep = getGuestDetailsTestCase.getTestStepByName("g
etGuestDetails")
log.info("Name of the TestStep: "+getGuestDetailssoapStep.getLabel())

//To get test step count
log.info("Number of TestSteps in getGuestDetails TestCase:
"+getGuestDetailsTestCase.getTestStepCount())

//To get all test steps
for(teststep in getGuestDetailsTestCase.getTestStepList())
log.info("Name of the TestStep in getGuestDetails TestCase:
"+teststep.getName())
```

Assuming that we have two TestSteps, **getGuestDetails** and **Delay**, in the **getGuestDetails** TestCase, the **script log** output will show results similar to the following:

```
INFO:Name of the TestStep: getGuestDetails
INFO:Number of TestSteps in getGuestDetails TestCase: 2
INFO:Name of the TestStep in getGuestDetails TestCase: getGuestDetails
INFO:Name of the TestStep in getGuestDetails TestCase: Delay
```

Once we get hold of the TestStep object as described above, we can try out many interesting things. Suppose we want to add an assertion to a specific step in a TestCase, we can obtain the required TestCase first, traverse through all the TestSteps of the TestCase and add the necessary assertion programmatically as shown in the following script:

```
import com.eviware.soapui.impl.wsdl.teststeps.*
def getGuestDetailsTestCase = testRunner.testCase.testSuite.project.te
stSuites["GuestManagementServiceTestSuite"].testCases["getGuestDetails
TestCase"]

//Define the type of assertion
def soapAssertion ="SOAP Response"
```

```
//Retrieve all TestSteps in getGuestDetailsTestCase
for(testStep in getGuestDetailsTestCase.getTestStepList()) {
  //Check whether the TestStep is a SOAP Request TestStep
    if(testStep instanceof WsdlTestRequestStep)
      testStep.addAssertion(soapAssertion)
}
```

As we accessed the child TestSteps of the **getGuestDetails** TestCase, the parent TestSuite can also be retrieved using `getGuestDetailsTestCase.getTestSuite()`.

We looked into some preliminary methods of soapUI ModelItems which can be used to manipulate various elements and operations in a soapUI project. So far, we have worked with scripts which have been inside Groovy Script TestSteps. However, Groovy Script step is not the only place where you can write your script. There are more:

- Setup and TearDown Scripts at TestCase, TestSuite level which can be used to initialize and clean up various resources used in a soapUI test
- Load Script at project level which is used to run a script after loading the project
- Script assertion to introduce arbitrary validation on response
- MockService-specific scripts

As we have already discussed the last scripting option, MockService-specific scripts during *Chapter 6, Web Service Simulation with soapUI*, we will continue our discussion based on the rest of the scripting options.

Setup and TearDown scripts in soapUI

Setup and TearDown scripts can be used for many purposes. In particular, if you want to initialize something which is applicable for the whole TestSuite or TestCase, the Setup script will be the most appropriate option. Let's look at how we can initialize database connection in **RoomManagementServiceTestSuite** using **Setup Script**:

1. Right-click on **RoomManagementServiceTestSuite** and select Show **TestSuiteEditor**.

2. Select **Setup Script** at the bottom pane and add the following script:

```
import groovy.sql.Sql;
def DBdriver="com.mysql.jdbc.Driver"
def DBpath="jdbc:mysql://localhost:3306/HOTEL_RESERVATION_DB"
def username='root'
def password='root'
```

```
try {
DBconnection = Sql.newInstance(DBpath, username, password,
DBdriver);
context.setProperty("dbConProp", DBconnection)
} catch (Exception e) {
log.error "Could not establish connection to the database."
}
```

Here, we used Groovy SQL library to establish a database connection to our sample HOTEL_RESERVATION_DB. Once the connection is established, in order to use the connection from anywhere in the TestSuite, we set the connection as a context property, dbConProp:

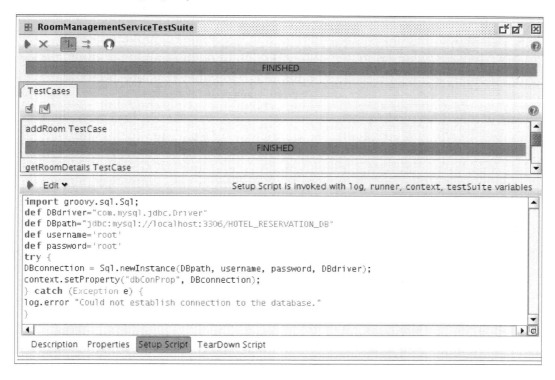

3. Now, we can use this connection within the **RoomManagementTestSuite**. In order to demonstrate the usage of the connection, let's add a simple Groovy Script TestStep under the **addRoom** TestCase:

```
def statement = "insert into ROOM_T values(500, 'Luxury',
'Double')"
def DBCon = context.getProperty("dbConProp")
DBCon.execute(statement)
```

Here, we simply used the `dbConProp` context property to execute a SQL query. Run **RoomManagementServiceTestSuite** and query the `ROOM_T` table. You will find the query has been executed successfully.

Similarly, TearDown Scripts can be used to close database connections at the end of the TestSuite execution.

4. Click on the **TearDown Script** tab at the bottom pane of **RoomManagementServiceTestSuite** and add the following script to close the database connection:

```
def DBCon = context.getProperty("dbConProp")
DBCon.close()
```

Load Script at soapUI project level

If we need to do something common for the whole project, we can invoke a script at the project level. In the soapUI project view, you will find **Load Script** and **Save Script** tabs at the bottom pane, where you can specify a script at the project level and run it just after loading the project.

In SOA testing, we usually need to use the same soapUI project in multiple environments. Before deploying the web services in the QA environment, developers may execute the whole set of test suites in the development environment. Similarly, the same tests will be executed in the staging environment before moving the services into production. Usually, in all these cases, nothing but the service endpoints are changed. Therefore, it will be necessary to change all endpoint URLs when moving the TestSuites among different environments. To address that, we can use a simple Groovy script at the project level and run it before deploying the test in different test environments.

Assume the following are the URLs of three of our sample web services when they are deployed in the QA environment:

*   `http://QAServer:8080/axis2/services/GuestManagementService`
*   `http://QAServer:8080/axis2/services/RoomManagementService`
*   `http://QAServer:8080/axis2/services/ReservationService`

Let's look at how we can change the existing endpoints of the SOAP request TestSteps in our sample project when moving the test into the QA environment.

1. Right-click on **HotelReservationProject** and select **Show Project View**. Then click on the **Load Script** tab on the bottom pane to open the script editor.

2. Add the following script:

```
//Define three web service endpoints
def GuestQAEndpoint = "http://QAServer:8080/axis2/services/
GuestManagementService"
def RoomQAEndpoint = "http://QAServer:8080/axis2/services/
RoomManagementService"
def ReservationQAEndpoint = "http://QAServer:8080/axis2/services/
ReservationService"
 //Get all TestSuites inside HotelReservationProject
 testSuiteList = project.getTestSuites()
 //Iterate through each TestSuite
 testSuiteList.each
 {
 //Rerieve a particular TestSuite by its name
 testSuite = project.getTestSuiteByName(it.key)
 //Get all TestCases inside particular TestSuite
 testCaseList = testSuite.getTestCases()
//Iterate over each TestCase of a particular TestSuite
 testCaseList.each
   {
   //Retrieve specific TestCase by its name
   testCase = testSuite.getTestCaseByName(it.key)
   //We do not want to set endponts for all TestSteps in a
// TestCase. So, get only the SOAP Request TestSteps
   soapTestStepsList = testCase.getTestStepsOfType(com.eviware.
soapui.impl.wsdl.teststeps.WsdlTestRequestStep.class)
   //Iterate over each SOAP Request TestStep in a TestCase
   soapTestStepsList.each
    {
    //Assign the relevant endpoint
    if(testSuite.name == "GuestManagementServiceTestSuite"){
    it.properties['Endpoint'].value = GuestQAEndpoint
    } else if (testSuite.name == "RoomManagementServiceTestSuite"){
       it.properties['Endpoint'].value = RoomQAEndpoint
    }else {
       it.properties['Endpoint'].value = ReservationQAEndpoint
    }
   }
   }
 }
```

We will not go through each line in the previous script as everything is explained as inline comments. Note that we used Groovy closure style looping and the keyword it (it.key) to get the specific TestCase and TestSuite names from the list objects.

3. Run the script by clicking on the green arrow icon at the upper-left corner of the Script window. Check the SOAP Request TestSteps of each TestSuite. You will notice that the default endpoints of all SOAP requests are changed accordingly.

We will discuss the Script assertion as part of response handling through scripts.

Request and response handling using Scripts

So far, we have discussed about manipulating individual elements such as projects, test cases, and test steps of a soapUI project. However, we have not specifically looked into the different operations which can be carried out on request and response messages. soapUI provides us with a few important APIs to use with request and response messages:

- com.eviware.soapui.support.GroovyUtils: The API documentation of the GroovyUtils class (http://www.soapui.org/apidocs/com/eviware/soapui/support/GroovyUtils.html) provides us with all the necessary information to use this API.

- com.eviware.soapui.support.XmlHolder: This is a very useful API to act upon XML request and response messages. More details about the API can be found at the official API documentation (http://www.soapui.org/apidocs/com/eviware/soapui/support/XmlHolder.html)

- com.eviware.soapui.model.iface.MessageExchange: This interface represents an exchange of request and response messages using various API methods. For more details, visit http://www.soapui.org/apidocs/com/eviware/soapui/model/iface/MessageExchange.html.

Let's find out the basic usage of each of these classes using our sample project.

1. Add a new Groovy Script TestStep under the **getRoomDetails** TestCase of **RoomManagementServiceTestSuite**.

2. Add the following script:
   ```
   def xmlHolder = new com.eviware.soapui.support.XmlHolder(context,
   "getRoomDetails#Response")
   log.info xmlHolder.getXml()
   ```

Here, we created a new `XmlHolder` object which makes use of `WsdlTestStep` context variable and response of `getRoomDetails` request through property expansion. Submit the **getRoomDetails** TestStep once so that we will have a valid response in context. Then, run the Groovy script which will execute the script against the last received response message. You will find the response SOAP message in the script log.

3. We can get hold of the response XML message using the `GroovyUtils` class as follows:

```
def groovyUtils = new com.eviware.soapui.support.
GroovyUtils(context)
def xmlHolder = groovyUtils.getXmlHolder("getRoomDetails#Respon
se")
log.info xmlHolder.getXml()
```

4. Similarly, the request message can also be accessed:

```
def xmlHolder = new com.eviware.soapui.support.XmlHolder(context,
"getRoomDetails#Request")
```

Once you get hold of request and response messages, you can do various XML manipulations through the methods included in the `XmlHolder` class such as `getDomNode(xpath)` and `getNodeValue(xpath)`.

Script assertion

Script assertion is another type of assertion that can be used to validate the responses. The major advantage of using script assertion over the other assertions is you have much more control over the messages exchanged. Thus, you can validate the message content or headers using Groovy or JavaScript.

1. Open the **getRoomDetails** test request editor. Click on the **Assertions** tab at the bottom pane and select the **Adds an assertion to this item** option. Select **Script Assertion** and click on **OK**:

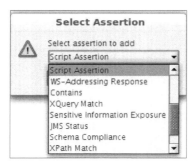

2. At the upper-right of the script editor, you will notice the message, "Script is invoked with log, context and messageExchange variables". Thus, you can use these variables to access request and response messages to do various content level validations.

3. The `com.eviware.soapui.model.iface.MessageExchange` interface represents an exchange of request and response message in a test run. Therefore, we can use the methods exposed by this interface such as `getResponseContent()` and `getResponseHeaders()` to access the request and response messages.

4. Add the following script in the script assertion editor and run the **getRoomDetails** TestCase:

```
import com.eviware.soapui.support.XmlHolder
def responseHolder = new XmlHolder(messageExchange.
getResponseContentAsXml())
def requestHolder = new XmlHolder(messageExchange.
getRequestContentAsXml())
assert responseHolder["//ns:roomNumber"] == requestHolder["//
typ:roomNumber"]
```

We used two `XmlHolder` objects to hold request and response. Request and response messages were retrieved by calling the `getReponseContentAsXml` and `getRequestContentAsXml` methods of the `messageExchange` object.

This is a trivial example which we used to demonstrate the usage of script assertion in a soapUI project. By using the `context` and `messageExchange` variables, you can try out much advanced and comprehensive operations on request and response messages.

Summary

The default behavior of tests can be extended by scripting facilities included in soapUI. Using Groovy or JavaScript, more control over the tests can be gained and hence, custom functionalities for your soapUI tests can be introduced. As the soapUI APIs are accessible through scripting, many useful methods can be used in your soapUI tests. In this chapter, we looked into the scripting possibilities of soapUI using the Groovy scripting language. First, we had a glance at the fundamentals of the Groovy scripting language. We discussed many reasons for using scripts in a soapUI project. The two important context-related variables—context and testRunner - have been introduced and explained using simple examples. We also looked into the ModelItems, the preliminary categorization of elements in a soapUI project. Finally, we went through examples of using scripts at various levels of a soapUI project.

12
Automated Testing with soapUI

Automated testing is the process of executing the existing manual tests using software. As we discussed throughout the book, the soapUI tests can simply be triggered via the intuitive user interface of soapUI. Will that be sufficient when testing the components including web services in your service-oriented solution? Isn't it a tedious and time-consuming task for your Quality Assurance (QA) team to run the soapUI TestSuites manually through user interface against each build? Can we minimize the human intervention when running soapUI tests?

The automated execution of soapUI tests can be considered as a possible answer for most of these questions. Even if we have an approach to run the soapUI tests automatically, we cannot gain the complete advantage of test automation, if we do not integrate the tests in to the build process and triggering them automatically with each build cycle. There are various mechanisms that can be adopted to achieve much ROI (Return-On-Investment) from test automation. This chapter will give you a quick overview on the test automation possibilities of soapUI projects by taking you through the following topics:

- An introduction to automated testing
- Continuous Integration
- soapUI JUnit integration
- Command-line execution of soapUI tests
- Maven soapUI plugin

Test automation

According to Wikipedia (`http://en.wikipedia.org/wiki/Test_automation`);

> *Test automation is the use of software to control the execution of tests, the comparison of actual outcomes to predicted outcomes, the setting up of test preconditions, and other test control and test reporting functions.*

We do not want to stress the fact that manual execution of tests is an exhausting, time consuming, and tedious process. In modern agile projects, the separation between independent Quality Assurance teams and development teams has become too narrowed. Quality is not the sole responsibility of a separate QA team. Everyone in a project equally owns the quality of the deliverables and contributes to the testing process. Therefore, Quality Assurance is no longer an independent or isolated activity, which used to happen at the final phases of a product release. Instead, more rigorous and agile testing processes are becoming popular among software development teams. One of the reasons for adopting more agile processes is the demand of frequent product/project releases. As we discussed in *Chapter 1, Web Services Testing and soapUI*, quickly adapting to business, process, or integration changes are one of the key promises of SOA. Therefore, it is evident that the SOA projects should follow an agile software development and testing approach to facilitate frequent releases and gain faster feedback by sharing products early with the relevant stakeholders.

How does test automation help in agile SOA projects? The common benefits of test automation are equally applicable for SOA as well. We are not going to spend time discussing the benefits of test automation in general because it is a well-known and popular topic which can easily be found out by browsing the Internet.

Why is test automation essential in SOA?

Regardless of the nature of the architectural style, which you use in your projects, test automation gives you a lot of benefits. However, test automation is an absolutely necessary factor in SOA.

1. Service-oriented solutions comprise of geographically distributed and heterogeneous components. Therefore, manual testing of individual components as well as the interactions among each other is not always possible.

2. The frequency of releases is comparatively high in service-oriented projects. Due to the demand of quickly reacting to the business, process, or technological changes, the releases occur quite often. Thus, a fast approach is required to provide the feedback about the system under test.

3. Majority of the components of a service oriented solution are headless. In other words, the components do not include a user interface for human interaction but the machine-processable interfaces. Therefore, these components are naturally fit into automated testing.

4. Re-usability is one of the key principles of SOA. Therefore, one service (or component in general) can be used by many different consumers. Most of the times, the potential consumers cannot be predicted in advance and the usage pattern of services can be varied. The automated TestSuites are the only solution to address large number of integration combinations in such a dynamically changing system.

5. The low-level components such as web services are totally message-oriented applications. To test these components need access to the message level and work with various message types (for example, SOAP, JSON) as well as transports (HTTP(S), JMS, VFS, FTP, and so on). Though you can capture the test scenarios and carry out the first round of functional tests manually using a tool such as soapUI, regression testing of message-oriented tests is an unnecessarily time consuming and tedious task if the tests are not triggered automatically.

Test automation frees up the tester's time to do more effective and exploratory tests which are crucial for the success of quality assurance of service oriented solutions. Because of the complexity due to the integrations and heterogeneous nature, deriving test scenarios of a service oriented solution is not a simple and straightforward task. Hence, the automated tests must be used as a time saver for testers to think about end-to-end system test cases and more exploratory testing. Based on these facts, we can conclude that the test automation is just not another nice-to-have activity when it comes to SOA. As we have discussed so far in this book, we can use soapUI to build a comprehensive functional or non-functional test suite to test web services included in Service-oriented solutions. The web services in our solution will not just be delivered after one test cycle but will go through multiple iterations which involve bug fixes as well as various enhancements. Therefore, we must plan to repeat the tests in multiple cycles. In order to do that, just having a soapUI project with multiple TestSuites is not necessary. We need to find a mechanism to automatically execute the tests and report results.

The automatic execution of soapUI tests can be done in two different approaches. Once the web services, which are under test, are built and ready for testing, we can automatically trigger the tests separately from the build environment. Or else, test automation can be combined with the build automation process and trigger the soapUI tests as part of the build process. The latter approach is commonly referred to as **continuous testing** and which can be considered as the ideal approach for automating tests in SOA. Continuous testing is a part of a more generic process, **Continuous Integration (CI)** where pieces of the software components integrate early and often to improve the overall quality and effectiveness of the software development process.

Continuous Integration (CI)

Continuous Integration, as the term implies, is the process of integrating individual units of source code in frequent cycles. During these frequent integration cycles, automated builds and tests are used to detect integration errors as early as possible and prevent them from introducing into the mainstream software product.

The summarized representation of the functions of a continuous integration system can be shown as follows:

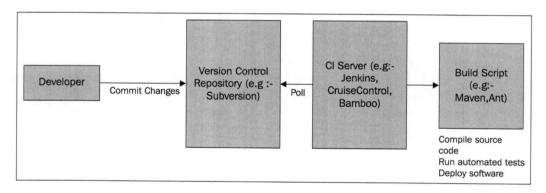

 The previous image and the introductory discussions on Continuous Integration are based on the book, *Continuous Integration – Improving Software Quality and Reducing Risk* by *Paul Duvall, Steve Matyas, Andrew Glover* (http://www.integratebutton.com/). I would recommend you to read that book to learn more about continuous integration and the related topics. We will only discuss the basic components of Continuous Integration systems in this chapter.

In general, any continuous integration system performs the following tasks:

1. Developers commit the code changes to the version control repository such as SVN, CVS, or VisualSourceSafe.

2. The Continuous Integration (CI) server is configured to poll the version control repository for changes in pre-defined time intervals (hourly, nightly, or at every commit based on the nature and complexity of the code base of your project).

3. The CI server detects the changes in version control repository, thus it retrieves the latest copy of the code base from the repository.

4. The CI server executes the build script (for example, in the case of Apache maven, the `pom.xml` file, or `build.xml` if the build tool is Apache Ant) which involves compilation of source code, preparing the databases, running automated tests, deploying the software into the deployment servers.

5. Finally, the CI server notifies the relevant parties about the status of the build through an email.

As we can understand from these steps, automated tests play a key role in a CI system. Since SOA is based on agile methodologies, it is extremely important to have a properly managed CI system in your SOA projects. The continuous testing of a CI system is not merely the unit tests which automatically validate the functionality of the logic of individual pieces of code in your service oriented solutions. The continuous testing must be performed to verify the functionalities of individual web services, service integrations, as well as business processes which are formed by multiple service compositions.

In order to test the services as well as service compositions in a service oriented project, the web service test suites must also be executed as part of the build cycle without maintaining them separately. soapUI provides us with various integration facilities with build tools, such as Apache Maven and Apache Ant, as well as the test frameworks, such as JUnit, which allow us to execute soapUI tests as part of a Continuous Integration system.

Let's proceed with discussing each of these integration facilities one by one.

soapUI JUnit integration

JUnit (http://junit.org/) is a framework to write repeatable tests in Java. As the name implies, the primary purpose of JUnit is to verify the functionality of individual units of code. However, by integrating with the external libraries, JUnit tests can be extended to verify integration as well as system tests.

Since the examples are the best way to describe something, without spending time on abstract descriptions, let's look into adding a JUnit test into our sample `HotelReservation` project.

1. Open the `hotel_reservation` project in your favorite **Integrated Development Environment (IDE)**. (Please revisit *Chapter 2, The Sample Project* to recap your memory on the project structure and location.)

2. Create a `test` directory at the root of the project, that is, `SAMPLE_PROJECT_HOME/test`(for example, `/home/charitha/soapui-projects/sample-project/hotel_reservation-1.0/test`).

3. Add a new package, `com.test.soapuitest` under the `test` directory and add a new JUnit TestCase with a single test method as follows:

```
package com.test.soapuitest;

import junit.framework.TestCase;

public class HotelReservationSoapUITest extends TestCase {

    public void testSoapUITestRunner() {
        //Run soapUI TestSuites
    }

}
```

 Make sure to download the latest version of JUnit jar (at the time of writing, `Junit-4.10.jar`) from `https://github.com/KentBeck/junit/downloads` and add it to the classpath of your sample project.

4. soapUI provides us with a standalone `testrunner` class called `SoapUITestCaseRunner` (`http://www.soapui.org/apidocs/com/eviware/soapui/tools/SoapUITestCaseRunner.html`) which can be used to run soapUI tests from any class, command line, or from the Apache Maven build script. We will instantiate an object of this class inside our JUnit test and invoke the methods to run the soapUI TestSuites or whole project at once.

 Before referring to the soapUI libraries from JUnit, make sure to add the `SOAPUI_HOME/lib` directory and `SOAPUI_HOME/bin/soapui-4.0.1.jar` library into the classpath of the sample project.

5. Let's implement the `testSoapUITestRunner()` method in our JUnit TestCase. First, we will initialize an object of the `SoapUITestCaseRunner` class. By looking at the API documentation of this class, we can find out all the methods of it. Out of them, we will use the `setProjectFile(String projectFile)` method to define the soapUI project file which contains the tests to be run. We will also use the `run()` method to execute the whole tests included in our soapUI project.

```
public void testSoapUITestRunner() {
        SoapUITestCaseRunner soapUITestCaseRunner = new
SoapUITestCaseRunner();
        soapUITestCaseRunner.setProjectFile("/home/charitha/
soapui-projects/HotelReservationProject-soapui-project.xml");
        try {
            soapUITestCaseRunner.run();
        } catch (Exception e) {
            e.printStackTrace();
        }
    }
```

Note that, in the `setProjectFile()` method, the absolute path of the location of our sample hotel reservation soapUI project has been given.

6. Now, run this JUnit test case. You will notice a set of log messages as follows:

```
[SoapUITestCaseRunner] Finished running soapUI testcase [addGuest
TestCase], time taken: 137ms, status: FINISHED

[SoapUITestCaseRunner] Running soapUI testcase [deleteGuest
TestCase]

[SoapUITestCaseRunner] running step [deleteGuest]

[SoapUITestCaseRunner] Finished running soapUI testcase
[deleteGuest TestCase], time taken: 50ms, status: FINISHED
........

[SoapUITestCaseRunner] Finished running soapUI testcase
[getGuestDetails TestCase], time taken: 50ms, status: FINISHED

[SoapUITestCaseRunner] Project [HotelReservationProject] finished
with status [FINISHED] in 481ms
```

Also, if any of the soapUI tests fail or errors occur, the `run()` method throws an exception and the details of the failed test step will be logged, shown as follows:

```
java.lang.Exception: Not SOAP Fault in [deleteGuest] failed;
[null/empty response]
Status: FAILED
Time Taken: 20
Size: 0
```

Obviously, you do not have much control over the test execution if you just execute the whole soapUI project in the previous approach. We should be able to run individual TestCases via JUnit.

7. soapUI provides us with various API classes to deal with individual test elements of a soapUI project. One of the most useful implementations is `com.eviware.soapui.impl.wsdl.WsdlProject` (see the API documentation, `http://www.soapui.org/apidocs/com/eviware/soapui/impl/wsdl/WsdlProject.html`) which can be used to retrieve individual TestSuites and TestCases from a given soapUI project so that they can be executed as we wish through any Java class.

8. Let's redo our first test in a different manner without just executing all TestCases. Create another test method shown as follows:

```java
public void testSoapUIHotelReservation()
        throws XmlException, IOException, SoapUIException {
    //Create a new WsdlProject instance by specifying the
    //absolute path of sample HotelReservation soapUI project
    WsdlProject project = new WsdlProject("/home/charitha/
soapui-projects/HotelReservationProject-soapui-project.xml");
    //Retrieve all TestSuites included in the sample
    //HotelReservation soapUI project
    List<TestSuite> testSuiteList = project.
getTestSuiteList();
    //Iterate over all TestSuites in the project
    for (TestSuite ts : testSuiteList) {
        System.out.println("******Running " + ts.getName() +
"***********");
        //Retrieve all TestCases under a particular TestSuite
        List<com.eviware.soapui.model.testsuite.TestCase>
testCaseList = ts.getTestCaseList();
        //Iterate over all TestCases in the particular
//TestSuite
        for (com.eviware.soapui.model.testsuite.TestCase
testcase : testCaseList) {
            System.out.println("******Running " + testcase.
getName() + "***********");
            //Run the specific TestCase
            TestRunner testCaseRunner = testcase.run(new
PropertiesMap(), false);
            //Verify whether the testCase is finished
//successfully or failed due to the assertion failures
            assertEquals(TestRunner.Status.FINISHED,
testCaseRunner.getStatus());
        }
    }
}
```

As the inline code comments explained, we first created an instance of the
`WsdlProject` class by passing the absolute path of our sample hotel reservation
soapUI project as a constructor argument. Then we iterate over the TestSuites
and TestCases to run TestCases individually. Once you run the above method,
you will notice that all twelve TestCases of the `HotelReservation` soapUI project
will be run sequentially. If there are any assertion failures, you will see an output
similar to the following:

```
******Running addRoom TestCase***********
junit.framework.AssertionFailedError: expected:<FINISHED> but
was:<FAILED>
```

In the previous test method, if we want to run a specific TestCase of a TestSuite, we
can simply call the `getTestCaseByName` (`String TestCaseName`) method as follows:

```
com.eviware.soapui.model.testsuite.TestCase getRoomDetailsTestCase =
ts.getTestCaseByName("getRoomDetails TestCase");
```

Now, you may possess some understanding about how soapUI tests can be invoked
from a JUnit TestCase. By integrating your soapUI tests into the mainstream test
framework (JUnit) of your Service-oriented solution in this manner, you could let the
soapUI tests run as part of the build process very easily.

Depending on your build tool, you can invoke JUnit tests automatically as part of the
build process. In Apache Ant, JUnit tests can be launched using the JUnit task. You
can refer to the official documentation of the Apache Ant JUnit task at `http://ant.
apache.org/manual/Tasks/junit.html`.

Here is an excerpt from a `build.xml` that can be used to launch the previous
`HotelReservationSoapUITest` class.

We should define the classpath libraries to compile the source code of the JUnit test
and refer from Ant JUnit task.

```
<path id="test.lib.class.path">
        <pathelement location="/home/charitha/soapui-projects/
sample-project/junit-4.10.jar" />
        <pathelement location="/home/charitha/soapui-projects/
soapui-4.0.1/bin/soapui-4.0.1.jar" />
        <fileset dir="/home/charitha/soapui-projects/soapui-4.0.1/
lib">
                <include name="**/*.jar"/>
        </fileset>
        <pathelement location="${build.dir}" />
    </path>
```

The JUnit task will be similar to the following. Note that the plain formatter is used to generate a test report in text format.

```
<target name="junit" depends="compile">
        <junit printsummary="on" fork="true" haltonfailure="no">
                <classpath refid="test.lib.class.path" />
                <formatter type="plain" />
                <batchtest todir="${test.report.dir}">
                        <fileset dir="${t est.src.dir}">
                                <include name="**/*SoapUI*.java" />
                        </fileset>
                </batchtest>
        </junit>
    </target>
```

We looked into the possibility of running soapUI tests through the JUnit test framework and how those tests can be launched using the Apache Ant build tool. If you are using Apache Ant as the build tool in your continuous integration system, now you should be able to integrate your soapUI tests into your build system very easily.

In the previous examples, we launched soapUI `testrunners` programmatically from the JUnit TestCases. However, without using any test automation framework, you can directly run your soapUI tests using the command line scripts which are shipped with soapUI distribution. We will discuss the command line execution of the soapUI tests in the following section.

soapUI command line executions

soapUI provides us with a set of easy-to-use batch scripts to launch soapUI tests from the command line so that the tests can be invoked without opening the soapUI graphical interface separately. This is very useful in test automation because you can just call the batch scripts from your automated build scripts (Ant or any other script) and integrate into your build system right-away.

You will find the following runner scripts inside the SOAPUI_HOME/bin directory:

- `testrunner.sh {bat}`: This can be used to run any soapUI functional test from command line
- `loadtestrunner.sh {bat}`: Any soapUI load test can be launched from the command line through this script
- `mockservicerunner.sh{bat}`: soapUI mock services can be run straightaway from the command line using this script

- `toolrunner.sh {bat}`: This can be used to launch the tools included in soapUI such as Axis2, CXF, and so on
- `securitytestrunner.sh{bat}`: This can be used to run the security tests such as SQL injection, boundary scan, cross-site scripting, and so on from the command line

Invoking a soapUI command line functional test runner

Since all of the command line tools follow a common pattern, by studying one script, we should be able to use the others in a similar manner. Therefore, let's focus on a functional `testrunner` script and its usage.

1. Go to `SOAPUI_HOME/bin` and just run `testrunner.sh` or `testrunner.bat` depending on your operating system.

   - In Windows, open a command window and type `testrunner.bat` and press *Enter*
   - In Linux, open a shell, type `sh testrunner.sh` and press *Enter*

   This will print the usage of the `testrunner` script shown as follows. All the available options of the `testrunner` script can be found when you run the command.

   ```
   /soapui-projects/soapui-4.0.1/bin $ sh testrunner.sh


   ==================================

   =

   = SOAPUI_HOME = /home/charitha/soapui-projects/soapui-4.0.1

   =

   ==================================

   soapUI 4.0.1 TestCase Runner

   usage: testrunner [options] <soapui-project-file>

    -v     Sets password for soapui-settings.xml file
   ```

```
-t      Sets the soapui-settings.xml file to use

-A      Turns on exporting of all results using folders instead of
long filenames
```

 You can find a clear and detailed description about all these options in the soapUI official documentation (http://www.soapui.org/ Test-Automation/functional-tests.html). Therefore we will not spend time to go through each of them.

2. Let's launch the `testrunner` script without any options and look at the output.

```
sh testrunner.sh /home/charitha/soapui-projects/
HotelReservationProject-soapui-project.xml
```

3. Here, the `testrunner` executes all the TestSuites and TestCases included in the specified soapUI project file. You will see the output of the test in the `testrunner` console as follows:

```
09:28:48,262 INFO    [log] GuestManagementServiceTestSuite

09:28:48,322 INFO    [log] ReservationServiceTestSuite

09:28:48,322 INFO    [log] RoomManagementServiceTestSuite

09:28:48,342 INFO    [SoapUITestCaseRunner] Running soapUI tests in
project [HotelReservationProject]

09:28:48,343 INFO    [SoapUITestCaseRunner] Running Project
[HotelReservationProject], runType = SEQUENTIAL

09:28:48,434 INFO    [SoapUITestCaseRunner] Running soapUI testcase
[addGuest TestCase]

09:28:48,440 INFO    [SoapUITestCaseRunner] running step [addGuest]

09:28:48,655 INFO    [SoapUITestCaseRunner] Assertion [Not SOAP
Fault] has status VALID

09:28:48,656 INFO    [SoapUITestCaseRunner] Finished running soapUI
testcase [addGuest TestCase], time taken: 211ms, status: FINISHED
```

```
09:28:48,656 INFO  [SoapUITestCaseRunner] Running soapUI testcase
[deleteGuest TestCase]

09:28:48,657 INFO  [SoapUITestCaseRunner] Finished running soapUI
testcase [deleteGuest TestCase], time taken: 0ms, status: FINISHED

09:28:48,657 INFO  [SoapUITestCaseRunner] Running soapUI testcase
[getGuestDetails TestCase]

09:28:48,657 INFO  [SoapUITestCaseRunner] running step
[getGuestDetails]

09:28:48,697 INFO  [SoapUITestCaseRunner] Assertion [SOAP
Response] has status VALID

09:28:48,697 INFO  [SoapUITestCaseRunner] Assertion [SOAP
Response] has status VALID

09:28:48,697 INFO  [SoapUITestCaseRunner] Assertion [SOAP Response
1] has status VALID

09:28:48,697 INFO  [SoapUITestCaseRunner] Assertion [SOAP Response
2] has status VALID

09:28:48,697 INFO  [SoapUITestCaseRunner] Finished running soapUI
testcase [getGuestDetails TestCase], time taken: 39ms, status:
FINISHED

09:28:48,698 INFO  [SoapUITestCaseRunner] Project
[HotelReservationProject] finished with status [FINISHED] in 352ms
```

> Note that, we have disabled some TestSuites in
> `HotelReservationProject` for the demonstration
> purposes, hence you may observe a different output
> than the one mentioned previously.

4. With the command line `testrunner`, we can selectively run TestSuites as well as TestCases. For example, we can run the `getGuestDetails` TestCase directly from the `testrunner` script.

```
sh testrunner.sh -c "getGuestDetails TestCase"  -r /home/charitha/
soapui-projects/HotelReservationProject-soapui-project.xml
```

5. Since we inserted the -r option, soapUI prints a simple summary report at the end of the test execution shown as follows:

```
SoapUI 4.0.1 TestCaseRunner Summary

------------------------------

Time Taken: 169ms

Total TestSuites: 0

Total TestCases: 1 (0 failed)

Total TestSteps: 1

Total Request Assertions: 4

Total Failed Assertions: 0

Total Exported Results: 0
```

By specifying the -j option in the previous command, we can generate a JUnit compatible XML report (in our example, a report called TEST-GuestManagementServiceTestSuite.xml will be created at SOAPUI_HOME/ bin directory where you launched the previous command) which can then be directly integrated with the rest of your JUnit based test reports.

Invoking test runners from the soapUI graphical user interface

SoapUI TestRunners are just not for the purpose of running through the command line. They can even be launched within the soapUI graphical interface. Let's see how the functional TestRunner can be invoked from the soapUI interface.

1. Right-click on HotelReservationProject in the soapUI navigator pane and select **Launch TestRunner**.

2. The **Launch TestRunner** window will be opened as shown in the following screenshot:

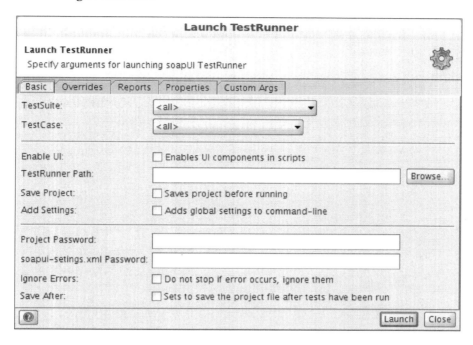

3. The same command line arguments which we used in the `testrunner` scripts can be specified in the previous window. Use the following argument values to run the `getGuestDetails` TestCase from the TestRunner:

    ◦   **TestSuite**: GuestManagementServiceTestSuite

    ◦   **TestCase**: `getGuestDetails` TestCase

    ◦   **TestRunner path**: `/home/charitha/soapui-projects/` `soapui-4.0.1/bin` (Browse or type the location of `SOAPUI_HOME/` `bin`)

4. Apart from the aforementioned set of arguments, we can specify the additional options from the other tabs of the **Launch TestRunner** window (**Overrides**, **Reports**, **Properties**, and **Custom Args** tabs). For our example, let's select the **Reports** tab and select the **Print Report** option.

5. Finally, click on the **Launch** button to run the `testrunner` file. You will see the output similar to the following:

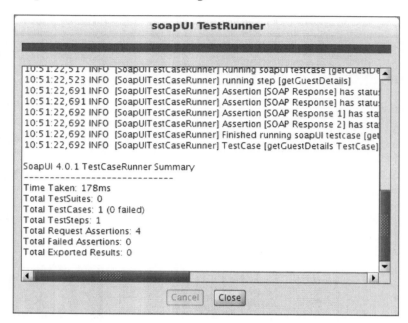

We looked at launching the functional `testrunner` from the command line as well as a soapUI graphical interface. Similarly, we can use the other runners (`loadtestrunner.sh{bat}` and so on) as well. You can find more information about the other runners from the soapUI official documentation.

Depending on your requirements, you can either use the command line `testrunner` scripts or launch your soapUI tests from JUnit when you need to integrate soapUI into your continuous integration systems. Launching soapUI tests from `testrunner` scripts can be comparatively easier for novice users because they do not want to learn soapUI API methods to invoke soapUI tests. Also, the `testrunner` invocation is pretty straightforward. If you decide to launch soapUI tests from the command line `testrunner` then your build tool can be configured to run the script with arguments. In the case of Apache Ant, the exec task which is used to execute system commands can be used as shown in the following example:

```
<project name="Ant-soapUITestRunner" default="soapui-tests-cmdline"
basedir=".">
<target name="soapui-tests-cmdline">
        <exec executable="/home/charitha/soapui-projects/soapui-4.0.1/
bin/testrunner.sh" failonerror="yes">
                <arg value="-r"/>
```

```
        <arg path="/home/charitha/soapui-book/
HotelReservationProject-soapui-project.xml"/>
        </exec>
</target>
</project>
```

Maven soapUI plugin

Apache Maven (`http://maven.apache.org/`) is a Java-based project management and build tool which is used by a plethora of commercial and open source Java applications. Maven does almost all of its build and project management tasks using various plugins. There are some core plugins maintained by the Apache Maven project, such as complier plugin which compiles the Java source, surefire plugin which executes JUnit tests, site plugin which generates website for a project, and so on.

Apart from the plugins supported by the Maven project, there are plugins developed by other parties. The Maven selenium plugin (`http://mojo.codehaus.org/selenium-maven-plugin/`) for launching and running selenium tests from the Maven build process, Maven clover plugin (`http://maven.apache.org/plugins/maven-clover-plugin/2.4/index.html`) to find the code coverage are some of the popular Maven plugins which are supported by respective tooling projects. Because of the popularity of Maven in Java projects, when a testing tool is released, the associated Maven plugin will also be made available. This is true for soapUI too.

The Maven soapUI plugin is used to execute soapUI tests as part of a Maven build cycle. If you are already familiar with Maven, integrating the soapUI plugin will be surprisingly easy. For the benefit of everyone, let's proceed with our sample `HotelReservation` soapUI project and see how the Maven soapUI plugin can be used.

Maven projects have their own structure. Note that we did not use Maven for building our sample `HotelReservation` project in *Chapter 2, The Sample Project*. Without going back and modifying the sample project to build using Maven, just for the purpose of demonstrating soapUI maven plugin, we will create a separate Maven project. By using the Maven Archetype plugin (`http://maven.apache.org/archetype/maven-archetype-plugin/`), we can create a working Maven project structure in a matter of seconds. Let's go through each step in detail:

1. If you do not have Maven running in your system, download and install Apache Maven2 or Maven3 latest build from `http://maven.apache.org/download.html`.

2. Once Maven is installed, verify whether it is running by issuing an `mvn` version command.

3. Create a new root directory for the sample Maven project in your file system. (for example, `/home/charitha/soapui-projects/maven-project`).

4. Go to the newly created directory and enter the following command to create a standard Maven project structure:

```
mvn archetype:create -DgroupId=com.soapui.test -DartifactId=HotelR
eservationSoapUITests
```

This will generate a Maven project structure similar to the following:

```
  └── HotelReservationSoapUITests
      ├── pom.xml
      └── src
          ├── main
          │   └── java
          │       └── com
          │           └── soapui
          │               └── test
          │                   └── App.java
          └── test
              └── java
                  └── com
                      └── soapui
                          └── test
                              └── AppTest.java
```

5. The Maven archetype plugin creates the required project structure as well as a root POM file.

   Since we are not going to use the auto-generated test class (`AppTest.java`) and the sample application (`App.java`), remove the main directory as well as the `HotelReservationSoapUITests/src/test/java` sub directory. Create a new sub directory, `resources` under `HotelReservationSoapUITests/src/test` and copy our sample `HotelReservation` soapUI project file (`HotelReservationProject-soapui-project.xml`) to the `resources` directory.

6. Now, open the generated `pom.xml` file and remove the JUnit dependency. (We do not run any JUnit tests hence the JUnit dependency is not required.)

7. Then, we need to do the configurations specific to the Maven soapUI plugin. First, add the eviware Maven2 repository to the `pom.xml`.

```
<pluginRepositories>
        <pluginRepository>
                <id>eviwarePluginRepository</id>
                <url>http://www.eviware.com/repository/maven2/
</url>
        </pluginRepository>
</pluginRepositories>
```

8. Next, add the soapUI plugin configuration to pom.xml.

```xml
<build>

<plugins>

 <plugin>

        <groupId>eviware</groupId>

        <artifactId>maven-soapui-plugin</artifactId>

        <version>4.0.1</version>

        <configuration>

        <projectFile>src/test/resources/HotelReservationProject-soapui-project.xml</projectFile>

        </configuration>

        <executions>

          <execution>

            <id>soap-webservice-test</id>

            <phase>integration-test</phase>

            <goals>

              <goal>test</goal>

            </goals>

          </execution>

        </executions>

    </plugin>

</plugins>

</build>
```

9. Here, we used the 4.0.1 version of the Maven soapUI plugin, which was the latest at the time of writing. The `<configuration>` element is used to define the soapUI specific settings associated with the plugin such as projectFile, testSuite, testCase, and so on. In this example, we run all TestSuites in the soapUI project without selection. Therefore, we just specified the `<projectFile>` element.

   soapUI tests can be executed as part of the integration test phase. Thus, we have given `<phase>integration-test</phase>` as the phase where the plugin is executed.

10. Save the `pom.xml` and run the following Maven goal:

    `mvn eviware:maven-soapui-plugin:test`

    This will run all soapUI tests included in `HotelReservationProject-soapui-project.xml` and return the output similar to the following (note that, I have enabled only the `GuestManagementServiceTestSuite` in the project to simplify the demonstration):

    ```
    ~/soapui-projects/maven-project/HotelReservationSoapUITests $ mvn
    eviware:maven-soapui-plugin:test

    [INFO] Scanning for projects...


    [INFO] ------------------------------------------------------------
    -------------

    [INFO] Building HotelReservationSoapUITests 1.0-SNAPSHOT

    [INFO] ------------------------------------------------------------
    -------------

    soapUI 4.0.1 Maven2 TestCase Runner

    18:44:10,165 INFO  [WsdlProject] Loaded project from [file:/home/
    charitha/soapui-book/maven-project/HotelReservationSoapUITests/
    src/test/resources/HotelReservationProject-soapui-project.xml]

    18:44:11,037 INFO  [log] GuestManagementServiceTestSuite

    18:44:11,097 INFO  [SoapUITestCaseRunner] Running soapUI tests in
    project [HotelReservationProject]

    18:44:11,098 INFO  [SoapUITestCaseRunner] Running Project
    [HotelReservationProject], runType = SEQUENTIAL
    ```

```
18:44:11,166 INFO  [SoapUITestCaseRunner] Running soapUI testcase
[addGuest TestCase]

18:44:11,172 INFO  [SoapUITestCaseRunner] running step [addGuest]

18:44:11,337 INFO  [SoapUITestCaseRunner] Assertion [Not SOAP
Fault] has status VALID

18:44:11,339 INFO  [SoapUITestCaseRunner] running step
[getGuestDetails]

18:44:11,378 INFO  [SoapUITestCaseRunner] Assertion [SOAP
Response] has status VALID

18:44:11,378 INFO  [SoapUITestCaseRunner] Assertion [SOAP
Response] has status VALID

18:44:11,379 INFO  [SoapUITestCaseRunner] Assertion [SOAP Response
1] has status VALID

18:44:11,379 INFO  [SoapUITestCaseRunner] Assertion [SOAP Response
2] has status VALID

18:44:11,379 INFO  [SoapUITestCaseRunner] Finished running soapUI
testcase [getGuestDetails TestCase], time taken: 39ms, status:
FINISHED

18:44:11,379 INFO  [SoapUITestCaseRunner] Project
[HotelReservationProject] finished with status [FINISHED] in 278ms
```

11. If we want to gain more control over test execution, we can configure the
    Maven soapUI plugin with various settings. Simply specify the following
    property under the `<configuration>` element of the soapUI plugin to
    invoke the `getGuestDetails` TestCase.

```
<configuration>

        <projectFile>src/test/resources/HotelReservationProject-
soapui-project.xml</projectFile>

        <testCase>getGuestDetails TestCase</testCase>

</configuration>
```

Similarly, you can run a specific TestSuite.

```
<testSuite>RoomManagementServiceTestSuite</testSuite>
```

> You can find all the settings of the Maven soapUI plugin at
> `http://www.soapui.org/Test-Automation/maven-`
> `2x.html` which explains the usage of each setting.

We looked at one of the goals out of the four different goals provided by the Maven soapUI plugin. The `maven-soapui-plugin:test` goal can be used to execute soapUI functional tests as part of the Maven build process as explained in the previous example. Apart from that, the `maven-soapui-plugin:loadtest` goal is used to run soapUI load tests. `Maven-soapui-plugin:tool` and `maven-soapui-plugin:mock` goals can be used to execute soapUI tools such as Axis2 Wsdl2Java and mock services respectively.

You can also execute multiple soapUI projects within a particular Maven build process. In order to do that, multiple executions of the plugin can be defined and include in a common life cycle phase.

- Suppose we have two soapUI project files, `HotelReservationProject-soapui-project1.xml` and `HotelReservationProject-soapui-project2.xml`. Then, we can include them in two different executions with a unique ID as shown in the following code:

```
<plugin>

  <groupId>eviware</groupId>

  <artifactId>maven-soapui-plugin</artifactId>

  <version>4.0.1</version>

  <executions>

    <execution>

      <id>soap-webservice-test1</id>

      <phase>integration-test</phase>

      <goals>

        <goal>test</goal>

      </goals>
```

```
<configuration>

<projectFile>${basedir}/src/test/resources/
HotelReservationProject-soapui-project1.xml</projectFile>

</configuration>

</execution>

<execution>

<id>soap-webservice-test2</id>

<phase>integration-test</phase>

<goals>

<goal>test</goal>

</goals>

<configuration>

<projectFile>${basedir}/src/test/resources/
HotelReservationProject-soapui-project2.xml</projectFile>

</configuration>

</execution>

</executions>

</plugin>
```

- Now, if you run a `mvn integration-test` goal, both soapUI projects will be executed sequentially in the order they were defined inside the plugin.

Summary

Test automation is not another *Nice-to-Have* task when it comes to service-oriented solutions. In order to achieve the real advantages of SOA adoption, automated testing should play a key role and it must be part of the mainstream build process. In this chapter, we discussed the necessities of having automated tests in SOA projects. Then, we summarized the steps involved in Continuous Integration (CI) systems and why CI is important in SOA. soapUI facilitates the automatic execution of tests using multiple approaches. First, we looked into the integration of soapUI with the JUnit test framework and invoked soapUI tests as part of JUnit tests. Then, we discussed how those JUnit tests can be run continuously from Apache Ant. We also looked into the command line `testrunner` scripts provided by soapUI. Finally, we went through a sample Maven project to demonstrate how the Maven soapUI plugin can be used to run soapUI tests as part of the Maven build cycle.

13
Miscellaneous Topics

Starting from a sample hotel reservation application, we explored most of the key features provided by the world's leading web services testing tool, soapUI. At the beginning of the book, we discussed the key elements of a soapUI project such as TestSuites, TestCases, and TestSteps. Our discussions have not just been limited to functional testing. We looked into the use of soapUI in load and performance testing as well. Then, we moved forward with the topics such as web service simulation, RESTful services testing, JMS testing, JDBC testing, and test automation. In between, we discussed about the scripting capabilities of soapUI and the advanced web services testing topics, such as WS-Security.

There are some useful topics which we did not include in the previous chapters, but we believe they must be discussed separately before concluding the book. For example, most SOA developers and testers prefer to use soapUI directly from their preferred **Integrated Development Environments (IDEs)** instead of using a separate soapUI installation. Also, there are some general features such as external web service framework integrations, which we cannot categorize into one particular chapter of the book. Therefore, we dedicate this chapter to discussing some useful auxiliary features of soapUI. We will focus on the following miscellaneous topics in this chapter:

- soapUI Eclipse plugin
- soapUI Intellij IDEA plugin
- WS-I validation using soapUI
- soapUI integration with external web services frameworks
- Sending attachments with SOAP messages using soapUI

soapUI IDE plugins

IDE plugins are software components that add functional extensions on top of a particular IDE. In particular, the IDE plugins are used by developers to run various tools inside the development environment which is more effective than launching tools separately. soapUI provides us with a few IDE plugins which allow us to build and run soapUI tests from within popular IDEs such as **Eclipse** (`http://www.eclipse.org`), **Intellij IDEA** (`http://www.jetbrains.com/idea/`), or **NetBeans** (`http://netbeans.org/`).

soapUI Eclipse plugin

The soapUI eclipse plugin brings all the features provided by the standard soapUI desktop application into Eclipse IDE. Adding the soapUI plugin into Eclipse is pretty straightforward; follow these steps:

1. Open Eclipse IDE (this plugin supports Eclipse version 3.4 or later).
2. Go to **Help | Install New Software ...**.
3. Enter `http://www.soapui.org/eclipse/update` as the update site in the **Work with:** textbox and click on **Add**.
4. Enter the name of the installation as soapUI and click on **OK**.

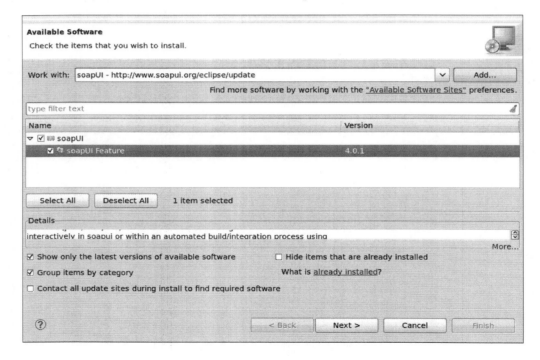

5. Select **soapUI Feature**, as shown in the preceding screenshot, and click on **Next**. Review the installation and licenses in the next screen of the wizard and click on **Finish**. After a few minutes, depending on the speed of your Internet connection, the soapUI plugin will be installed.

6. Restart Eclipse to take effect on the new plugin installation.

7. In the Eclipse main toolbar, go to **Window | Open Perspective | Other** and select soapUI. This will open our familiar soapUI project explorer, as shown in the following screenshot:

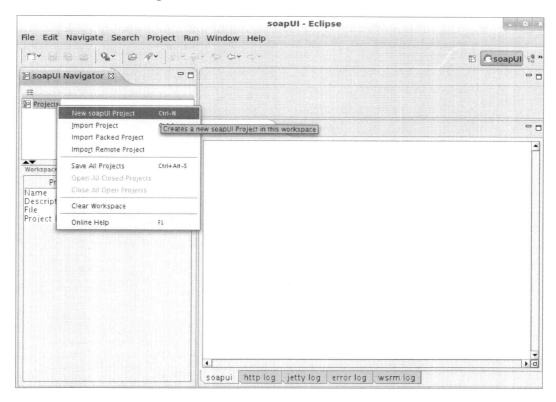

Now, we can create new soapUI projects and proceed with the usual soapUI features inside Eclipse. In addition to the general preferences, we can configure the soapUI settings in the Eclipse preferences editor by navigating to **Window | Preferences | soapUI**.

soapUI IntelliJ IDEA plug-in

IntelliJ IDEA (http://www.jetbrains.com/idea/) is a commercial IDE which is widely popular among developers due to its extremely rich set of features and productivity enhancements. The soapUI IntelliJ IDEA plugin is also similar to the Eclipse plugin, which can be used to integrate soapUI into the IDE and launch any soapUI project from within the IDE.

There are multiple ways to install plugins in IDEA:

- Downloading the soapUI IntelliJ plugin from http://sourceforge.net/ projects/soapui/files/soapui-intellij-plugin/ and installing it in IDEA

- Installing the plugin using the IntelliJ IDEA plugin manager UI

 Note that the direct link for installing the soapUI plugin is available only in IntelliJ IDEA 8.0 or later versions.

In the following demonstration, we will install the soapUI plugin using a third approach, the direct link of the soapUI plugin install option:

1. Open IntelliJ IDEA and select **Tools** from the top menu and go to **Webservices | Install SoapUI**. This will download the latest version of the soapUI plugin from the plugin repository and install it in your IDE.

2. Restart IDE. You will see a "SoapUI" option under the **Tools** menu, as shown in the following screenshot:

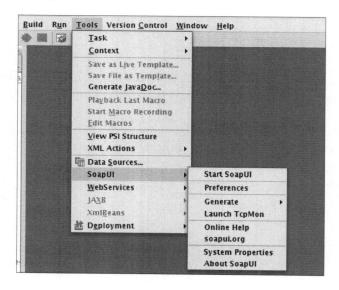

3. Select **Start SoapUI** to start soapUI inside IntelliJ IDEA. Once soapUI is started, the **Start SoapUI** menu option will be changed to **Close SoapUI**.

4. Now, select **Window** in the top menu and go to **Tool Windows | soapUI Navigator**. This will open the soapUI navigator which we are familiar with, in the soapUI desktop version, inside IntelliJ IDEA:

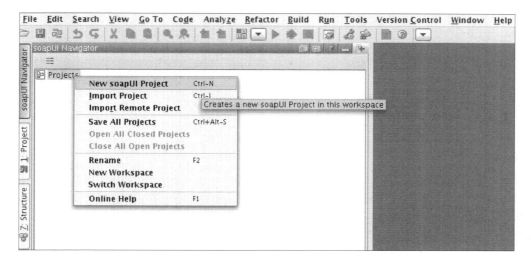

WS-I validation using soapUI

The ability to work with heterogeneous systems in a seamless manner is one of the key promises of SOA and web services. In order for multiple vendor platforms to operate with each other, every participant of a heterogeneous system should follow a common set of standards and rules. The **Web Services Interoperability Organization (WS-I)** `http://www.ws-i.org`, which recently became part of the **Organization for the Advancement of Structured Information Standards (OASIS)**, defines the best practices for web services' interoperability. WS-I provides web services' developers with various deliverables such as **profiles**, **sample applications**, and **testing tools**.

According to Wikipedia, **WS-I profile** is a set of named web services specifications at specific revision levels, together with a set of implementation and interoperability guidelines recommending how the specifications may be used to develop interoperable web services.

Among the multiple profiles defined by WS-I, the basic profile (`http://www.ws-i.org/deliverables/workinggroup.aspx?wg=basicprofile`) defines the best practices and guidelines for the interoperability of core web services specifications such as SOAP and WSDL. Therefore, the basic profile can be used to validate WSDLs and SOAP messages in service-oriented solutions. To validate the conformance with WS-I profiles, WS-I develops multiple testing tools, which can be downloaded from `http://www.ws-i.org/deliverables/workinggroup.aspx?wg=testingtools`.

These WS-I conformance testing tools are embedded into soapUI distribution by default. You can find the WS-I Testing Tools V1.1, which can be used to validate the conformance against the Basic Profile V1.0 and 1.1 as well as Simple Soap Binding Profile V1.0 inside the `SOAPUI_HOME/wsi-test-tools` directory.

In this section, we will look at how one of the WSDLs of our sample hotel reservation soapUI project can be validated using WS-I testing tools:

1. Right-click on **GuestManagementServiceSoap11Binding** in the hotel reservation soapUI project and select **Show Interface Viewer**. You will see the **WS-I Compliance** tab in the interface viewer which allows us to create a WS-I conformance report for the selected interface.

2. Before generating the report, let's have a look at various options which can be used in report generation. Click on the **Sets WS-I report creation options** icon, which brings up the **soapUI Preferences** dialog box as shown in the following screenshot:

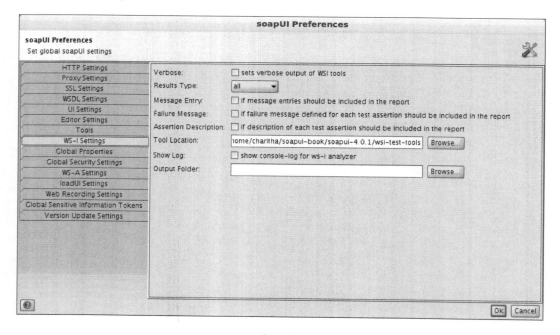

3. The default location of the WSI tool kit is shown in the preceding preferences dialog box. Select an output directory for the report. You can also modify some of the WS-I analyzer configuration options through this dialog. Keep those options intact and click on **OK**. This will generate a WSI compliance report and save it in the location that we specified. The report will also be shown under the WS-I compliance tab as shown in the following screenshot:

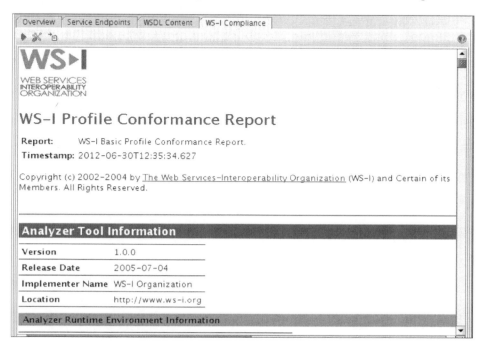

In the soapUI version that we used in this book (soapUI-4.0.1), the WS-I compliance report is saved in the /tmp directory if the WS-I validation generates non-conformance errors of the WSDL. You will experience this with our sample **GuestManagementService**. After the validation of WSDL, if you open the generated XML report, which can be found in the /tmp directory of your filesystem (for example, /tmp/wsi-report4252591991256058421), you will come across the assertion failures similar to the following:

```
<assertionResult id="BP2703" result="failed">

    <failureDetail xml:lang="en" >Exception:

org.xml.sax.SAXException: Error: cvc-complex-type.2.4.a: Invalid
content was found starting with element &apos;wsdl:fault&apos;. One of
&apos;{&quot;http://schemas.xmlsoap.org/wsdl/&quot;:output}&apos; is
expected.
```

Now, in order for you to understand the exact meaning of these types of errors, check the given `assertionResult` ID in the **Basic Profile-1.1 Test Assertion Document (TAD)**, which can be found in the `SOAPUI_HOME/wsi-test-tools/common/profiles` directory. According to that document, the `assertionID` value `BP2703` will represent the following WS-I basic profile conformance assertion:

```
<!--                            BP2703                          -->


    <testAssertion id="BP2703" entryType="definitions" type="required"
enabled="true">


      <context>For a candidate description within a WSDL document</
context>


        <assertionDescription>If it uses the WSDL namespace, then
it conforms to the schema located at http://schemas.xmlsoap.org/
wsdl/2003-02-11.xsd, and if it uses the WSDL-SOAP binding namespace
then it conforms to the schema located at http://schemas.xmlsoap.org/
wsdl/soap/2003-02-11.xsd.</assertionDescription>


        <failureMessage>WSDL definition does not conform to the schema
located at http://schemas.xmlsoap.org/wsdl/soap/2003-02-11.xsd for
some element using the WSDL-SOAP binding namespace, or does not
conform to the schema located at http://schemas.xmlsoap.org/wsdl/2003-
02-11.xsd for some element using the WSDL namespace.</failureMessage>


        <failureDetailDescription>Error message from the XML parser.</
failureDetailDescription>
```

Similarly, you can find out the conformity errors of your WSDL and correct them as suggested in the assertion results.

soapUI integration with external web services' frameworks

soapUI cannot only be considered as purely a web service testing tool. As we discussed in previous chapters, soapUI provides us with the features to work with both client and server side of the general web service equation. SOAP message transmission over HTTP or JMS, RESTful service invocations are the obvious examples of using soapUI as a web service client. The mock service generation can be considered a good example for service hosting capabilities provided by soapUI.

In SOA, services are built using various commercial or open source web services frameworks. For example, one may use **Apache CXF** (http://cxf.apache.org) to develop and host the web services whereas another may use **Jboss** (http://www.jboss.org/jbossws/) or Apache Axis2 for the same purpose. Many of these web service frameworks provide web service developers with numerous tools to assist them in web service development and testing tasks. With soapUI, you can directly make use of the tools provided by your favorite web services framework. In this section, we will look into integrating soapUI with some of the external tools.

If you select the **Tools** option from the top menu of soapUI, you will find a number of utilities provided by external web service frameworks:

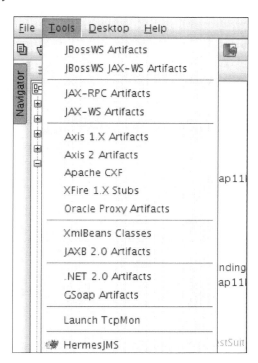

All these options directly invoke the tools such as WSDL2Java, associated with a particular web services' framework and return the results. To make use of a tool included in a particular web services' framework, you must first configure the location of the web services framework in **soapUI Preferences**:

1. As we have already used the Apache Axis2 web services framework in our sample project, let's specify its location in the **soapUI Preferences** dialog box, as shown in the following screenshot:

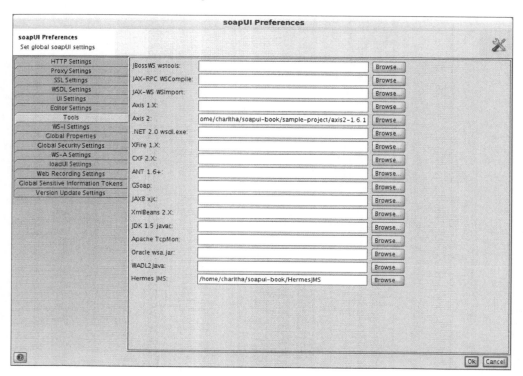

2. **WSDL2Java** is a tool given by most of the web services frameworks to generate client-side artifacts (**stubs**) or **service skeletons** from WSDLs. We are going to create client-side artifacts from WSDL of **GuestManagementService** using the Axis2 WSDL2Java tool. Click on the **Tools** option in top menu and select **Axis2 Artifacts**.

3. The **Axis2 artifacts** window will be opened as shown in the following screenshot. Enter the URL of the **GuestManagementService** WSDL and specify an output directory. Keeping the other options intact, click on **Generate**.

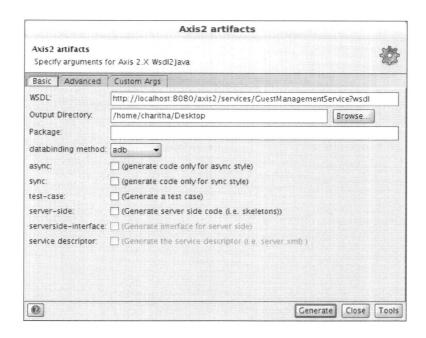

When you click on **Generate**, soapUI invokes the `wsdl2Java.sh` or `wsdl2java.bat` script located in the `AXIS2_HOME/bin` directory. You will find the generated artifacts in the specified output directory.

Axis2 WSDL2Java script generates the `src` directory and an ant `build.xml` file when you run the script with the default options. The `src` directory contains the stub classes which can be imported when creating a Java client to invoke web services programmatically.

 Make sure to set executable permissions for `AXIS2_HOME/bin/`
`wsdl2java.sh` script if you come across a "permission denied"
error when running Axis2 WSDL2Java tool from soapUI.

Depending on the web services framework you use, follow a similar approach with the other tools such as Apache CXF, Axis2 1.1, or .NET 2.0.

Sending attachments with SOAP messages using soapUI

Attachments are one of the important aspects of any message transmission facility. Attachments are commonly used in transport mechanisms such as MAIL (for example, SMTP) where the attachments are included as part of the mail message. In all our examples which we have discussed so far, the payload of SOAP messages represented simple XML elements with primitive data types. However, in the real world, we do not just transmit raw XML through SOAP messages. SOAP messages are transmitted along with images, PDF documents, or some other binary data. There are multiple approaches used to send attachments with SOAP messages:

- **Base64 encoding**: Data is embedded as an element or attribute value inside the payload of the SOAP message using Base64 encoding. (http://en.wikipedia.org/wiki/Base64).

  For example:

  ```
  <x:data xmlns:x="http://test.data.com" >
    <image>/ayQKWWWa=</image>
  </x:data>
  ```

  Because of its inefficiency and performance concerns of decoding the messages, this mechanism is not considered as a good solution for attachment transmission in SOAP messaging.

- **SOAP with Attachments (SwA)**: SOAP with Attachments (http://www.w3.org/TR/SOAP-attachments) is an approach that is analogous to attaching binary files to e-mails. Binary data is put completely outside of the SOAP envelope by including a reference to the binary file:

  ```
  Content-Type: multipart/related

  type="text/xml"


  --MIME_boundary

  Content-Type:text/xml; charset=UTF-8

  Content-Transfer-Encoding: binary

  Content-id=<main>


  <?xml version="1.0" encoding="UTF-8"?>
  ```

```
<soapenv:Envelope>

...

<data href="cid:attachment"/>

...

</soapenv:Envelope>

--MIME_boundary

Content-Type:application/octet-stream

Content-Transfer-Encoding: binary

Content-id=<attachment>

--MIME_boundary
```

The attachment is referred using the content ID (CID) or content location as shown in the preceding code. Though many web service frameworks support SOAP with Attachments, it has now been superseded by the much enhanced attachment processing mechanisms such as the **SOAP Message Transmission Optimization Mechanism (MTOM)**.

- **MTOM (SOAP Message Transmission Optimization Mechanism)**: MTOM (`http://www.w3.org/TR/soap12-mtom/`) is a more efficient method of sending binary data to and from web services with combining Base64 encoding and SOAP With Attachments. In MTOM, binary data does not reside outside SOAP envelope as in SOAP With Attachments. This is achieved through a technology known as XML-binary Optimized Packaging (XOP).

  soapUI supports all of the above attachment-handling mechanisms. You can find more details about how soapUI supports these approaches in the soapUI official documentation (`http://www.soapui.org/SOAP-and-WSDL/adding-headers-and-attachments.html`). In this section, we will look into using soapUI to attach a binary file to a SOAP message using MTOM as it is the commonly used attachment transmission mechanism.

Deploying an MTOM-enabled web service

Apache Axis2 includes an MTOM sample service that we can use out of the box to demonstrate our scenario:

1. Go to the `AXIS2_HOME/samples/mtom` directory and follow the `README.txt` to deploy `sample-mtom.aar` in axis2server.

2. Once the service is deployed, access `http://localhost:8080/axis2/services/MTOMSample?wsdl` and check whether you can retrieve the auto-generated WSDL of the service.

   This web service consists of a single operation, **attachment**, that accepts a string value as file name/file path, and a binary attachment. This service will save the content of the attachment into a new file at the given file path.

Using soapUI to send an attachment to the web service

As we have the service ready, let's see how we can use soapUI to send a SOAP request to the above web service with an attachment:

1. Create a new soapUI project, MTOM Test Project. Enter `http://localhost:8080/axis2/services/MTOMSample?wsdl` as the initial WSDL.

2. Once the project is created, look at the generated SOAP request under **MTOMServiceSOAP11Binding**:

   ```
   <soapenv:Envelope xmlns:soapenv="http://schemas.xmlsoap.org/soap/
   envelope/" xmlns:mtom="http://ws.apache.org/axis2/mtomsample/"
   xmlns:xm="http://www.w3.org/2005/05/xmlmime">
      <soapenv:Header/>
      <soapenv:Body>
         <mtom:AttachmentRequest>
            <mtom:fileName>?</mtom:fileName>
             <mtom:binaryData xm:contentType="application/?">c
   id:228548525934</mtom:binaryData>
         </mtom:AttachmentRequest>
      </soapenv:Body>
   </soapenv:Envelope>
   ```

   The SOAP payload of the request consists of two elements — `fileName` and `binaryData`.

   As the `fileName` value is just a string, we can give any string value as the filename. But how should we specify the second parameter of the payload — the binary attachment?

3. SoapUI allows us to add attachments to SOAP requests through a separate **Attachments** tab that can be found at the bottom of the request editor. Select the **Attachments** tab and click on the **Adds an attachment** icon that is at the upper-left corner of the **Attachments** tab.

4. A file browser will be launched where we can select a file to be attached. Browse to a file in your filesystem (for example, a PNG or GIF image).

5. A message box will appear, requesting to cache the attachment in the request. If we click on **Yes**, the attachment is cached by creating a local copy of the attachment inside soapUI, so that the subsequent requests do not read the attachment from the absolute file path. Otherwise, the absolute path of the attachment is stored by soapUI in the **Name** column of the **Attachment** table. In our example, click on **Yes** to cache the attachments in the requests.

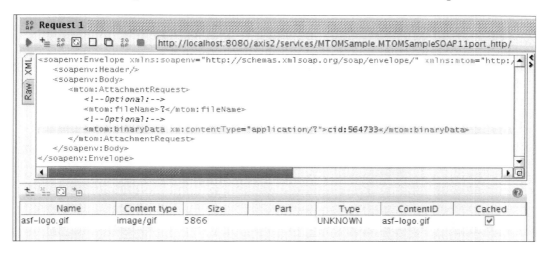

The name of the file which is to be attached to the request is given in the first column in the attachments table. The content type of the attachment is captured according to the selected binary file.

In this example, we are using a GIF image, hence **image/gif** is the content type of the attachment. The size of the attachment is given in bytes under the **Size** column. The **Part** column shows the MIME part as defined by the binding of the WSDL of the web service. MIME part value should explicitly be chosen if the operation is defined to use MIME attachments in the corresponding WSDL. As we are using MTOM, this can be kept blank.

The type column shows the attachment type, which can be **CONTENT**, **MIME**, **SWAREF**, **XOP**, or **UNKNOWN**. The type is a read-only value, hence it cannot be changed for a particular request. For MTOM, the attachment type will be XOP. ContentID represents the content ID as given in the MIME part definition of the associated WSDL of the service. In our example, as we use MTOM attachment transmission, the ContentID of the attachment can be the same as the attachment name.

6. Replace ? of the `<mtom:fileName>` element with a target file path (for example, `/home/user/logo.gif`) (if you just specify file name without specifying the file path, it will be saved in the `AXIS2_HOME/bin` directory).

7. We must change the CID value of the `<mtom:binaryData>` element with the ContentID of the attachment, shown as follows:

```
<mtom:binaryData xm:contentType="application/?">cid:asf-logo.gif</
mtom:binaryData>
```

8. Now, we have included an attachment to the SOAP request. However, we have not instructed soapUI to use the MTOM attachment transmission mechanism. If you look at the **Request Properties** at the left pane, you will find multiple attachment-specific properties:

Enable MTOM	true
Force MTOM	false
Inline Response Attachments	false
Expand MTOM Attachments	false
Disable multiparts	false
Encode Attachments	false
Enable Inline Files	false

Some of these properties are applicable only for the response attachments.

- **Enable MTOM**: This property instructs soapUI to use MTOM in transferring binary data.

- **Force MTOM**: This property is used to enforce soapUI to use MTOM for any SOAP request regardless of having any attachment. If the SOAP response message includes an attachment, it is separately shown in the **Attachments** tab of response editor. Instead of that, the complete response can be shown with attachments inline in the XML view of response editor by setting the **Inline Response Attachments** property to **true**.

- **Expand MTOM Attachments**: This property can be used to extract the binary data of the response and include it as a child of the payload of the response. The attachment will be separately shown under the response's **Attachments** tab as shown in the following screenshot:

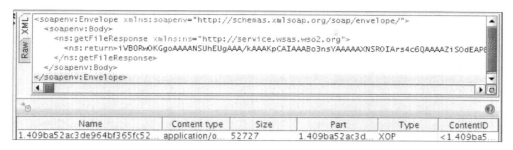

```
<soapenv:Envelope xmlns:soapenv="http://schemas.xmlsoap.org/soap/envelope/">
  <soapenv:Body>
    <ns:getFileResponse xmlns:ns="http://service.wsas.wso2.org">
      <ns:return>iVBORwOKGgoAAAANSUhEUgAAA/kAAAKpCAIAAABo3nsYAAAAAXNSROIArs4c6QAAAAZiSOdEAP8
    </ns:getFileResponse>
  </soapenv:Body>
</soapenv:Envelope>
```

Name	Content type	Size	Part	Type	ContentID
1.409ba52ac3de964bf365fc52...	application/o...	52727	1.409ba52ac3d...	XOP	<1.409ba5...

- ○ **Disable multiparts**: This property can be used when sending or receiving multiple attachments to pack attachments with the same type into a multipart attachment.

9. To encode the MTOM attachment in accordance with the corresponding binary type defined in WSDL (base64Binary or hexBinary), we can set the **Encode Attachments** property to **true**.

10. By setting the **Enable Inline Files** property to **true**, a file can be attached to a request just by specifying `file:<file name>`.

    Note that the description just given is a very brief description of the attachment related properties. You can find more information about these properties in `http://www.soapui.org/SOAP-and-WSDL/adding-headers-and-attachments.html`.

11. In our example, we just set the **Enable MTOM** property to **true** and keep the other options as they are. Now, submit the request by clicking on the arrow icon at the top of the request editor.

12. You will get the following response:

```
<soapenv:Envelope xmlns:soapenv="http://schemas.xmlsoap.org/soap/
envelope/">
    <soapenv:Body>
        <ns2:AttachmentResponse xmlns:ns2="http://
ws.apache.org/axis2/mtomsample/">File saved succesfully.</
ns2:AttachmentResponse>
    </soapenv:Body>
</soapenv:Envelope>
```

Check that a file with the name given in the request will be saved in the specified location. Have a detailed look at the request message by selecting the **Raw** view. You can see the `<inc:include>` element inside the payload which is used to mark where the binary data is, as follows:

```
POST http://localhost:8080/axis2/services/MTOMSample.
MTOMSampleSOAP11port_http/ HTTP/1.1

Accept-Encoding: gzip,deflate

SOAPAction: "attachment"

Content-Type: multipart/related; type="application/xop+xml";
start="<rootpart@soapui.org>"; start-info="text/xml";
boundary="----=_Part_60_92678960.1341151455014"

MIME-Version: 1.0

User-Agent: Jakarta Commons-HttpClient/3.1

Host: localhost:8080

Content-Length: 6910



------=_Part_60_92678960.1341151455014

Content-Type: application/xop+xml; charset=UTF-8; type="text/xml"

Content-Transfer-Encoding: 8bit

Content-ID: <rootpart@soapui.org>



<soapenv:Envelope xmlns:soapenv="http://schemas.xmlsoap.org/soap/
envelope/" xmlns:mtom="http://ws.apache.org/axis2/mtomsample/"
xmlns:xm="http://www.w3.org/2005/05/xmlmime">
    <soapenv:Header/>
    <soapenv:Body>
        <mtom:AttachmentRequest>
            <!--Optional:-->
            <mtom:fileName>/home/charitha/my.gif</mtom:fileName>
            <!--Optional:-->
        <mtom:binaryData xm:contentType="application/?"><inc:Inclu
de href="cid:asf-logo.gif" xmlns:inc="http://www.w3.org/2004/08/xop/
include"/></mtom:binaryData>
```

```
        </mtom:AttachmentRequest>
    </soapenv:Body>
</soapenv:Envelope>

-------=_Part_60_92678960.1341151455014

Content-Type: image/gif; name=asf-logo.gif

Content-Transfer-Encoding: binary

Content-ID: <asf-logo.gif>

Content-Disposition: attachment; name="asf-logo.gif";
filename="asf-logo.gif"
```

Summary

In this chapter, we discussed some important topics which in a way did not fit in neatly in the previous chapters. We started off by looking into two important plug-ins, which allow us to integrate soapUI into Eclipse and IntelliJ IDEA **Integrated Development Environments (IDEs)**. Then, we discussed validating WSDLs against WS-I Basic Profile using the embedded WS-I validation tool. We also looked at the options provided by soapUI to consume some useful tools such as WSDL2Java, which are included in popular web services frameworks such as Apache Axis2, CXF, and .NET 2.0. Finally, we had a brief look at the attachment processing capabilities of soapUI by focusing on the MTOM attachment transmission mechanism.

Index

broker 10
burst load strategy 107, 108
bytes message 226

C

CI
  about 260
  functions, representing 260
  tasks 261
class declaration, Groovy 240
ClasspathGroups dialog box 220
Classpath Groups tab 219
Close connections between each request,
     LoadTest option 117
com.eviware.soapui.model.iface.
     MessageExchange API 254
com.eviware.soapui.support.GroovyUtils
     API 254
com.eviware.soapui.support.XmlHolder
     API 254
command line executions, soapUI
  about 266
  soapUI command-line functional test
     runner, invoking 267-270
  test runners from soapUI graphical user
     interface, invoking 270-272
composition 10, 11
Contains assertion 88
context.expand (<String>) method 244
context object 242-245
Continuous integration. *See* CI
continuous testing 260
contract-first methodology 121
contract-first web service development 120
control structures, Groovy 239
Create Requests check box 76
Create Requests option 62
Creates and opens request option 186
Create TestSuite option 76
CRUD (Create Read Update Delete) 45

D

data
  testing, in isolation 202
data handling 201
Default outgoing WSS property 125

def keyword 238
DELETE 179
deleteGuest operation 67, 70, 77
deleteRoom TestCase 81
Destination properties dialog box 221
detail element 17
digest 162
Disable multiparts property 297
domain property 156
dynamic responses
  using 131-137

E

Eclipse
  URL 282
Enable Inline Files property 297
Enable MTOM property 296
endpoint references 142
end-to-end JMS message delivery
  verifying, sample project used 228
Enterprise Service Buses. *See* ESB
Enterprise Service Bus. *See* ESB
envelope, SOAP 12
ESB 10, 121, 130, 201
Expand MTOM Attachments property 296
external web services frameworks
  soapUI, integrating with 288-291
Extract Params button 185

F

faultcode element 17
faultstring element 17
Fetch Size property 207
fire and forget pattern, MEP 16
Force MTOM property 296
functional testing
  about 19, 23
  of REST services 197, 198

G

Generate TestSuite dialog box 200
GET 179
getGuestDetails operation 67, 136, 223
getGuestDetails TestStep 227
getRoomDetails TestCase 81

Thank you for buying
Web Services Testing with soapUI

About Packt Publishing

Packt, pronounced 'packed', published its first book "*Mastering phpMyAdmin for Effective MySQL Management*" in April 2004 and subsequently continued to specialize in publishing highly focused books on specific technologies and solutions.

Our books and publications share the experiences of your fellow IT professionals in adapting and customizing today's systems, applications, and frameworks. Our solution based books give you the knowledge and power to customize the software and technologies you're using to get the job done. Packt books are more specific and less general than the IT books you have seen in the past. Our unique business model allows us to bring you more focused information, giving you more of what you need to know, and less of what you don't.

Packt is a modern, yet unique publishing company, which focuses on producing quality, cutting-edge books for communities of developers, administrators, and newbies alike. For more information, please visit our website: www.packtpub.com.

About Packt Open Source

In 2010, Packt launched two new brands, Packt Open Source and Packt Enterprise, in order to continue its focus on specialization. This book is part of the Packt Open Source brand, home to books published on software built around Open Source licences, and offering information to anybody from advanced developers to budding web designers. The Open Source brand also runs Packt's Open Source Royalty Scheme, by which Packt gives a royalty to each Open Source project about whose software a book is sold.

Writing for Packt

We welcome all inquiries from people who are interested in authoring. Book proposals should be sent to author@packtpub.com. If your book idea is still at an early stage and you would like to discuss it first before writing a formal book proposal, contact us; one of our commissioning editors will get in touch with you.

We're not just looking for published authors; if you have strong technical skills but no writing experience, our experienced editors can help you develop a writing career, or simply get some additional reward for your expertise.

Selenium 1.0 Testing Tools: Beginner's Guide

ISBN: 978-1-84951-026-4   Paperback: 232 pages

Test your web applications with multiple browsers using the selenium Framework to ensure the quality of web applications

1. Save your valuable time by using Selenium to record, tweak and replay your test scripts

2. Get rid of any bugs deteriorating the quality of your web applications

3. Take your web applications one step closer to perfection using Selenium tests

4. Packed with detailed working examples that illustrate the techniques and tools for debugging

Python Testing Cookbook

ISBN: 978-1-84951-466-8   Paperback: 364 pages

Over 70 simple but incredibly effective recipes for taking control of automated testing using powerful Python testing tools

1. Learn to write tests at every level using a variety of Python testing tools

2. The first book to include detailed screenshots and recipes for using Jenkins continuous integration server (formerly known as Hudson)

3. Explore innovative ways to introduce automated testing to legacy systems

4. Written by Greg L. Turnquist – senior software engineer and author of Spring Python 1.1

Please check **www.PacktPub.com** for information on our titles

PUBLISHING

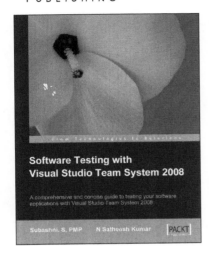

Software Testing with Visual Studio Team System 2008

ISBN: 978-1-84719-558-6   Paperback: 356 pages

A comprehensive and concise guide to testing your software applications with Visual Studio Team System 2008

1. Test your software applications with Visual Studio Team System 2008 and rest assured of its quality

2. Create a structured testing environment for your applications to produce reliable products

3. Comprehensive yet concise guide with a lot of examples and clear explanations

4. No knowledge of software testing is required, only basic knowledge of Visual Studio 2008 operation is expected

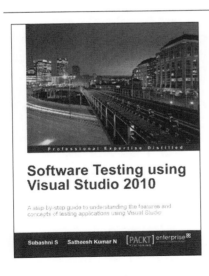

Software Testing using Visual Studio 2010

ISBN: 978-1-84968-140-7   Paperback: 400 pages

A step by step guide understand the features and concepts of testing applications using Visual Studio

1. Master all the new tools and techniques in Visual Studio 2010 and the Team Foundation Server for testing applications

2. Customize reports with Team foundation server.

3. Get to grips with the new Test Manager tool for maintaining Test cases

4. Take full advantage of new Visual Studio features for testing an application's User Interface

Please check **www.PacktPub.com** for information on our titles

14645171R00184

Printed in Great Britain
by Amazon.co.uk, Ltd.,
Marston Gate.